D0481383

PRESENT INDICATIVE

Books By
NOEL COWARD

PLAYS

TONIGHT AT 8:30: *Plays*
POINT VALAINE: *A Play in Three Acts*
CONVERSATION PIECE: *A Romantic Comedy*

PLAY PARADE

DESIGN FOR LIVING: *A Comedy in Three Acts*
CAVALCADE: *A Play in Three Acts*
POST-MORTEM: *A Play in Eight Scenes*
PRIVATE LIVES: *An Intimate Comedy in Three Acts*
BITTER SWEET: *A Play in Three Acts*
THE VORTEX: *A Play in Three Acts*
HAY FEVER: *A Light Comedy in Three Acts*
"THIS WAS A MAN": *A Comedy in Three Acts*
EASY VIRTUE: *A Play in Three Acts*

SKETCHES

COLLECTED SKETCHES AND LYRICS

PARODIES ·

SPANGLED UNICORN

AUTOBIOGRAPHY

PRESENT INDICATIVE

NOEL COWARD

PRESENT
INDICATIVE

Noel Coward

Garden City   New York

DOUBLEDAY, DORAN AND COMPANY, INC.

MCMXXXVII

PRINTED AT THE *Country Life Press*, GARDEN CITY, N. Y., U. S. A.

COPYRIGHT, 1937
BY NOEL COWARD
ALL RIGHTS RESERVED

To
My Mother

ILLUSTRATIONS

[vii]

ILLUSTRATIONS

PART ONE

I WAS PHOTOGRAPHED naked on a cushion very early in life, an insane, toothless smile slitting my face and pleats of fat overlapping me like an ill-fitting overcoat. Later, at the age of two, I was photographed again. This time in a lace dress, leaning against a garden roller and laughing hysterically. If these photographs can be found they will adorn this book.

In due course I was baptized into the Church of England and, I believe, behaved admirably at the font. No undignified gurglings and screamings. I was carried to the church, damped, and carried back home, preserving throughout an attitude of serene resignation.

Two years later, laced and beribboned, I was conveyed to church again, and was unimpressed by everything except the music to which I danced immediately in the aisle before anyone could stop me, and, upon being hoisted back into the pew, fell into such an ungovernable rage that I had to be taken home.

There are many other small incidents of my infancy, some based on hearsay, and some that I actually recall, but I will try to employ a selective economy in setting them down, for it is a tricky business tracing the development of a character along the avenues of reminiscence. Too much detailed accuracy makes dull reading. I don't believe that my own childhood, until I went on the stage at the age of ten, was very different from that of any other little boy of the middle-classes, except perhaps that certain embryonic talents may have made me more precocious than the average, and more difficult to manage. Several characteristics which have been commented upon in later years evinced themselves early. I was self-assured from the first, and intolerant of

[3]

undue piety. I was also uncompromising in my attitude towards people I disliked, attempting to strike them in the face, or, failing this, going off into screaming fits which frequently lasted long enough for the doctor to be sent for, but invariably gave place to chubby cluckings and smiles by the time he arrived.

I cherished a woolly monkey called 'Doris' for many years. She shared my bed until I was five, despite the fact that time and friction had denuded her of her fur, her tail, and one eye. I was also excessively fond of fish.

My mother came from what is known as 'Good Family', which means that she had been brought up in the tradition of being a gentlewoman, a difficult tradition to uphold with very little money in a small suburb, and liable to degenerate into refined gentility unless carefully watched.

The family name was Veitch, and there is a genealogical tree and a crest and engravings of the house in Scotland which my mother and her sisters never saw as it passed into alien hands before they were born. My grandfather was a captain in the Navy, and the photographs we have of him show a handsome head with curly hair, wide eyes, and side-whiskers. He was, I believe, rather short, which doesn't show in the photographs, as in all of them he is sitting down. He painted a lot in his spare time, mostly water colours, some of them very large indeed. He was good at mountains and clouds and ships, and reflections in the sea, but consciously bad at figures, so he frequently cut these out from coloured prints, and stuck them, singly and in groups, on to his blue mountains, to give the landscapes 'life.'

He died in Madeira, comparatively young, and his wife and children came home to England where my mother was born soon afterwards. There were, in addition to Mother, three girls and two boys, and an extra relation called Barbara or 'Borby' who had fallen out of a port-hole on her head at the age of two, and was consequently a little peculiar. In course of time both the brothers died, and two of the sisters married, one well, the other not so well, and in the year 1883 my grandmother, Aunt Borby, Aunt Vida, and my mother, came to Teddington, still quite a small village on the banks of the Thames, where they lived gently and, I think, a trifle sadly, making over last year's dresses and keeping up appearances.

The social activities of Teddington swirled around St. Alban's Church. It was an imposing building rearing high from the ground, secure in the possession of a copper roof which had turned bright green, and a militant vicar, the Rev. Mr. Boyd, who was given to furious outbursts from the pulpit, in course of which his eyes flashed fire and his fingers pointed accusingly at old ladies in the congregation. He calmed down in after years and became vicar of St. Paul's, Knightsbridge. Apart from him and the copper roof, the church's greatest asset was the Coward family which was enormous, active, and fiercely musical. My Uncle Jim played the organ, while my father, together with my Uncles Randolph, Walter, Percy and Gordon, and my Aunts Hilda, Myrrha, Ida and Nellie, graced the choir. Aunt Hilda, indeed, achieved such distinction as a 'coloratura' that she ultimately became known as 'The Twickenham Nightingale.'

It was during choir practice that my mother (also musical) met my father. He courted her for a long time through many services. I like to think of him peeping through his fingers at her during the Litany, and winking fearfully at her under cover of Mr. Boyd's vitriolic sermons. They appeared together also in various discreet theatricals, notably a performance of *The Gondoliers* at the Town Hall, in which all the Cowards played principal parts, and Mother demurely tra-la-la'd in the chorus.

When they were married they continued to live at Teddington. Father was very spruce. He always wore a blue cornflower in his buttonhole, and was justly proud of having a cold bath every morning, winter and summer. He went every day to London where he worked for Metzler's, the music publishers. A boy was born and christened Russell, but he died of meningitis at the age of six, a year and a half before I appeared on the morning of December 16th, 1899.

Teddington grew steadily. A new lock was built. There was a swifter train service to London, and electric trams began to screech along the High Street. There were lots more houses everywhere, with lots more people in them, and with this onset of urban progress the Coward glory began to fade. Nearly all the sisters married and dispersed, the brothers also; Uncle Percy, indeed, actually dispersed all the way to Toronto where he married a professional pianist, had a daughter by her, deserted them both in almost record time, and has never been heard of since, with the exception of a few vague rumours from Australia.

In 1905 we moved to a small villa in Sutton, Surrey. It had bow windows in the front, and a slim straight garden at the back. It also had coloured glass let into the front door. Father had left Metzler's and joined a piano firm which was just beginning. His position in the firm was at first not clearly defined, but on closer analysis proved to be that of a traveller. This necessitated his being away from home a good deal. Once he even went as far afield as Naples. I remember this distinctly, because post-cards of Vesuvius fluttered daily through the letter-box.

A little while after we arrived in Sutton, my brother Eric was born. Emma, our beloved 'General' who had been with us since before my birth, took me round to have tea with some friends, and when I got back I was led upstairs by Auntie Vida to see my 'new little brother.' He seemed to me to be bright red and singularly unattractive, but everybody else was delighted with him. Various things of minor importance happened to me in Sutton. I was run over by a bicycle and had concussion. The calf of my leg was practically torn off by a bull terrier, and I was brave when it was cauterised.

When I was six I was sent to a day school which was kept by a Miss Willington who wore blouses with puffed sleeves, plaid skirts, and her hair done over a pad. I didn't care for her. On one occasion when she had been irritating me over some little question of English grammar I bit her arm right through to the bone, an action which I have never for an instant regretted.

I made my first public appearance at a prize-giving concert at the end of the term. I was dressed in a white sailor suit and sang, 'Coo' from *The Country Girl,* followed by a piping little song

[6]

about the spring for which I accompanied myself on the piano. This feat brought down the house, and I had to repeat it. I remember leaning over to Mother and Father in the front row and hissing exultantly: 'I've got to sing again.' The evening ended in tears, however, because I was not given a prize. Mother tried vainly to explain to me that the prizes were for hard work during the term and not for vocal prowess, but I refused to be comforted, and was led away weeping.

Mother had an old school friend who came to stay with us sometimes. Her name was Gwen Kelly, and she was a darling. She had large mournful Irish eyes, and a white tailor-made coat and skirt, and she sang and played exquisitely. Her voice was a husky contralto with a brogue in it, and it is to her that I owe the first real enthusiasm I ever had for music. She is dead now, after devoting her life to genteel poverty and an invalid mother, but she was the first artist I knew and I shall never forget her.

We went to the seaside every summer for a fortnight. Broadstairs or Brighton or Bognor. It was at Bognor that I met Uncle George's Concert Party. I shall always remember Uncle George and his 'Merrie Men' with tenderness. They held for me a romantic attraction in their straw hats, coloured blazers, and grubby white flannel trousers. They had a small wooden stage on the sands on which they performed every afternoon and evening. Uncle George himself was the comedian and Uncle Bob, I think, was the serious vocalist. I forget the names of the others excepting Uncle Jack, who was very jaunty and sang 'Put a little bit away for a rainy day', swaggering up and down the stage and jingling coins in his trouser pocket.

Uncle George gave a song-and-dance competition every week for the 'Kiddies' for which I entered my name. I don't think Mother was keen on the idea, but she gave in when she saw how eager I was. On the evening of the competition I put on my sailor suit and waited in a sort of pen with several other aspirants, noting with satisfaction that those who appeared before me were inept and clumsy. When my turn came I sang, 'Come Along with Me to the Zoo, Dear' and 'Liza Ann' from *The Orchid*. I also danced violently. The applause was highly gratifying, and even Mother forgot her distaste of Uncle George's vulgarity somewhat and permitted herself to bridle. At the end of the performance Uncle George made a speech and presented me with the first prize, a large box of chocolates, which when opened in our lodgings proved to be three parts shavings.

From the age of five onwards Mother always took me to a theatre on my birthday. We went up to London in the morning and waited in the pit queue. I saw *The Dairymaids* and *The Blue Moon,* and a Spectacle at the London Hippodrome with a dam bursting and tons of water pouring into the arena. We also went to the pantomime at Croydon which I enjoyed ecstatically from the first moment when the orchestra tuned up and the advertisement-covered safety curtain rose, disclosing the faded old red tabs lit with an orange glow from the footlights, to the very end of the Harlequinade, when crackers were thrown by the clown and pantaloon to those fortunate enough to be in the expensive seats.

One Christmas I was given a toy theatre complete with two sets of scenery. One scene was a thick wood with a cottage in the distance, and the other was the interior of the cottage with a lot of painted beams. I used to augment this meagre décor with penny pantomime sheets which in those days were obtainable at any newspaper shop. There was *Cinderella, The Forty Thieves,* and a lurid melodrama called *Black-Eyed Susan,* and many others as well. There were generally three scenes to each sheet with all the characters brilliantly coloured and marked for each act. These had to be cut out with scissors and mounted on cardboard. I remember 'Fatima Act III' of the *Bluebeard* sheet was one of my favourites. She was a bulbous girl with a turban. I was also very partial to 'Dandini Act I' in the *Cinderella* set. Later on I had a bigger theatre, and Father painted me some excellent scenery, and I used dolls on wires instead of the pasteboard figures, but in my heart I liked the pantomime sheets best.

When I was seven I spent the summer with my Aunt Laura in

MYSELF
aged
TWO YEARS

Aged
ABOUT FIVE YEARS

Cornwall. She was kind, pretty and vain, and I was very fond of her. Her garden was lovely, and there was a large lake, very deep, with an island in the middle and jungle all around with small hidden waterfalls and secret paths. There was a swing, too, and a small blue punt which sank immediately if touched.

In 1908 we moved to Number 70, Prince of Wales Mansions, Battersea Park. It was a top flat with a little balcony looking out over the park to where the iron framework of Albert Bridge and Chelsea Bridge rose in the distance above the trees. I made a few friends in the adjacent flats and together we harassed the park-keepers, rang bells and ran away, and roller-skated up and down the pavements. Sometimes in the summer we skated all the way to St. George's Baths in Buckingham Palace Road and back again, with our wet bathing dresses flapping round our necks.

At this period money worries were oppressing my parents considerably. Father's income from Payne's pianos was small, and Eric and I were both growing fast and had to be clothed and fed. Mother, realising that something had to be done in order to pay off the swiftly mounting debts, decided to take in paying guests. And so a Mr. Baker and a Mr. Denston came to live with us, and everybody dressed for dinner for the first time for years. This was really quite a jolly period. Emma was still with us and she was a good cook. Gwen Kelly often came to dinner and played the piano afterwards. Father was gay and sang all his old songs with Mother playing his accompaniments. She would take off her rings and place them on the side of the piano and then embark with a flourish upon the introductory chords of 'Mary Adeane', or 'She and I Together', while I sat in an Eton collar on the sofa watching for her little grimace when she struck a wrong note, and listening to Mr. Baker whispering flirtatiously to Gwen Kelly in the corner.

Father had a light tenor voice of great sweetness, and he frequently shut his eyes tightly for the top notes, reliving, I am sure, in those moments, not only the past glories of Teddington drawing-rooms, but the more austere occasions when he, together with

Uncle Percy, Uncle Randolph, and Uncle Walter, had awakened the sophisticated echoes of the Caxton Hall, Westminster:

> *'So dainty fair, so gentle wise,*
> *Young love peeped forth from heaven blue eyes*
> *The lark poured rapture from the skies*
> *As we went through the heather.'*

(2)

A short while after we had settled in Battersea Park a great agitation was started as to whether or not I was to join the Chapel Royal choir. Uncle Walter, then an eminent member of it, was approached, also Dr. Alcock the organist. It was agreed that I should go to the Chapel Royal school to begin with until I was old enough to have my voice tried for the choir itself. The school was in Clapham, and was run by a Mr. Claude Selfe. It was small, consisting only of the twelve Chapel Royal boys, and seven or eight outside pupils of which I was one. Mr. Selfe was kind, sometimes jocular, and nearly always noisy. He had a slight paunch and the most tremendous calves which looked as though they were about to burst exuberantly through his trousers. Manliness was his strong suit, and he did everything in his power to foster this admirable quality in us. Boyishness was all right up to a certain age, but after that manliness was the thing. He wore a black gown and a mortar-board, and when he became in the least enthusiastic or excited over anything, bubbles of foam sprang from his lips like ping-pong balls.

I travelled to school daily by tram, or, rather, two trams, as I had to change half-way. The second one landed me at the Plough, Clapham, and from there I walked, in anguish in the mornings, and on wings of song in the afternoons when I was on my way home, loitering on autumn days to collect 'conkers', and occasionally ringing a few bells just to celebrate the joyful hours of freedom separating me from the next morning. There was a second-hand book-shop on the way where I could buy 'back numbers' of the *Strand Magazine* for a penny each, and I hoarded my pocket money until I could buy a whole year's worth in order to read the E. Nesbit story right through without having to wait for the next instalment. I read 'The Phœnix and the Carpet', and 'Five Children and It', also 'The Magic City', but there were a few numbers missing from that year, so I stole a coral necklace from a visiting friend of Mother's, pawned it for five shillings, and bought the complete book at the Army and Navy Stores. It cost four-and-six, so that including the fare (penny half return, Battersea Park to Victoria) I was fivepence to the good. In later years I told E. Nesbit of this little incident and I regret to say that she was delighted.

Three days a week at the Chapel Royal school the choir-boys were absent, either in the mornings or afternoons for choir practice. These days were blissfully quiet, the class-room seemed a pleasant place relaxed in a peaceful emptiness. When I arrived in the morning and saw that those horrible little mortar-boards were not on the pegs in the lobby I knew at once that lessons would be easier, that Mr. Selfe would be in an amiable mood, and that the quarter of an hour interval in the middle of the morning would be an interlude of rest rather than a strained evasion of games I didn't want to play.

On the days when the choir-boys were all present the entire atmosphere seemed charged with gloom and foreboding. They were nasty little brutes, as far as I can remember, and used to bully me mildly, putting ink pellets down my collar and forcing my head down the w.c. pan. Once during one of these boyish pranks I pretended to faint, having kicked one of them in the fork, an unmanly performance which frightened everyone very much indeed.

Eventually the day came when my voice was to be tried, a lot of assiduous practice having taken place beforehand with Mother at the piano and me hooting the praises of the Lord at her side.

I was dressed in my Eton suit with a slightly larger collar than usual in case of unforeseen throat expansion, and, with my hair suitably plastered, I set off clutching a roll of music and Mother's hand.

Dr. Alcock was distant and extremely superior. Perhaps his position as Chapel Royal organist, which automatically brought him into contact with the Royal Family as well as the Almighty, faintly upset his balance as a human being. However, undaunted by his forbidding expression, I sang Gounod's 'There Is a Green Hill Far Away' at him from beginning to end. My voice was very good and I sang it well, although perhaps a shade too dramatically. I remember giving way to a certain abandon on the line 'There was no other goo-oo-oo-ood enough to pay the price of sin', and, later, lashing myself into a frenzy over the far too often repeated 'Arnd terust in His redeeming blood.' I think, perhaps, it was this that settled my hash with Dr. Alcock, for we were ushered out rapidly with the parting words that not only was I far too young, but that there was no vacancy anyhow. Mother was bitterly disappointed, and I felt miserable at having failed, also offended that my assured talent should not have been immediately recognised, but deep down inside me I was conscious of a secret relief, a certain lifting of the heart when I reflected that my near future was not, after all, to be spent singing sacred music in company with those unpleasant choir-boys. Mother simmered with rage against Dr. Alcock and the whole Chapel Royal for weeks, ultimately arriving at the more comforting viewpoint that my not being accepted was a great stroke of good fortune as Dr. Alcock was silly and obviously didn't know a good voice when he heard one, and that the whole choir looked extremely common, including Uncle Walter.

(3)

Shortly after my failure for the Chapel Royal, our paying guests departed, and Mother made another of her sudden decisions. This time it was to let the flat for six months and take a small cottage in the country. I think that during all those years in

London and the suburbs she had been secretly yearning for some quieter place in which to be poor. Small poverty is a greater strain in a town than in a village, and Mother was country bred, and weary of whining Cockney tradesmen and crowded buses and genteel makeshifts. She often talked wistfully of Chobham where she had lived as a girl; where there had been a garden to the house, a real garden, not a ruled-off passage sown with a few nasturtiums. An advertisement was put in the paper and we waited anxiously for results. Fate was kindly prompt, and in a very few days a Mrs. Davis arrived without warning while we were having tea. She was gay and erratic and untidy, with a large green hat and a feather boa. She immediately joined us at tea, and intercepted Mother who was trying to nip into the kitchen in order to change the jam-jar for a more impressive glass dish.

After tea we went into the drawing-room which smelt rather frowsy as it hadn't been used for a long time, and Mrs. Davis sang 'Mifanwy' and 'My Dear Soul' in a piercing soprano, and then, encouraged, I think, by our obvious musical appreciation, said that she would like to take the flat on the dot providing that she could move in within three days. Mother assumed a dubious expression which wouldn't have deceived a kitten, and shook her head thoughtfully, trying hard to conceal the glint of excitement in her eyes and endeavouring not to appear too eager. I personally thought that she had gone raving mad. However, it was all fixed up satisfactorily, and we spent the next three days in a state of rapture, spring-cleaning, and having our meals off one end of the kitchen table.

We went first to stay with Grandmother, Auntie Borby, and Auntie Vida in rooms at Southsea, and Eric and I were left there while Mother and Father scoured Hampshire for a cottage. There were many enchanting things to do in Southsea. Trips backwards and forwards across Portsmouth Harbour in ferry-boats, sometimes expeditions as far as Ryde in bigger steamers, concerts on the Clarence Pier, and occasionally an actual play on the South Parade Pier. It was early April, and windy, and I frequently sat for hours watching the waves sliding up the slanting stone breakwaters just below the castle. I can remember, too, trudging home at dusk across the common after a long walk, with a flick of rain in the wind, and all the lights coming up along the parade. There is for me a certain romantic desolation about Southsea and I shall always be attached to it. Whenever I revisit it now it feels familiar and friendly. The South Parade Pier and the Clarence Pier may have shrunk a trifle, the Isle of Wight may seem a little less magical and not so far away, but the forts are still there patterned like chess-boards in the sea, and the castle, and Handleys, and the Cosham trams creaking round the corners; and there are still grey warships lying out at Spithead.

About this time I took a fancy for the most tremendously hearty schoolboy literature. I read avidly week by week *Chums, The Boy's Own Paper, The Magnet,* and *The Gem,* and loved particularly these last two. *The Gem* appeared on Thursday or Friday, and was devoted to the light-hearted adventures of Tom Merry and Co. *The Magnet* came out on Tuesdays, and dealt with the very similar adventures of Harry Wharton and Co. As far as I can remember, the dialogue of the two papers was almost identical, consisting largely of the words 'Jape' and 'Wheeze', and in moments of hilarity and pain respectively: 'Ha Ha Ha!' and 'Yow Yow Yow!' There was a fat boy in each. In *The Magnet* it was Billy Bunter, who, in addition to being very greedy and providing great opportunities for jam-tart fun ('Ha Ha Ha!—He He He!— Yow Yow Yow!'), was a ventriloquist of extraordinary ability, and could make sausages cry out when stabbed with a fork. They were awfully manly decent fellows, Harry Wharton and Co., and no suggestion of sex, even in its lighter forms, ever sullied their conversation. Considering their ages, their healthy-mindedness was almost frightening. I was delighted to find in a newspaper shop the other day that *The Magnet* was unchanged, excepting its cover, which used to be bright orange and is now white. I read a little of it with tender emotion. There they all were, Harry Wharton, Frank Nugent, and Billy Bunter, still Ha-Ha-Ha-ing and He-He-He-ing and still, after twenty-four years, hovering merrily on the verge of puberty.

Mother and Father finally discovered a minute cottage at a place called Meon in Hampshire, not far from the village of Tichfield. It had a thatch, and a lavatory at the end of the garden, the door of which always had to be kept shut because the goat liked to use it as well as the family. We lived there for six months completely happily. There was very little money, and at times I believe there wasn't quite enough food, but we were in the country, and so it didn't matter so much.

The sea, or rather the Solent, was only a mile away, and during Cowes Regatta Week we could see all the excitements going on just across the water. It was the year the German Emperor came and our Fleet saluted his yacht. For several nights all the warships were illuminated, and we had a moonlight picnic on the edge of the low sandy cliff, and let off some fireworks of our own that Father had bought in Fareham.

I learned a lot about the country during those six months. We went nutting and blackberrying and haymaking, and Mother and I were nearly caught stealing our landlord's plums after dark, and had to lie giggling in a ditch for half an hour.

Some little girls lived near by, and I forced them to act a tragedy that I had written, but they were very silly and during the performance forgot their lines and sniggered, so I hit the eldest one on the head with a wooden spade, the whole affair thus ending in tears and a furious quarrel between the mothers involved.

Mrs. Davis wished to keep our flat on in London for longer than she had originally intended, and at the end of our lease of the cottage we went back to Southsea for six weeks. A little while after Christmas Mother and Father became suddenly conscience-stricken over my lack of education, and so it was arranged for me to return to London a week before them in order to be in time for the first moment of the term. I was to stay with my Uncle Ran and Aunt Amy in St. George's Square, and I travelled up to Victoria bleak in spirit at the prospect, not only of staying in a strange house, but of getting up early in the morning and going back to school. Mr. Selfe loomed in my imagination like a black bat, the voluminous wings of his gown waiting to envelop me in the manly discipline from which I had been free for so long, and the day that I was to rejoin Mother in the flat seemed too far away in the future to be the least comfort.

That week more than came up to expectations; it was miserable beyond belief, although on looking back I am unable to discover exactly why I should have been so wretched. My aunt and uncle were kind, if somewhat remote in their attitude; perhaps if they had fussed over me a little at first and been less distantly correct in their manner towards me, or perhaps if I had not been so spoiled at home, I might have been happier there. As it was, I was conscious for the first time of being a very small boy indeed, forlorn, and badly mother-sick. There was a thick yellow fog throughout the whole week and school work was done with the gas on. The shadows of my snuffling classmates flickered over the walls, and the general smell of feet and linoleum smothered me. Mr. Selfe was irascible and more frothy than ever, and one day caned me lightly on the hand which shocked and frightened me immeasurably. I remember crying all the way home in the tram to Victoria, and groping my way through the fog to St. George's Square, where I managed to get to my bedroom at the top of the house without being seen by anyone but the housemaid who let me in. Once there I gave way to screaming hysterics. I was obsessed with the idea that Mother was going to have some sort of accident and die without my ever seeing her again. The dramatic scenes I visualised were terrifying: first the fatal telegram arriving at the house, and my aunt and uncle calling me into the drawing-room on the first floor to break the news, then a tear-sodden journey in the train and Auntie Vida meeting me at Fratton Junction, very small and morose, in black. Then, as a fitting climax, I imagined the front bedroom enshrouded in funereal twilight with the blinds down and Mother lying still and dead under a sheet like a waxwork. My Aunt Amy appeared presently and admonished me kindly; she must have been startled, poor woman, at the sight of such abandoned despair. However, there was in her manner a certain dry efficiency that eventually suffocated my tears and reduced me to stillness, and a little later I dined downstairs in a state of splendid calm, and talked tremulously to the various nurses from the Westminster Hospital, several of whom were always present at meal times. My aunt was then, and is still, a brisk dealer in nurses who, not being spoiled hysterical little boys, derive much comfort and warmth from that high clean house.

During the year 1909 my singing voice developed strongly. It was really a good voice, more full-blooded than the usual boyish treble. I occasionally sang anthems in churches but I hated doing this because the lack of applause depressed me. It irritated me when I had soared magnificently through 'God Is a Spirit' or 'Oh for the Wings of a Dove' to see the entire congregation scuffle on to their knees murmuring gloomy 'Amens' instead of clapping loudly and shouting 'Bravo.' Concerts were much more satisfactory, and I particularly enjoyed the annual church garden party at Teddington. It was a sort of fête and jumble sale, and there were stalls and amusements and a band. It was generally opened by someone suitably aristocratic, and my Aunt Myrrha ran the concerts, of which there were usually three or four in course of the afternoon. This was when I shone. I always sang a serious ballad to begin with, my principal successes being 'Through the Forest' and 'Cherry Blossom Time.' The latter invariably was a great favourite, possibly owing to the redundance of its 'Hey Nonnys' and 'Ho Nonnys' and its winsomely pastoral sentiments. After this, I returned, smiling to the applause, and rendered a light musical-comedy number with dance. It must have been surprising and, I should have thought, nauseating to see a little boy of nine in a white sailor suit flitting about a small wooden stage, employing, with instinctive accuracy, the gestures and tricks of a professional soubrette, but they seemed to love it and encored me vociferously. Perhaps my lack of self-consciousness and my youth mitigated a little the horror of the situation, but I am certain that could my adult self have been present in that stuffy tent, he would have crept out, at the first coy gurgle, and been mercifully sick outside. I do not mean that I wasn't good. I was certainly good, far and away too good. My assurance was nothing short of petrifying, and although I look back upon myself in that saucy sailor suit with a shudder of embarrassment, there is envy in my heart as well.

The reader will probably gather from the above description that I was a brazen, odious little prodigy, over-pleased with myself and precocious to a degree; perhaps I was, but I was learning a lot, even from those kindly old ladies in their garden-party finery; after all, I act to them still at matinées and I have a sad suspicion that I don't give them half as much pleasure now as I did then.

I was taken to *The King of Cadonia* on my ninth birthday, and fell in love with Gracie Leigh, and Mother bought me the *Play Pictorial,* and I cut out all the photographs and stuck them on my bedroom wall, where they remained until they turned yellow and curly at the edges and were replaced by new ones.

A little while after this, Mother, who was pleased but not surprised by my successes in public, decided that my natural gift for dancing could be improved by a few lessons. So far I had tripped and flitted with much grace but little technique, often, owing to an inadequate knowledge of balance, losing control in my turns, and on one unfortunate occasion actually finishing with my back to the audience on the final chord. The question of my going on the stage had been discussed several times. My talents and ambitions seemed obviously to lead towards it, but we were ignorant of the initial steps to take. Also, I was only nine years old, and, excepting a casual acquaintance with 'Mensa. A Table' in the first declension only, and a vivid mental picture of Flamborough Head, I was absolutely uneducated. The idea was therefore temporarily dismissed and lay fermenting in our minds waiting to jump out again the first moment a suitable opportunity offered itself. Meanwhile, the dancing lessons were a move in the right direction. It was no use concentrating on my voice, for that, alas, owing to certain processes in adolescence, would inevitably degenerate into humiliating croakings, and there was no physiological guarantee that when the raucous period passed, a silvery tenor would emerge in compensation for the lost soprano.

We interviewed a Miss Janet Thomas who ran a dancing

academy in Hanover Square. Her manner was professionally brusque but sympathetic, and she seemed to take a fancy to me and agreed to give me a course of twelve lessons at a minimum fee. So for the next six weeks I dispensed with school on Tuesday and Friday afternoons, and journeyed, first in the train from Battersea Park to Victoria, and then in a bus to the corner of Conduit Street.

It says a lot for Mother's self-control that she could sit at home, tortured by visions of street accidents, and allow me to gallivant about the town by myself at such a tender age; but she had fostered in me a spirit of independence, realising with remarkable foresight, considering how much she loved me, the valuable experience I should gain from learning to grapple early and alone with small adventures. This was brave wisdom and I profited by it. Long before I was twelve years old I was capable of buying tickets and counting change, ordering buns and glasses of milk in tea-shops, and battling in and out of trams and buses and trains. I could have found my way anywhere about London with ease, and, above all, I acquired the inestimable habit of being completely happy alone. I also found that conversation with casual strangers was stimulating to the imagination. I shocked many kindly interfering old ladies with picturesque descriptions of my appalling life at home, making them cluck and shudder with horror at the drunken brutality of my father, and the squalid misery of our tenement room filled with ill-nourished brothers and sisters, many of them suffering from lingering diseases. One old body, I believe, actually went to the police about me. At any rate, she said she was going, but as I had given her a false name and address, nothing ever came of it. It was also a pleasant game to be discovered sobbing wretchedly in the corners of railway carriages or buses in the hope that someone would take pity on me and perhaps give me tea at Fuller's. This was only rarely successful, the only two responses I can recall both being clergymen. One talked to me for a long time and told me to trust in God and everything would come right, and the other pinched my knee and gave me sixpence. Of the two, I preferred the latter.

I loved my dancing lessons with Miss Thomas. She started me

off herself and then passed me on to her assistant, Miss Alice Hall, who put me through the whole routine of ballet dancing, including even point work for which I wore block-toed shoes. The room was long and large and smelt dimly of Ronuk. There were enormous mirrors all along one wall, and I had a fascinating view of my own front and Miss Hall's behind, which, while she was showing me the fleeter steps, jumped up and down merrily inside her black satin bloomers. There was another assistant, too, named Enid, who had slightly projecting teeth and was a dear. When Miss Thomas wasn't there Miss Hall and Enid used to ask me to stay to tea which was brewed on a spirit lamp in a little curtained-off recess in the corner of the studio. This treat was only possible when I was the last pupil, and I was often bitterly disappointed when, just towards the end of my time, some gangling débutante would appear for her deportment lesson.

Frequently on my homeward journey I walked all the way from Hanover Square to Victoria, through Green Park, thereby saving a penny to buy fudge at a little shop in the Buckingham Palace Road. It was a stern principle with me never to buy the fudge at any other shop before I reached Victoria, in case I broke my leg and hadn't the penny for the bus fare.

(4)

One day, just before I had come to the end of my dancing course, a little advertisement appeared in the *Daily Mirror*. Mother read it aloud to me while I was having breakfast. It stated that a talented boy of attractive appearance was required by a Miss Lila Field to appear in her production of an all-children fairy play: *The Goldfish*. This seemed to dispose of all argument. I was a talented boy, God knows, and, when washed and smarmed down a bit, passably attractive. There appeared to be no earthly reason why Miss Lila Field shouldn't jump at me, and we both believed that she would be a fool indeed to miss such a magnificent opportunity.

I departed for school that morning late, leaving Mother to compose a not too effusive answer to the advertisement. In due course a letter arrived from Lila Field making an appointment for us to go and see her.

On the day specified we left the house in a flurry of grandeur, Mother very impressive in grey satin with a feather boa, and me burning bright in a new Norfolk suit with an Eton collar. Miss Field received us in a small bare room in George Street, Baker Street. She was smart and attractive, with a charming voice, and her large brown eyes smiled kindly at us over highly-rouged cheeks and a beauty spot. My heart sank when I noticed that there was no piano, but after a little polite conversation we surmounted that difficulty and I sang 'Liza Ann' unaccompanied, and Mother la-la'd for the dance. Miss Field was delighted and said that she would engage me for the part of Prince Mussel and that the fee would be a guinea and a half a week, upon which Mother became sadly red and said that she was afraid we couldn't afford to pay that. Miss Field laughed and said that the guinea and a half a week was what I would receive, and that she'd let us know soon when rehearsals started. Mother and I floated down the narrow staircase and out into the street. The moment was supreme, and we could scarcely breathe for excitement. We went straight to Selfridge's and celebrated our triumph with ice-cream sodas over which we calculated how much a year I should be earning at a guinea and a half a week. Father was impressed with our news when we reached home and we sat up very late inaccurately visualising my future. A letter was sent to Mr. Selfe announcing that my school attendance would be even more convulsive than it had been hitherto, as I was now a professional actor.

The rehearsals for *The Goldfish* took place about twice a week for many months; there seemed to be a hitch over the actual production and many mothers became impatient and snatched their children away, which naturally made holes in the cast and necessitated further rehearsals of the newcomers.

Ultimately a definite production date was announced and rehearsals became less spasmodic, the 'all-children' cast sang and danced, and tried on elaborate costumes at Debenham and Freebody's in a state of wild excitement. Even the most hardened and cynical of the mothers were moved to enthusiasm.

The Goldfish was a fairy play in three acts, written by Miss Field herself. I believe it had originally been produced the previous year at The Playhouse for special matinées, but the production in which I appeared was entirely reorganised.

I can only vaguely remember the plot. The first act was a children's garden party with a spirited opening chorus 'School School, Good-bye to School', which I led in company with a pretty fair girl, Little June Tripp (later June and, later still, June Inverclyde). After this came some gay provocative dialogue, only one line of which I can recall: 'Crumbs! How exciting.'

In the second act for some reason or other all the children from the first act had turned into fish. June was Princess Sole, Burford Hampden, King Starfish, and Alfred Willmore, King Goldfish. I, as Prince Mussel, did not appear until the third act. There were many other fish characters, and a large girl with big knees and a rich contralto voice who played The Spirit of the Shells. She sang a song at the beginning of the second act which always convulsed me; there was something about her strangely adult figure swathed in green tulle weaving up and down the stage, and that strong resonant voice bursting out of her, that was ridiculously at variance with the piping refinement of the rest of the cast. She also mouthed her words in a most peculiar manner.

> *'A so-unbeam fel-ler intew the sea*
> *Arnd waandered far arnd waide*
> *Oonteel eet found ar leetle shell*
> *Whoere eet coould safely haide.'*

As Prince Mussel, King Starfish's court jester, I had a good song in the last act. It was sure-fire sentiment as I was supposed to be torn between my duties as a jester and my unrequited love for the queen. I sang it with tremendous passion, and at the end tore off a top B flat with a Pagliacci sob in it. I was invariably encored, sometimes twice.

The play, having opened at the Little Theatre, ran a week of matinées, and during the following six months was revived twice, first at the Crystal Palace for two performances, and later at the Court Theatre for a week, matinées and evenings, when it was condensed into two acts and was part of a triple bill, the other two items of which were performed by adults.

During the over-long intervals between my public appearances I still attended school, but with even less enthusiasm than before. I developed the adventurous habit of playing truant which was made especially easy for me by the frequently genuine excuse of rehearsals. I used to leave the flat in the morning with a thrilling sensation of wickedness, and take quite a different tram and spend the whole day in Waterloo Station or Clapham Junction watching the trains. Once I bought a pennyworth of crêpe hair at a chemist's and walked up and down the embankment with a red beard.

(5)

After the Court Theatre engagement *The Goldfish* finally petered out, and as I had only received one week's salary I believe some acrimonious letters passed between Mother and Miss Field. My next appearance was in a less important role in a more professional atmosphere. I was sent for by Bellew and Stock, Theatrical Agents, and they (Mr. Bellew) led me to E. M. Tarver, Charles Hawtrey's stage manager at the Prince of Wales's Theatre, who engaged me at two pounds a week (ten per cent commission to Bellew and Stock) to play a page boy in the last act of a comedy called *The Great Name*. It was only three days before production so my first rehearsal was a dress rehearsal, which should by rights have frightened me considerably although I only had one line, but I was buoyed up by some painstaking rehearsals at home with Mother. My line was to be addressed to Charles Hawtrey himself, playing the piano in the artists' room at Queen's

Hall. I had to enter boldly in my buttoned suit and say: 'Stop that noise at once, please. In there they're playing *The Meistersingers*. Making such a horrible noise. We're used to good music here.' Mother and I did that scene over and over again in the dining-room of the flat with the table pushed against the wall. Mother, running the whole gamut of emotions, instructing me. 'STOP that noise at once, please' was to be said with tremendous force, then with a barely perceptible note of awe creeping into the voice 'in there (big gesture to the left) they're playing *The Meistersingers*' (pause for effect). Then (with biting contempt), 'Making such a horrible row,' then (swelling with pride), 'we're used to good music here!' (rising inflection on the word 'good'). Having finally mastered this vocally to Mother's satisfaction we achieved an entrance and exit that would have been a lesson in deportment to a Ziegfeld show girl, and thus primed I bounced on to my first meeting with Charles Hawtrey. I have seldom seen a human being so astounded. He swung round on the piano stool with a glaze of horror in his eyes, while the members of the company seated in the stalls roared with laughter. After I had made my dramatic exit there was a slight pause, and I heard Mr. Hawtrey say to the stage manager in a weary voice: 'Tarver, never let me see that boy again.'

He relented later, and I was re-rehearsed by Mr. Tarver, and ultimately gabbled the line hurriedly in Cockney, employing the minimum of gesture.

Charles Hawtrey smelt strongly of Eau-de-Cologne, was infinitely kind to me, and I worshipped him. On the strength of my association with him I bought an autograph book with glacé sweet-peas on the cover which he signed continually. I followed him about like a sheep, seizing every opportunity that offered for polite conversation. Whenever there was a vacant chair near him at the side of the stage I grabbed it and chattered at him shrilly. Once I distracted him so that he missed an entrance in the first act, after which I was not allowed on the stage at all until there was a legitimate excuse for me to be there. If I shut my eyes now his image is clear to me. I can smell the Eau-de-Cologne, see the

CORNWALL
1907

In THE GREAT NAME with LYDIA BILBROOKE and CHARLES HAWTREY
Prince of Wales Theatre, 1911

twinkle in his eye and the stripes on his Paris shirt, and hear his quiet voice edged with exasperation saying: 'Go away, boy, for God's sake leave me alone.'

The bugbear of the child actor is the business of being licensed. The law insists that no child under fourteen may appear on the professional stage without the sanction of a Bow Street magistrate; consequently, before each production, a miserable morning is spent by the business manager, the mother, and the child, standing about tortured with anxiety in draughty passages, oppressed by an atmosphere of criminality, and surrounded by policemen. The magistrates vary. Some are easy-going and give the license without any fuss, others are obtuse and disapproving, seemingly obsessed with the idea that the child is being forced against its will to act in order to support idle and dissolute parents.

We nearly failed to get a license for me to appear in *The Great Name* because the magistrate, who had several feet in the grave and looked like a macaw, could not be persuaded that the whole thing was not a case of sweated child labour of the worst variety. After considerable pleading on the part of Mr. Fitzgerald (Hawtrey's business manager), he squawked a refusal, whereupon I burst into loud sobs, and Mother, outraged beyond endurance, sprang to her feet and delivered a vehement protest to the effect that if the license were not granted I should be so heartbroken that I should probably go into a decline and have to be sent to a sanatorium, and that, far from using my meagre two pounds a week to support the home, she would willingly pay double that amount to ensure my happiness and peace of mind. After this she sat down, very red in the face and with her hat slightly on one side. The whole court waited expectantly in dead silence for her to be led to prison; but the old magistrate seemed crushed and, without further argument, granted the license and we left the court tearful with relief, after a dignified bow to everybody present.

The Great Name was not a success, and ran only two months, but before it finished I was already rehearsing for Hawtrey's production of *Where the Rainbow Ends* at the Savoy. Again I was playing a page boy, but this time a much more important part, although only in the first act.

The whole company assembled on the stage for the reading of the play.

Parts were dealt out to everybody, and we sat following them while Mr. Hawtrey read. He read beautifully and it was an afternoon of enchantment, only slightly clouded for me by the fact that I wasn't playing Crispian, the leading part. For this, however, Master Philip Tonge had been engaged. I scrutinised him enviously along the front row of chairs (where I had placed myself with the principals). He was the great boy actor of London. His only serious rival was Master Bobbie Andrews, who had appeared with considerable success the year previously in *Where Children Rule* at the Garrick. Philip Tonge had a fresh red face, a large woolly overcoat, a 'Burglar Bill' cap with ear-flaps tied up on the top, and a formidable mother who regarded the other young juvenile males of the cast balefully, as though she expected them to rise up and fell Philip to the ground in a fury of jealousy. She proved on closer acquaintance to be kind, although domineering, and once during the run she had to be requested by the management not to monopolise our dressing-room basin for washing out her gloves, a proceeding which had become so tedious to the rest of us that we had complained.

Where the Rainbow Ends that first year was a glamorous entertainment. The leading lady was Miss Esmé Wynne, a podgy, brown-haired little girl with a bleating voice. Also in the cast was a strange fragile little thing named Mavis Yorke. She played Will-o'-the-Wisp and was exquisite; she flitted through the woods and glades of the production to Roger Quilter's gentle music, and there was in her a quality of magic. She was in no way a winsome prodigy, and utterly unlike all the other little actress children with their pert voices and black satin coats and ringlets. I often wonder what became of her, whether that tiny supple body ever became set in maturity, or whether she just snuffed out, to be remembered only as a Will-o'-the-Wisp in a children's play.

During that run several large parties were given for us, which generally took place at the Savoy. There were enormous silver trays with rows and rows of little chocolate éclairs, and crackers and paper caps and games, and our evening performances were frequently the worse for them.

The ballet mistress was Miss Italia Conti. She supplied then, as she does still, all sorts of children for all sorts of productions. They used to come shuffling into rehearsals in a great troupe, all those fairies and elves and frogs and caterpillars, gauntly escorted either by Miss Conti herself or her sister, Mrs. Murray, a dragon in astrakhan. It was a matter of constant amazement to me that she could so surely remember all their names, but she undoubtedly could and did. Mr. Hawtrey winced many a time when suddenly in the middle of the ballet Miss Conti's commanding voice came shrilly out of the gloom of the dress-circle: 'Dorothy, do your coupé again,' or 'Grace, how many times have I told you never to push against Phyllis in your pirouette?'

Miss Conti insidiously suggested to me one day at the beginning of rehearsals that, as my part was over after the first act, I might like to appear as a hyena and a frog in the later scenes as well. I was delighted with the idea, and rehearsed three times in a dingy basement room under the Bay Malton Hotel in Great Portland Street. Mother, having been dubious over the plan from the first, came with me to the third rehearsal and I never went any more. I was disappointed, but Mother soon convinced me that it was better to be content with my small part, which was at least among the principals, than to lower my prestige by crawling about on all fours in a hot hyena skin.

(6)

After *Where the Rainbow Ends* finished I was out of work for a while, and I spent a good deal of time, now being an established actor, in writing in to the various theatres for free seats. I had had some professional cards printed with Master Noel Coward in the middle, and Mr. Charles Hawtrey's company *Where the Rainbow*

Ends, Savoy Theatre in the left-hand corner. These were sent to different managements with a stamped addressed envelope inside and a pompous little note in the third person, usually beginning 'Master Noel Coward would be so very much obliged,' etc.

Usually they returned with callous regrets, but every now and then, as though to keep up my spirits, two pink dress-circle tickets would arrive with 'Complimentary' stamped across them. These were gala days. Mother used to frizz her hair and put on her evening dress. I put on my black suit and Eton collar, and off we'd go in the train and bus, always arriving far too early, long before the safety curtain had risen, but content with a box of chocolates and a programme. We used to have supper when we got home and discuss the play over it. Our greatest favourite of all was Gertie Millar. We had naturally never been able to get free seats for anything in which she was appearing, but we went in the gallery. My bedroom was plastered with photographs of her, for ever since the first time I had seen her in *The Quaker Girl* I had adored her; and in my memory she is clearly the most graceful and charming artist I have ever seen. Now that I know her well I can never look at her gay unchanged face without a little stab of the heart to think that never again will she float down the stage, chuckling lightly and expressing with her hands a joy of living which was her own special charm. I often waited outside the Adelphi stage door for hours to see her come out. She always smiled at me and said good night. Once she gave me a flower from a bouquet she was carrying which I pressed carefully in a bound volume of *Chums.*

A little while ago a party was given by Gladys and Leslie Henson. A good higgledy-piggledy theatrical party with a magnificent star cast of yesterday and to-day. Lily Elsie was there and Maurice Chevalier and Violet Loraine, and everybody balanced vol-au-vents on their knees, and drank whatever they wanted, and gossiped and sang songs. Gertie Millar (the Countess of Dudley) sat on the stairs in chinchilla while I was at the piano strumming a few excerpts from bygone musical comedies in which everybody joined. Suddenly as I played 'Tony from America' the other

With PHILIP TONGE in Where The Rainbow Ends
Savoy Theatre, 1911

MASTER NOEL COWARD
"Charles Hawtrey's Company,"
1912

sounds fell away, and from the semi-gloom of the stairs came 'He guessed I was all alone, so that's why he came along and found me', in that funny, un-vocal little voice, bridging the years and for a strange instant filling our hearts with a pleasurable melancholy. Many of us cried because it was a most touching moment, and theatrical people are notoriously facile of emotion, and frequently victimised by their own foolish sentimentality.

(7)

During the spring of 1912 I spent a lot of time going the round of the agencies, a proceeding with which every struggling actor is bitterly well acquainted. Blackmore's, Denton's, Bellew and Stock's, crowded waiting-rooms, with spangled principal boys on the walls, triumphant in their stardom, leering down at their seedy brothers and sisters in the profession; character actors, old lady parts, straight juveniles, singing soubrettes, standing about or sitting on the few shiny chairs, talking softly to each other in corners, not so much to impress, as to bolster up their tremulous faith in themselves. Every now and then a man comes in and calls a name. There is a flutter of excitement and some wizened over-made-up little woman rises to her feet, gives a defiant tug to the frayed tulle round her neck, and minces into the inner office in tight glacé shoes smelling of petrol. When she comes out again she nods brightly and goes down the stairs; if her nod is too bright everybody knows that she hasn't got the job, and hope flutters anew in those that are left.

I passed hours in those horrid waiting-rooms. Twice a week I devoted a whole day to doing the rounds. I had sixpence to spend on lunch which I took, not in an ordinary Lyons, but in the Corner House. Macaroni and tomato sauce fourpence, a roll a penny, and a penny for the waitress. Sometimes I was fortunate enough to find fourpence under the plate when I arrived at the table. This meant a chocolate éclair extra and twopence for the waitress.

One day I was actually sent for by Blackmore's Agency and engaged at two pounds ten a week to play in the prologue of a big dramatic spectacle called *War in the Air* which was to be produced at the Palladium.

The writer and producer of the show was a little grey man, I think American. He was verbose and enthusiastic and seemed convinced that the production was going to revolutionise practically everything. I played the infant Aviator in the prologue and flew a small model aeroplane, which I was supposed to have made with my own chubby hands, backwards and forwards across the stage. Unfortunately it nearly always rushed into the stalls and had to be retrieved from under old ladies' seats while I waited politely for it to be returned to me by the musical director.

The end of my scene was deeply moving. I undressed and said a prayer at my mother's knee in a white spotlight. 'Please God, bless Mummy and Daddy and Violet (my slightly Cockney playmate) and make me a great big aviator one day,' whereupon the lights faded and all hell broke loose back stage. I was whisked violently backwards into the property room, bed and all, and my gentle grey-haired mother skipped about like a two-year-old in order to avoid being knocked down by moving scenery. The rest of the entertainment was devoted to my adventures as a 'Great Big Aviator', culminating in a tremendous aerial battle in which I (grown-up) and Violet (also grown-up and even more Cockney) swung out into the auditorium in an aeroplane amid a lot of banging and red fire. This hair-raising effect was spoiled at the third performance by the aeroplane becoming hitched on to the front of the upper-circle where it remained for three hours. It was finally dislodged, and slid back on to the stage, after the audience had gone home. Violet, I believe, disembarked in a fainting condition. After this the effect was resolutely cut by the management.

I always got to the theatre and made up before the performance started so that I could watch from the side the variety artistes who occupied the first part of the programme. Nellie Wallace was on the bill, and Phil Ray, and Maidie Scott whom I loved; she always gave me tea and cake in her dressing-room at matinées.

(8)

It was some time during this year, 1912, that I was engaged by Miss Ruby Ginner for some special performances of a ballet she was producing at the Savoy Theatre. It was an artistic little morsel arranged to a selection of Chopin melodies and entitled *An Autumn Idyll,* and was planned as a curtain raiser to precede a two-act operetta *The Cicada.* Ruby Ginner herself was the Première Danseuse, and the *motif* of the ballet, as far as I can remember, was a day in the life of an Autumn Leaf (Miss Ginner) in conflict with the winter mists (members of Miss Ginner's Dancing School). As a mushroom I provided a few of the more lighthearted moments together with a little girl called Joan Carrol as a toadstool. I wore grey silk skin tights, a large grey silk hat like a gargantuan muffin, and a diaphanous frill round my middle to conceal any unæsthetic protuberances. My entrance consisted of a series of abandoned high kicks, slightly higher with the right leg than with the left, typifying the carefree *joie de vivre* of the average mushroom, until upon observing the toadstool (Joan Carrol in pink) my mood changed from gaiety to tenderness, and there ensued a refined *pas de deux* and exit to tepid applause. The really big moment of the ballet was undoubtedly Miss Ginner's valiant fight with the mists and ultimate death as the lights faded, although the effect of this was marred for me by the fact that she seemed so much larger and better developed than the mists that vanquished her.

My next engagement was with Charles Hawtrey again in a sketch *A Little Fowl Play* at the Coliseum. The magistrate refused to license me for the evening performances as the sketch didn't come on until just before eleven o'clock. I was heartbroken, and used to stand nightly in the prompt corner and listen to the assistant stage manager playing my part (one line with a slight stutter to give character: 'I've brought the ch-ch-ch-chicken, sir'). It was typical of Hawtrey that he paid me my full salary for the whole four weeks' run when he could perfectly easily have dispensed with me altogether. I saw and learned a lot during that engagement. The entire bill was changed every Monday. The stage manager, Mr. Crocker, was kind, and allowed me to stand at the side except on Monday afternoons, when he was too harassed to bear me bobbing about under his feet. I had a close-up view of George Robey, Beattie and Babs, Mme. Alicia Adelaide Needham and her choir, The Grotesques, and a Wild West show with property grass matting and cowboys and horses. During the last week Pauline Chase was on the bill with Holman Clarke in Barrie's *Pantaloon*. In this also was a small girl called Moya Nugent who played the little clown. She was by then an experienced Barrie actress as she had played Liza in *Peter Pan,* I think, for two consecutive seasons. We became great friends and have remained so ever since.

In between the matinée and evening performances the Coliseum stage had an even greater allure for me; with only a few working lights left on here and there, it appeared vaster and more mysterious, like an empty echoing cathedral smelling faintly of dust. Sometimes the safety curtain was not lowered, and I used to stand down on the edge of the footlights singing shrilly into the shadowy auditorium. I also danced in the silence. Occasionally a cleaner appeared with a broom and pail, or a stagehand walked across the stage, but they never paid any attention to me. An empty theatre is romantic, every actor knows the feeling of it. Complete silence emphasised rather than broken by the dim traffic noises outside, apparently hundreds of miles away; the muffled sound of a motor-horn and the thin reedy wail of a penny whistle being played to the gallery queue. As a rule there are a few exit lights left burning, casting blue shadows across the rows of empty seats. It seems incredible that within an hour or two this stillness will awake to garish red-and-gilt splendour, and be shattered by the sibilance of hundreds of voices, and the exciting discords and trills of the orchestra tuning up.

(9)

After *A Little Fowl Play* I was re-engaged for my original part in *Where the Rainbow Ends*. This time it was produced at the Garrick, with more or less the same cast. The run was uneventful. There were the same parties given at the Savoy, and the same kindly clergyman eager to take the younger members of the cast to tea at Lyons' Corner House. As a step in my own development this engagement was negligible except for one all-important evening when I walked with Philip Tonge all the way to his home in Baker Street, and he told me the facts of life. I was tremendously excited, not only by the facts themselves, which were confined principally to the procreation of species, but also because it was a unique experience to be able to talk to Philip alone, without the didactic presence of his mother. I can't think what she could have been doing that night, but there we were on our own, trudging up Regent Street, along Oxford Street and down Orchard Street, Philip in his Sherlock Holmes's cap and overcoat, and me in a mackintosh, gloriously immersed in a sea of pornographic misinformation. We parted opposite the Baker Street tube station, and I climbed on to the top of the last bus to Victoria in an exalted frame of mind. Presently this heady intoxication of newly acquired knowledge began to wear off and give place to a fearful remorse. I felt smirched and unclean; I felt that God was angry with me and would probably visit me with some sharp punishment in the near future. By the time I arrived home I was in a state of hysteria. Mother was in bed, slightly anxious because I was so late, but reading a book in a sensible effort to calm her fears; her relief was obvious when I charged into her room, but her expression changed to alarm when she saw my face, as with perfect sense of the theatre I gripped the bedrail and cried in a tragic voice: 'Mother, I have lost my innocence!' She hoisted herself up on the pillows and after scrutinising me carefully for a moment did the very last thing in the world that I expected: she burst out

[33]

laughing. Upon looking back I consider that gesture was a brilliant stroke of psychological intuition. Her laugh pricked my swollen hysterical ego like a pin, and I am certain that it cost her a good deal to do it. I dissolved into healthy tears, and the story of my fall from spiritual grace was gradually coaxed out of me. She was wise and gentle and said that there was nothing at all for me to be upset about, and that I was bound to find out all those things sooner or later, and that the fact that it happened to be sooner was really just as well, as in order to become a good actor it was necessary to know about life as early and as thoroughly as possible. I retired to bed serene and happy after a hot cup of cocoa made on her spirit lamp.

(10)

In the spring of 1913 Italia Conti wrote to Mother and offered me a three weeks' engagement in Liverpool and Manchester with the Liverpool Repertory Company. Several other children were to be in it and we were all to travel together and live together under Miss Conti's personal vigilance. I was very keen to go although Mother was not enthusiastic, never having quite forgiven Miss Conti for trying to transform me into a hyena in *The Rainbow*. However, we went to interview a young man with a rasping voice and dark glasses, Basil Dean, who was to produce the play (*Hannele,* by Hauptman), and I was engaged at a salary of two pounds a week. In due course I was seen off by Mother at Euston, and in company of about ten other children and Miss Conti travelled to Liverpool. It was a pleasant journey. We ate sandwiches and chocolate and played card games on a travelling rug stretched across our knees. Some of the children I already knew. Gracie Seppings and two sisters, Ivy and Dorothy Moody, had been in *The Rainbow* with me, and a very perky little boy in a yachting cap called Roy Royston I had met at one or two parties. The others were strangers, and still are, with the exception of Harold French and a vivacious child with ringlets to whom I took an instant fancy. She wore a black satin coat and a black velvet military hat with a peak, her face was far from pretty, but tremendously alive. She was very *mondaine,* carried a handbag with a powder-puff, and frequently dabbed her generously turned-up nose. She confided to me that her name was Gertrude Lawrence, but that I was to call her Gert because everybody did, that she was fourteen, just over licensing age, that she had been in *The Miracle* at Olympia and *Fifinella* at the Gaiety, Manchester. She then gave me an orange and told me a few mildly dirty stories, and I loved her from then onwards.

We all lived together in the same digs at Liverpool, and I was violently, wretchedly homesick. Miss Conti dosed me with Epsom Salts, doubtless in the belief that the root of all woe lay in the bowels. This failed to cheer me at all and merely succeeded in making rehearsals extremely convulsive, to the great irritation of Basil Dean who was none too sweet-tempered at the best of times.

Roy Royston, Harold French and I were angels in the dream part of the play, then we did a quick change and became schoolchildren in blue smocks and hard black hats, and then back again to angels for the end of the play. The whole production was definitely advanced, in the best and worst traditions of the repertory movement. There were steps leading from the stage to the stalls, odd and not always successful lighting effects, and a lot of curtains. Gracie Seppings played Hannele, and Baliol Holloway, Gottwald, the schoolmaster.

Roy and Harold and I had a little scene of our own in the early part of the play. We appeared through the inevitable curtains at the back and read verses from scrolls. We wore short tunics with green and red hieroglyphics stencilled on them, small and uncomfortable gold fillets on our heads and bare feet, which were usually pretty dirty because we nearly always forgot the slippers which we were supposed to wear down from the dressing-room.

My homesickness got a little better after the first few days, although it never entirely left me. When once the play had opened distractions were provided for us in the shape of trips to New Brighton on the Mersey steamers, personally conducted tours around the docks, and games of rounders in the park; in course of one of these, Gertie distinguished herself by striking Miss Conti's sister, Bianca Murray, a sharp blow on the head with a wooden bat, presumably by accident.

When we had played a week in Liverpool we went to Manchester. We arrived in the afternoon and settled into rooms in Ackers Street, and after a substantial high tea went off to the theatre in the tram for an evening rehearsal. That was my first view of the little Gaiety Theatre, and whenever I face it nowadays and see the garish movie posters outside, I shudder in my heart to think that it should have fallen so sadly from the grace and quality of its early years.

On Monday morning those of us who were under fourteen were led to the police court, where a singularly disagreeable magistrate refused to grant us a license unless we attended school every day during the week we were in Manchester. Then ensued a flustered consultation between Mrs. Murray and the manager of the theatre, and we left the court dismal and anxious. In the course of the day a school was discovered which agreed to take us in. Saturday of course was a whole holiday and Monday had gone already, so it was only for four days that we were to be incarcerated. What high cultural grace the magistrate imagined we could acquire in that time I fail to see. Anyhow, the next morning we were taken to a large red board school in the Oxford Road. Harold and Roy and I were put in a class-room and questioned by a little master with pince-nez, and when it came to my turn to answer whatever it was he asked me I stood up and announced, quivering with rage, that I had not the faintest intention of answering that question or indeed any questions, and that I was not going to learn a lesson of any sort during the four days I was forced to come to the school, and that if I was caned or punished in any way I should go straight home to London. This tirade, oddly enough, was effective, and for the rest of the day I sat at the back of the class-room doing nothing at all but stare with distaste at the rest of my class-mates. The next day, in spite of Mrs. Murray's remonstrances (Miss Conti was in London), I took a book with me, nobody spoke to me in the school, and I was allowed to

With JOAN CARROLL
in AN AUTUMN IDYLL
Savoy Theatre, 1912

Slightly
in PETER PAN
Duke of York's Theatre, 1913

keep it. Roy and Harold, more democratic-spirited, entered into everything with admirable zest and in the ten minutes' morning interval rushed out in the playground and fought and played football with the others. I think they were a trifle ashamed of me and felt self-consciously that perhaps a whole-hearted participation in everything absolved them somehow from the stigma of association with me. On the Saturday night I went to bed deliriously happy. It was all over and I was going home. The journey the next day seemed interminable, but at last, as the train slid into St. Pancras Station, I saw Mother standing on the platform and knew that the purgatory of those three weeks was ended.

(11)

While I had been away a long-discussed move had taken place, and the flat at Battersea Park had been left in favour of an upper maisonette on the south side of Clapham Common. It was a very tall house called Ben Lomond, and was owned by a Mrs. White and Miss Pitney, her sister, who inhabited the ground floor and basement while we had the rest of the house. The rooms were much bigger than those we had had in the flat, and looked straight out across the common in the front, and on to a large private garden at the back. I had a tiny bedroom at the very top, situated next door to the kitchen in which we usually had our meals, because we couldn't afford a servant. Mother, I think, was unhappy but she didn't show it, and for my benefit treated the cooking and washing and floor-scrubbing as a lark. Eric, my brother, then aged eight, and I helped with the washing-up, and enjoyed it, anyhow for the first few days.

Clapham Common was a nice place to live. There was a pond opposite the house on which Father used to indulge his passion for sailing a model yacht in the intervals of travelling for Payne's pianos. He never succeeded in infecting me with enough enthusiasm to last out longer than a quarter of an hour. Eric, however, was more docile, and used to squat on the opposite side of the pond from Father and turn the boat round with a walking-stick every time it crossed successfully. We used to take our tea out under the trees during the summer and play bat-and-ball afterwards.

There were pleasant walks in Clapham along tree-shaded roads, neatly spaced with refined suburban houses, secure in small prosperity with their conservatories and stained-glass windows and croquet lawns. From the Plough onwards down the Clapham Road the atmosphere became palpably commoner, but it was very lively on Saturday nights, particularly at Christmas time when the shop windows were gay with tinsel and crackers and paper-chains, and the poulterers and butchers and greengrocers were glaring yellow caves of light, with the slow-moving crowds on the shining pavements silhouetted against them.

In order to get from Clapham Common to the West End you travelled either in a Number 88 bus which took a long time, or in the City and South London Tube, changing at the Elephant and Castle into the Bakerloo, which was quicker.

The City and South London has now been transformed into a spacious network of efficiency, but then it was unique in uncomfortable charm. The trains were smaller than any of the other tubes and rattled alarmingly, and over it all there brooded a peculiar pungent stink which will live somewhere in the back of my nostrils for ever. I am dwelling upon this particularly because for several years it was an integral part of my life. I went through every sort of emotion in the City and South London Railway. Exaltation, having been sent for by some agent. Utter despair, returning home in the evening having failed to get the job. Or else hysterical delight with a typewritten part clutched in my hand and 'Rehearsal Monday morning at 11 o'clock' flashing before my eyes like an electric-light sign along the walls of the tunnel. I also managed to get through a lot of reading during those journeys back and forth from Trafalgar Square to the Plough: French Revolution stories whenever possible, and a welter of Guy Boothby, Phillips Oppenheim, William Le Queux, Stanley Weyman, and the early novels of Edgar Wallace.

I can close my eyes and ears now and conjure up completely the picture of Mother and myself late at night on our way home from some theatre, Mother in a dust-coloured cloak over her evening dress, with a small diamanté butterfly in her hair, and me in a scrupulously pressed dinner-jacket suit (Lockwood and Bradley in the Clapham Road), rushing from the Bakerloo side at Elephant and Castle, down tiled passages with hot draughts flying up our legs until the well-known fœtid City and South London smell met our noses and a distant screeching and rumbling soothed us with the knowledge that we had not after all missed the last train.

(12)

In the summer of 1913 Auntie Vida and Auntie Borby took a small house at Lee-on-the-Solent, and we all went down to spend a month with them. It was lovely to be able to look across at the Isle of Wight again and watch the warships and liners steaming up and down the Solent. There was nothing to do at Lee but bathe and go for bicycle rides. My favourite occupation was to spend hours on the railway embankment waiting for the rare appearance of the fussy little train which connected Lee with Fort Brockhurst and put halfpennies on the line for it to flatten into pennies, after which I tried to coax them into the slot machine on the pier, with only occasional success.

A concert party called 'The Poppy Pierrots' played twice daily on the end of the pier. The stage was under cover, but the audience sat sparsely beneath the sky and scurried to the shelters at the side whenever it rained. Miss Maud Watson ran the company. She was dark-skinned and slightly *passée* and sang a number in the second part of the programme called 'Hush-a-bye, My Little Papoose', during which she perpetually rocked an imaginary child in her arms until the dance, when she callously discarded it. There were two comedians, Teddy Baird and Fred Benton, and a soprano with the fanciful name of Betley Delacoste. I forget the names of the others, but I swiftly made friends with

[39]

them all and was allowed to appear with them on benefit nights and sing a couple of songs.

One day in August a post-card arrived asking me to go and see Charles Hawtrey at his office at eleven-thirty. We looked at the postmark and discovered that Mrs. White must have been negligent in forwarding it, because it was four days late. Nevertheless, Mother and I went pelting up to London in an excursion train and found that Hawtrey, having tried vainly to locate me, had engaged another boy for a good part in his new comedy, *Never Say Die,* which was already in rehearsal. He was sympathetic and charming as always, and when he saw my face fall told me that he would engage me as understudy. This was definitely better than nothing, because anyhow it meant that I should be in the theatre, and be earning two pounds ten a week; so we accepted gladly, and I started attending rehearsals right away. My natural hatred of Reggie Sheffield, the boy whom I was understudying, evaporated quite soon and we became great friends, although I never ceased to pray in my heart that he would be run over by a bus. Unfortunately he was a remarkably healthy little boy and remained uninjured and in the pink of condition throughout the entire run. Doris Lytton was in the play and Winifred Emery, and there was a good dinner scene in the second act during which real asparagus was devoured nightly. Hawtrey always loved eating on the stage and I must say the food in his productions was invariably excellent. In *Never Say Die* I used to share the remains with Nelly Ayr, the wardrobe mistress.

(13)

In November I satisfied a long-cherished desire to be in *Peter Pan,* which was the Mecca of all child actors. I was engaged by Dion Boucicault at four pounds a week to play Slightly. It was Mother who beat him up to such a high figure, flushed with nervousness and horribly conscious of my agonised expression; she argued and insisted and finally won, and we sailed out into St.

Martin's Lane dizzy with triumph. Playing in *Peter Pan* was all that I hoped it would be and more, and after the London run the entire company went out on tour.

Mother's travelling expenses were paid on condition that she undertook to look after a little boy called Donald Buckley, who played Michael, and allow him to share digs with me. He was nice really, but I was highly delighted when it was discovered that he had caught lice in his head at Newcastle. He had to be tooth-combed and disinfected while I remained aloof, clean and maddeningly superior.

We played at Glasgow, Edinburgh, Newcastle and Birmingham, and all the suburban dates such as Wimbledon and Hammersmith and Kennington. When we were at Kennington Mother invited a lot of the company to tea between a matinée and evening performance and we were very excited when Pauline Chase consented to come. It's only a little way from Kennington Theatre to Clapham Common, most of us went by tram, but Pauline Chase and her great friend Miss Berri (who played the mermaid) drove to our house in a shining and smart yellow two-seater which threw Miss Pitney, who was peering through the ground-floor lace curtains, into transports of excitement. The tea was elaborate, the white Worcester cups (wedding present) were brought out, and Mother insisted proudly that I should sing, which I did, to my own and everybody else's acute embarrassment.

The tea-party, however, on the whole was considered a great success and the remains of the home-made coffee sponge with walnuts and the Fuller's almond cake brightened our lives for the rest of the week.

(14)

After the run of *Peter Pan* I was out of an engagement for a long while. These periods in my memory are difficult to recapture. They seem oddly jumbled and nebulous without the chain of the theatre to hold them together. I couldn't have been very happy really, because I was never completely happy when I wasn't working.

I met an artist named Philip Streatfield who had a studio in Glebe Place, Chelsea. He was painting a picture of Phyllis Monkman and I used to go to tea and watch it being finished. I don't really believe it could have been a very good picture, but I was most impressed by it. She was wearing the pink velvet dress in which she appeared in the Pom-Pom dance in the Alhambra revue; also, I think, a white feather head-dress. I met her once leaving the studio wrapped in fox fur and debated anxiously in my mind whether or not to ask her for her autograph, but by the time I had decided that I would she had hopped into a taxi and driven away. Philip also painted a model called Doris something-or-other, a pretty girl who posed casually in the nude and made tea afterwards. I soon became accustomed to the whole affair and spoke of it at home in a worldly manner.

It was about this time that an important friendship began, a friendship which for several years influenced me profoundly and is still clear to-day in spite of the fact that our two paths have diverged so definitely in opposite directions. Esmé Wynne was the little girl with the faintly bleating voice who had played the leading part in *Where the Rainbow Ends*. During the first two seasons of *The Rainbow* I had no idea that she could ever mean anything to me in the future; in fact, I always found her pompous, podgy, and slightly superior, and although she sometimes betrayed a latent sense of humour by a misplaced giggle or so at rehearsals, these occasions were rare and her majestic deportment at parties filled me with awe and a certain indefinite dislike. In the spring of 1914 she suddenly appeared at 50, South Side, Clapham Common, wearing a white knitted jumper and skirt and hat and wheeling a brand-new bicycle of which she seemed extremely proud. She confessed that she didn't ride it very well and was terrified out of her life on any but the quietest thoroughfares. After tea I cycled back with her to Stansfield Road, Stockwell, where she lived with her family. It was a smug little road and the houses squatted back from contamination with the pavements, from which they were protected by grey strips of garden, barely enlivened here and there by dusty shrubs. The family consisted of Mother, Father and

Auntie Mona. Auntie Mona was seldom present as she was generally away on tour. But although corporeally absent, her successful aura pervaded every corner of the home and she was discussed with pride over the supper table. Esmé's mother herself was a handsome woman, who at one time had been in the original troupe of 'The Palace Girls.' I was certainly englamoured by the thought of this, but could never completely visualise her darting on and off the stage in line and waving her matronly legs with meticulous clockwork abandon, but of course my first view of her was when she was approaching fifty, and middle-age had coaxed her figure into heavier shapes. I rode home that evening through the dim suburban roads, ecstatic in the thrill of new friendship, planning adventures for the future. Bicycle excursions into the country, matinées at the Coliseum (early doors ninepence with tea in the interval threepence extra). Long amicable evenings playing word games and listening to the gramophone (I had a new one that played flat disc records instead of the old-fashioned cylinders), and joyful shopping expeditions to the Woolworth's Threepenny and Sixpenny Bazaar in the Brixton Road, finishing up with the weekly melodrama at the Brixton Theatre. These romantic visions were realised quickly. Esmé and I became inseparable. Almost at the outset we gave each other nicknames, embarrassing now with the weight of years upon them, but at the time highly enjoyable. I was Poj and she was Stoj. We alternated between childishness and strange maturity. The theatre had led us far in precocity and we discussed life and death and sex and religion with sublime sophistication. We also dressed in each other's clothes and paraded the West End, rode for miles on the London and Brighton and South Coast Railway without tickets, evading station-masters, ticket-collectors and frequently even policemen. We stole chocolates from sweet-shops and cakes of soap from chemists; once Stoj got a large bottle of Phul-Nana scent. We extracted, with the aid of bent hair-pins and latchkeys, packets of Snake Charmer cigarettes from slot-machines and smoked them publicly with outward flamboyance and inward nausea. We explored the West End, the East End, the suburbs, and the near country with minute thorough-

[43]

ness. We even had baths together for the simple reason that we didn't wish to waste a moment's companionship and because it seemed affected to stop short in the middle of some vital discussion for such a paltry reason as conventional modesty. We quarrelled bitterly, usually over religion, Stoj at that time being given to spiritual ecstasies which fortunately seldom lasted long, but were remarkable alike for their violence and variety. Finally after many intensive arguments we evolved a list of rules for our 'Palship' which certainly saved us many unhappinesses and misunderstandings and was strictly adhered to for many years.

One of the most important aspects of this relationship was the fact that Stoj was determined to be a writer, an ambition that filled me with competitive fervour. She wrote poems. Reams and reams of them, love songs, sonnets and vilanelles: alive with elves, mermaids, leafy glades, and Pan (a good deal of Pan). Not to be outdone in artistic endeavour, I set many of the poems to music, sometimes, owing to the exigencies of my inspiration, changing her original scansion with disastrous results. One instance of this ruthlessness concerned a poem of which she was particularly proud, and an ugly battle ensued. The first lines were:

> '*Our little Love is dying*
> *On his head are lately crimson petals*
> *Faded quite*
> *The breath of Passion withered them last night . . .*'

I set these words to a merry lilt beginning: 'Our little Love is dying on his head . . .'

Very soon I began to write short stories, beastly little whimsies, also about Pan, and fauns and cloven hooves. We read a lot of Oscar Wilde and Omar Khayyam and Laurence Hope. Stoj even went so far as to sing 'The Indian Love Lyrics' for a short period until I put a stop to it, not so much from æsthetic principle, but because I knew with every instinct in me that her voice was quite horrid. Apart from these small skirmishings our mutual admiration was sincere and touching. Our egos were battling for recog-

nition and encouragement and we supplied one another generously with praise and mild, very mild, criticism.

(15)

In the early part of May Philip Streatfield, who had been discussing for a long time the possibility of taking a cottage somewhere suitably picturesque where he could paint landscapes, decided to make a motor tour through the west country and to my
intense excitement invited me to go, too. The car belonged to a
friend of Philip's, Sidney Lomer, who was kind enough not to
resent my inclusion in the party, and so, in due course, on a misty
drizzling afternoon we set forth, slipping out of London over
glassy roads, myself bouncing blissfully about at the back among
the bags. The whole two weeks' trip was enchanting, doubly so
for me as I had never been in a fast car in my life. We stopped in
farms and inns along the coasts of Devon and Cornwall and lingered in small fishing villages while Philip made water-colour
sketches, surrounded by admiring natives.

After a fortnight of the road I was dropped off at my aunt's
house in Charlestown. Philip and Sidney Lomer stayed to lunch
and I suffered tortures of apprehension in case my aunt should
embarrass me with over-solicitude, but she behaved beautifully
and was charming and social and, I hoped, impressive. When
lunch was over I waved them away in the car and spent the rest
of the day exploring the lake and the garden. Everything seemed
to look smaller than when I was there as a little boy, but the spell
of its beauty was as strong as ever and I was very happy. There
was the old blue punt, still water-logged, the deep wide lake,
coffee-coloured on account of the clay soil, and the mysterious
damp-smelling jungle surrounding it. I walked down every path,
crossed and re-crossed all the little bridges, rowed myself out to
the island in the dinghy, swung myself sick in the swing, and
made up little verses, gay, winsome fragments redolent of Stoj's
woodland influence and rife with whimsical pixie allusion. I fancied

myself for a little as a half-wild creature and darted about among the trees, occasionally crouching in the bracken in faun-like attitudes. This peculiar behaviour was, of course, 'play-acting', although at the time I failed to recognise it. Intermixed with this self-conscious enjoyment of myself was a completely un-selfconscious enjoyment of the country and, above all, of the sea. Perhaps a few drops of quarter-deck blood had seeped into my veins from my naval ancestors; at any rate, I remember feeling a deep indefinable satisfaction, even when I was quite small, whenever I was taken on to a beach and could watch the waves sliding in over the shingle. The Cornish seas were much more exciting than the refined Sunny South Coast variety. Here were no neat breakwaters and trim stone esplanades, no rompered children patting at sand castles, while fat mothers lolled near by in deck chairs reading novels and knitting; there was no discreet band music here to interfere with the sound of the waves. The waves had it all their own way in Cornwall; grey and formidable, they hurled themselves endlessly against the rocks and swirled into the little sandy coves, leaving yellow suds of foam high up on the beach among the crushed shells and thick ridges of brown seaweed. There were sea birds, too: cormorants and gulls in hundreds, wheeling and squawking round their nests on the cliffs, and diving for fish far out beyond where the waves curled and broke.

I was happy by myself in those days, a habit which I mislaid in later years, but have fortunately regained since. I spent many hours wandering along the cliffs, frequently returning drenched to the skin to eat large teas in my aunt's kitchen. Dripping-toast and splits and saffron cake, this last bright yellow and delicious.

On certain days I plastered my hair down, put on my best suit, and went driving with my aunt in the dog-cart to pay calls. I was proud of her extreme prettiness and delighted that my extra years had made me more companionable to her. My uncle was seldom visible, as he was a determined invalid and preferred to stay in his room most of the time.

Later on in the same year I went again to Cornwall, this time to stay with Philip at Polperro where he had found a pleasant little house perched up on the cliff overlooking the harbour. It was a lovely summer, hot and placid. There was nothing to do but bathe and lie on the rocks, or wander about the narrow streets of the village and talk to the fishermen. On the fourth of August we read in the paper that war had been declared, and later on in the day we saw three warships steaming slowly by, quite close in to the shore. They looked proud and invulnerable and almost smug, as though they were secretly pleased.

The peace of the holiday broke at once, and I was sent back to London immediately where I was to spend one night at an hotel and then join the family and Auntie Vida at Lee-on-the-Solent. Philip saw me off at Looe and put me in the charge of Hugh Walpole, who treated me to lunch on the train and tipped me half a crown at parting.

(16)

The rest of that year, so eventful for the world, was quite uneventful for me. We stayed at Lee for a few weeks and I bicycled about the country and read books and went off by myself for whole-day excursions into Portsmouth and Southsea. Presently we went back to Clapham and I set about looking for a Christmas engagement, a disheartening business because I was just reaching the awkward age midway between boy parts and young juveniles. I was tall for my years and my voice was breaking, which made me croak unexpectedly in the middle of conversations, to my own mortification and Stoj's great amusement.

I was dreadfully disappointed when I heard that A. W. Baskcomb was going to play Slightly in *Peter Pan* (his original part). This was my last hope gone and so I resigned myself miserably to the first Christmas I had spent without work for a long while. Mother did her best to cheer me up as much as possible and we went to one or two pantomimes, but I was really wretched until a sudden telegram arrived from Boucicault saying that Baskcomb was ill and that I could take his place immediately. It was heaven to be back in the theatre again, and I squeezed myself into my last year's furs (Act II, Never-Never Land) and pink-and-black striped boots, and sniffed the grease-paint and the 'size' and that particular burnt-paper smell which always permeates every production of *Peter Pan* and is caused by the fire that the Indians make in the second act. I was immensely elated at the thought of actually appearing on the same stage with Madge Titheradge who was playing Peter; I had seen her in *Tiger Cub* at the Garrick and was deeply in love with her husky voice and swift, alert charm. That first matinée when I rejoined the company I was going down the stairs on to the stage for the underground scene when I met her face to face; she shook hands warmly with me and said: 'My name's Madge, what's yours?' A never-to-be-forgotten, most characteristic gesture.

(17)

For the whole of the following year I did not work as I developed a strange cough, which upon examination proved to be caused by a tubercular gland in my chest. Mother was very frightened, but Dr. Etlinger, an old friend of the family's, assured her that it would be easily cured by a few months in the country away from theatres and smoky atmospheres. I spent a little time at the Pinewood Sanatorium at Wokingham. I was not an actual inmate of the sanatorium but stayed in Dr. Etlinger's private house in the grounds. He was extremely kind to me and allowed me to accompany him on his rounds in the morning, play croquet with the patients, and help him with small errands. He was a short weather-beaten man with twinkling blue eyes and a passion for Russian tea, which we used to brew at all hours of the day and night and drink out of long glasses. I learned a good deal about T.B. and its various symptoms and stages and became deeply interested. Most of the patients were officers and they were all extraordinarily cheerful, particularly the more hopeless ones. They played tennis and bowls and croquet on the lawn, dressed only in bathing trunks whenever the sun came out and in light sweaters when it didn't. It was strange to listen to these dying men talking so gaily of the future. They nearly all looked sunburned and well, and there was no trace of illness about them until they began to cough, and then in a moment their colour and vitality faded, and they seemed to shrink piteously. I remember sitting for hours in the doctor's library after dinner discussing their possible chances of recovery, and new cures and treatments and lung deflations, and the experiments of Professor Sparlinger. Then I would retire to bed, rather bleakly comforting myself with the reflection that if I ever contracted T.B. seriously, I should at least know enough about it not to be fooled by false illusion when the time came for me to face the truth of dying.

My cough rapidly disappeared, and by the summer I was stronger and healthier than I had ever been in my life. The time passed slowly for me, but not really unhappily. Of course I had moments of irritable yearning for the theatre, but the sight of so much disease at close quarters had scared a lot of commonsense into me, and I would have stayed away willingly for years rather than risk my cough recurring.

In June, entirely to please Mother, I consented to be confirmed and was duly prepared for this rite by Mr. Tower, our Clapham vicar. I went to tea with him two or three times a week in his study and he was very affectionate and biblical.

Soon after my confirmation I received a letter written in a slanting illegible hand from Mrs. Astley-Cooper, a friend of Philip Streatfield's. He had joined up and was training with the Sherwood Foresters in Essex and he had asked her to have me down to stay in the country. He seemed to think that she would like me and that I would not only derive much material benefit from her country air and excellent living, but also profit by the astringent wisdom of her friendship. He died the following year without ever realising to the full the great kindness he had done me.

I accepted her invitation to stay, and Mother came to see me off at St. Pancras and left her bag in the tube, with all the money she had scraped together for my return ticket. It was a dreadful moment. Mother, however, rose above it as usual and, depositing me in the waiting-room with my rather cheap suitcase, darted out of the station and asked a policeman the way to the nearest pawnshop. There happened to be one practically opposite and within five minutes she was back, without her only remaining diamond ring but with enough money for the ticket. She stood on the platform waving as the train slid away, triumphantly pink in the face but with the suspicion of tears in her eyes. The whole thing ended up well because she regained her bag miraculously within two days and so the ring was with her for a little while longer.

Mrs. Cooper lived at Hambleton in Rutland, about three miles from Oakham in the middle of the Cottesmore country. The village stands on a hill rising abruptly out of chequered fields, polite and green and neatly hedged. The whole county of Rutland is compact and tidy. In summer it sleeps gently and a little stuffily, but in winter it wakes for hunting.

Mrs. Cooper was gay company. Her principal pleasure was to lie flat on her back upon a mattress in front of the fire and shoot off witticisms in a sort of petulant wail. She draped scarves over all mirrors because she said she could find no charm in her own appearance whatever. The principal characters in the house were Uncle Clem (Captain Astley-Cooper) and Fred. Uncle Clem was handsome, charming and vague. An aura of military distinction still clung to him as he passed to and fro through the village and read the lessons in church on Sunday mornings. The status of Fred when I first saw him was difficult to define. He was too young and unimposing to be a butler, but he undoubtedly ran the house thoroughly and efficiently, Mrs. Cooper with it.

It was a pleasant experience staying in a well-run country house. The trappings of life there were new to me. A fire in my bedroom every night, dinner clothes laid out neatly on the bed, brass cans of hot water, and deep baths encased in shiny brown wood. People came over and lunched or dined occasionally. A flurry of wheels in the drive announced them and the murmur of different voices echoed up from the hall as I grandly descended the polished oak staircase, very careful not to slip in my new patent-leather shoes.

During my winter visits I used to go to meets in the dog-cart, driving myself and following the hunt for as long as the pony consented to gallop. It was never amenable for more than an hour or so and had a disconcerting habit of standing stock still for no reason at all, completely obstructing the road, and quite impervious to my shoutings and belabourings. Later on in the war Mrs. Cooper and Fred ran Hambleton as a convalescent hospital and I used to go down whenever I could, sometimes only for Sunday night when I was acting, and sing and play to the soldiers.

(18)

Just before Christmas 1915 *Where the Rainbow Ends* was produced again at the Garrick, its fourth consecutive season. Most of the original cast were re-engaged: Esmé Wynne (Stoj), Philip Tonge, Sidney Sherwood, Mavis Yorke and myself. This time I had grown too big for the page boy and was still apparently unacceptable for either Crispian or Jim Blunders, so I played a character part, The Slacker, who was a cross between a man and a dragon. I wore a greeny-beige costume with a tail, and put on an elaborate make-up, masses of number five (yellow), cheeks carefully emaciated with blue pencil, and glittering green sequins on my eyelids. The part was short but showy, and I gave a macabre performance, leading up to one of those hysterically laughing exits which never fail to get a round of applause.

After this Stoj and I were engaged to play Amy and Charley in the spring tour of *Charley's Aunt* at salaries of two pounds and two pounds ten a week respectively. The men of the company were required to provide their own clothes, which from the point of view of elegance was an unwise decision of the management's. My undergraduate flannels in act two, which were remarkable both in cut and texture, shrank degradingly in the first week's wash and by the end of the tour were practically cycling knickers. The company was then, is now, and always will be run by Mr. Cecil Barth, a kind man with an unbridled passion for respectability. He told us at the outset that Stoj and I were not to share rooms together because it would give the company a bad name, so I was paired off reluctantly with the leading juvenile, Arnold Raynor, who never cared for me much, while Stoj lived with a fair girl with long hair and a round face, called Norah Howard. In this Stoj was lucky, because Norah was the only other unmorose member of that exceedingly morose troupe. Kathleen Barbor (now Mrs. Ernie Lotinga) was the Walking Understudy and was a little less under the pall of self-satisfied gloom that enveloped the rest, but it got her down eventually and she was only seen to smile about once a fortnight. Many of the cast, of course, had played the play month in, month out for years and years and years, notably James Page (Mr. Spettigue), Sidney Compton (Brasset) and J. R. Crawford (Colonel whatever it was). Mr. Crawford also directed rehearsals with all the airy deftness of a rheumatic deacon producing *Macbeth* for a church social. Sidney Compton had a deep rasping voice and unfolded his mouth like an Inverness cape. James Page was the gayest of these three veterans, a gossipy, slightly bibulous old thing.

In my opinion, of all the parts in that least funny of all plays Charley is the worst. Jack and Lord Fancourt Babberley are the ones who get all the laughs and the wretched Charley supplies the cues. I tried desperately at first to invest this high-spirited congenital idiot with some reality, but after a while I gave up the struggle and just bounded on to the stage nightly and said the lines with as much conviction as possible. We seemed to me to play interminably everywhere, frequently split weeks in smaller towns such as Rugby and Peterborough. These split weeks were very expensive owing to changing rooms so rapidly. Often I had only enough money for one meal a day and was forced to make do with buns and glasses of milk until after the show at night when I stuffed myself with fish and chips. The whole tour was alive with incident. In Peterborough we played during a blizzard to exactly six people. In Chester Stoj and Norah and I went rowing up the river for a picnic completely forgetting that there was a matinée. In Manchester I had a row with Arnold Raynor about the bath water and decided to share with Stoj and Norah henceforward and risk Mr. Barth's disapproval.

The three of us started our alliance the following week in Hanley. The town was filthy, the rooms were filthy, and the other inmates of the house were four acrobats who used the bathroom at the same time for economy's sake and invariably left a rim of grey horror round the inside of the bath which we tried to rub off with wads of toilet paper.

Altogether, that week was far from successful. No night passed without one or other of us retiring to bed in tears. I drove Stoj mad by strumming the piano and she lacerated my nerves by strumming the typewriter. I forget what poor Norah did to irritate us, but I expect she whistled, or didn't quite understand our jokes. At any rate, we all quarrelled furiously to such an extent that Stoj and I (temporarily on the same side against Norah) defiantly determined to live alone together the next week and to give in our notices if there were any managerial objections.

We arrived in Chester late on Sunday afternoon in a downpour of rain. Norah, wearing a faintly superior smile, got herself and her luggage into a taxi and drove off to her combined room which she had had the forethought to reserve in advance. We left our bags at the station and set out in the rain. We trudged for miles, soaked to the skin. There was apparently only one street where theatrical rooms were available, and every room in every house seemed to be taken. We walked endlessly up and down it, averting our eyes as we passed Norah's window which was on the ground floor front. She had thoughtfully left the blind up so that we shouldn't miss the sight of her sitting by a crackling fire, cramming down hot cocoa and steak-and-kidney pudding and self-consciously reading a book propped up against the cruet. Finally we gave up the theatrical street entirely and found at the end of a lane a nice-looking house with an 'Apartments' board in the window. A flashily-dressed woman opened the door and greeted us with surprising enthusiasm. She showed us two well-furnished bedrooms and said that we could use her dining-room and that dinner was just ready. Absolutely delighted, we rushed back to the station, retrieved our luggage, and within half an hour were cosily installed in pyjamas and dressing-gowns eating roast mutton and red currant jelly. It was not until three different men had walked into Stoj's room in the middle of the night that we realised that we were in a brothel. Even then we were quite eager to stay because, as I truly remarked, Stoj's appearance at night with her hair scragged back in Hinde's curlers and layers of Icilma cream plastered all over her face was so repellent that she could pass unscathed through fifty brothels. Mr. Barth, however, inevitably found out and back we went to Norah, Stoj sharing her 'combined', and I sharing meals and inhabiting a lonely single attic down the road.

The tour pursued its dreary way through February, March, April and May. In Bristol I had a religious mania lasting exactly one day and based upon an inexplicable fear of death which descended upon me abruptly in the middle of a matinée. Homesickness started it, I think, a black nostalgia for Mother and the dear familiarity of my bedroom at Clapham Common. I felt definitely that I should never see my home again. I had been away too many weeks in frowsy lodging-houses and my nerves were raw with sudden loneliness. There was thunder in the air as well, and during that night a terrific storm broke, convincing me that this was my destined finish. I wept thoroughly at the vivid picture of Mother's face when she heard how the sharp lightning had struck her darling through the window of the second floor back. I murmured incoherent prayers, vowed many vows, and promised many promises, if only I might live a little longer. These were apparently granted, for I woke up the next morning as bright as a button and rapidly forgot the entire episode, promises and all.

In Torquay we had charming rooms. It was May and the weather and sea were warm enough for bathing, so Stoj and I reverted to the 'Woodland' again and went for long picnics on non-matinée days. We frolicked in secluded coves and danced naked in little woods fringing the shore, shutting our æsthetic eyes to the fact that Stoj's hair always went straight as string when even slightly damped, and that, owing to recent indulgences in sweets, my back was generously pimpled.

In Wolverhampton Arnold Raynor finally lost his temper with me and knocked me down just before my entrance in the last act. I had no time to retaliate even if I had wished to, and I tottered on to the stage with my collar torn and my white tie under my left ear.

In the dressing-room afterwards he said in sinister tones: 'Now we'll have this out,' and hit me again, upon which I lost all control and threw my tin make-up box at him. He was shorter than I and much stronger. He then hit me again and I fell down and banged my head against the wall. As I did so I had the presence of mind to yell with what I hoped was enough volume and tone to indicate anger rather than stark terror; anyhow, it was effective enough to bring Stoj flying into the room dressed in a brief camisole and a pair of knickers and waving a hair-brush with which she struck my aggressor so hard on the back of the head that he fell down, too, whereupon everyone cried and apologised and we all went out affectionately to supper.

(19)

The tour came to an end in June and we said good-bye to the company with unqualified delight and rejoined our various families. The autumn tour started early in August gratefully shorn of our presence. Meanwhile, I was busily preparing a single turn for the halls consisting of imitations of famous stars. This never amounted to anything as it was quite impossible for the acutest perception to distinguish one imitation from the other. I appeared at several auditions in evening clothes accompanied on the piano by Auntie Kitty (deserted in Toronto by Uncle Percy) in a black lace dress and a diamond slide in her hair. All we were ever offered was a trial week somewhere at our own expense, which I sadly and expediently refused.

A year or two before this I had met, I forget exactly where, a boy named John Ekins. He was a year older than I and had been at school at Walthamstow where I remember visiting him with

[55]

Stoj and taking him a box of chocolates. We had procured this by the simple means of buying an empty box for threepence and going from sweet-shop to sweet-shop in the Clapham Road and stealing the chocolates off the counters while one of us distracted the shopkeeper's attention by asking for sweets which we knew he didn't stock. The chocolates suffered rather from joggling about in our pockets, so when we got home we rubbed them with margarine to restore their vanished shine. Anyhow, they looked alluring enough when arranged neatly with paper shavings, and John was becomingly enthusiastic about them and ate the lot. He was the son of the rector of Rame in Cornwall and was more thoroughly stage-struck even than I. He knew what every actor and actress had played in for the last thirty years, also what they had worn and whom they had married. We used to sit in the garden of the rectory overlooking the summer sea with our noses buried in back numbers of the *Play Pictorial,* staring avidly at Lily Elsie wearing a hat like a tea-cosy in *The Count of Luxembourg,* putting her hand through a screen and being married to Bertram Wallis in a velvet coat; Kate Cutler in *Bellamy the Magnificent,* clutching her neck with both hands and looking extremely agitated; Charles Wyndham and Miss Compton in *Eccentric Lord Comberdene,* very uneasy in yachting caps; and, best of all, our beloved Gertie Millar in *Our Miss Gibbs,* wearing a beehive and talking to Robert Nainby as a Duke. On Wednesdays or Saturdays we used to go into Plymouth to see the matinée at the Theatre Royal. This meant walking a mile or so into Cawsand Village and catching the morning bus, which sometimes missed the ferry, forcing us to wait on the wrong side of the harbour in a fever of impatience for fear we should miss the beginning of the first act. After the matinée we always had tea in the Palm Court of the Royal, very casual and grand in our carefully pressed navy-blue suits and coloured silk socks. Coming home to Rame in the late evening was lovely except for the last drag up the hill which covered our shoes with dust and generally made us slightly irritable. The scenery all the way was beautiful, particularly in the dusk with the different coloured lights springing up behind us in

With
STOJ and
JOHN EKINS
1915

OUT OF WORK
1916

the harbour, and, through the giant trees of Mount Edgecombe Park, the regular flash of the Eddystone fifteen miles out to sea.

The rectory itself was cosy and lamp-lit and rather faded; all the rooms felt lived-in except the drawing-room, which retained an aloof atmosphere and smelt of moth balls. Mr. Ekins, Mrs. Ekins, Christine, Audrey and John comprised the family, and it was one of the nicest households I have ever known. Audrey was consumptive and we used to have tea-parties in her room to cheer her up, although she seemed to me to be happier than most people in the best of health. John finally prevailed upon his parents to allow him to live with his uncle in Lewisham and try for a stage engagement, which he succeeded in getting remarkably quickly. He appeared with Hawtrey in *Anthony in Wonderland,* played my longed-for Crispian in *Where the Rainbow Ends,* and was in a melodrama at Drury Lane called *The Best of Luck,* in which Madge Titheradge was the leading lady. I often used to walk on in the crowd scenes just to give myself the feeling of being in a job. We were inseparable friends until one morning in 1917 when a letter arrived from him from Farnborough where he was training as an Air Force cadet, explaining that he had a day's leave and asking me to go to a matinée with him. By the same post there was also a letter from his mother telling me that he had died suddenly of spinal meningitis. The violence of the shock robbed the day and myself of all reality, and I went to the matinée alone, remotely cheerful and feeling myself brave. It wasn't until the second entr'acte that I began to cry foolishly and had to go home. Memory is viciously insistent on such occasions. The City and South London Tube plunged through its tunnels interminably, while I bicycled down from Rame to Cawsand with John, picnicked with him below the fort on the rocks, slid wildly up and down the frozen pond on Clapham Common, and made tea late at night in his uncle's kitchen at Lewisham. The finality of death is bewildering on first acquaintance and the words 'never again' too sad to believe entirely. It took a long while for my unhappiness to disperse and even now I feel a shadow of it when I think of him.

Tragedy certainly descended swiftly on that gentle, harmless rectory. Within a year or so Christine, the healthy elder daughter, had married and died in childbirth, and there was only Audrey left to linger on for a few months. Mr. and Mrs. Ekins live there still and Christine's daughter is with them, but even so the house must feel empty.

(20)

In the summer of 1916 Robert Courtneidge engaged me to play a small part in a new musical comedy, *The Light Blues,* which was to be tried out for three weeks in Cardiff, Newcastle and Glasgow, before coming to the Shaftesbury Theatre. The play was very clean-limbed and jaunty and good-fellowish and dealt with the excruciating adventures of a jolly actress called Topsy Devigne, who dressed up as an undergraduate at Cambridge during May week and got herself into a series of roguish scrapes. Cicely Debenham played Topsy and Albert Chevalier was somebody's father, and Cicely Courtneidge and Jack Hulbert supplied a second-string love interest with a couple of dance duets. I can still recall fragments of the lyrics, as for example the finale of the first act when Topsy, having successfully squeezed herself into a navy-blue suit, sang:

> *'I'm Cuthbert the Coconut*
> *The smartest on the tree,*
> *Any girl who isn't shy,*
> *Can try a shy at me . . .' etc.*

And later on, Cynthia (Cicely Courtneidge) in a pink silk dress with panniers and a Dolly Varden hat, flitting backwards and forwards across the stage and singing with incredible archness:

> *'Don't you go a-counting of your chickens*
> *Wait 'til they're all hatched out,*
> *For you never never know*

What's going to happen next,
And you may be vexed,
And a little bit perplexed . . .' etc.

There was also a sentimental number sung by Albert Chevalier assisted by *bouche ferme* refrains from the whole company during which he paraded up and down in an angry white wig and sang with intense feeling:

'I see Life through rose-coloured glashes,
I see Lovers in ro-oshy light
Billing and coo-ooing,
Tenderly woo-ooing,
Oh, if you only would tesht your shight.'

This song was extremely long, and there was ample time for Chevalier himself and the company and the whole of Cambridge to change from amber to deep pink and back again to amber before the end of it.

I played what is technically described as a 'dude' part. Morning clothes, silk hat and false moustache (insecure). I was on for about five minutes in the first act and four in the second, and I was offended at not being included in any of the musical numbers, but I was given the understudy of Jack Hulbert and learned all his dances quickly in the forlorn hope that he would be seized with some disease on the opening night, giving me the chance to rush on and become a star immediately.

I enjoyed the three weeks' tour and shared rooms with Stephanie Stephens and her mother, who were old friends of mine. I didn't have much opportunity to enjoy the London run, as it only lasted a little while, but on the whole I learned a good deal. Mr. Courtneidge was violent at rehearsals and lost his temper gloriously. On one occasion when he was reviling me for being unable to peel a banana correctly, he actually flung his hat on the stage and jumped on it, which sent me into a flurry of nervous laughter. With all his rages he was really kind and just to everybody, but he happened to belong to that school of production which considers no later rehearsal complete without tears from someone.

In Glasgow I had a painful but salutary experience. There was a full rehearsal called and I went down to the theatre with Stephanie, sublimely unaware of the trouble in store for me. I have never been able to look at the bare stage of the King's Theatre since without a shudder of remembrance. On that particular morning it seemed normal enough at first with pieces of scenery littered about and the company waiting expectantly for the arrival of Mr. Courtneidge. I remember being gay and jocular myself and doing a saucy imitation of somebody or other to amuse some of the minor members of the cast. Presently the 'Guv'nor' arrived and the atmosphere changed somewhat, laughter dwindled into polite smiles and there was the usual silence while he stood by the prompt table talking to the stage manager. I must explain here that during the course of the second act I played a little scene with Shaun Glenville, who used to gag a good deal and say anything that came into his head. I was never particularly amused by these 'impromptus' but I frequently allowed myself to be convulsed with ill-repressed laughter, because I felt that it was quite a good plan to be suitably responsive to the leading comedian. Before that miserable rehearsal started Mr. Courtneidge called me out before the entire company and mortified me to the dust. He informed me that I was not only a very young actor but a very bad actor, and that in addition to this I was practically a criminal for accepting a salary of four pounds a week (I had told Stephanie I was getting five) when all I did to earn it was to fool about and giggle on the stage, and that if it wasn't for the fact that we were opening in London the following week he would sack me on the spot. He said a lot more which I forget now, but it was all in the same vein, and I slunk away more utterly humiliated than I had ever been in my life. Cicely Debenham, however, lent me her handkerchief, and Cicely Courtneidge patted me on the back and said: 'You mustn't mind Father.'

The play opened in London with the mark of death emblazoned

upon it, and although there were calls for author and several people made speeches, it actually ran only two weeks.

Just after this I became, briefly, a professional dancer. Not in the true 'gigolo' sense, for, alas, my adolescence was too apparent, my figure too gangling and coltish to promote evil desire in even the most debauched night-club habitués. I partnered a girl named Eileen Dennis, and we were engaged by the Elysée Restaurant (now the Café de Paris) to appear during dinner and supper. A slow waltz, a tango, and a rather untidy one-step made up our programme. Later, owing to popular demand (from Eileen Dennis's mother), we introduced a pierrot fantasia for which we changed into cherry-coloured sateen and tulle ruffs. No South African millionaires threw diamond sunbursts at Eileen's feet. We were neither of us ever invited to appear naked out of pies at private supper parties; in fact, the whole engagement from the point of view of worldly experience was decidedly disappointing.

Another brief engagement somewhere in those years was as a 'super' in a D. W. Griffith's film. I was paid, I think, a pound a day, for which I wheeled a wheelbarrow up and down a village street in Worcestershire with Lillian Gish. The name of the film was *Hearts of the World,* and it left little mark on me beyond a most unpleasant memory of getting up at five every morning and making my face bright yellow, and a most pleasant memory of Lillian, Dorothy and Mrs. Gish who were remarkably friendly and kind to me.

(21)

In December 1916 I was engaged for a Christmas play by Cecil Aldin, *The Happy Family,* in which I played a Sandhurst cadet in a red-and-white striped blazer and a pill-box hat. In the second act everybody turned into animals except Mimi Crawford and me, and I rendered a dashing military number: 'Sentry Go,' with a full chorus of ducks and pigs, which I drilled resonantly in the third refrain. In this play I was allowed to dance and sing for the first time since *The Goldfish,* so I was very happy. The steps I had learned from understudying Jack Hulbert came in useful, and a critic in one of the more obscure weeklies wrote that I combined the grace and movement of a Russian dancer with the looks and manner of an English schoolboy. This thrilled me, although I couldn't help regretting that *The Times* or the *Daily Mail* hadn't displayed the same acute perception.

The first act of *The Happy Family* was remarkable for a hilarious concerted number in which every member of the company took part and sang with enthusiasm:

> *'Isn't it awfully jolly*
> *Doing a little revue?*
> *Never could be a more happy idea*
> *It's nobby and nutty and new.*
> *Laughter and frolic and folly*
> *Won't we be going ahead?*
> *None of us stopping*
> *Until we are dropping*
> *And then we'll have breakfast in bed.'*

Ten years later I quoted this to C. B. Cochran after a twenty-seven-hour dress rehearsal of *On with the Dance* in Manchester, and he smiled dimly.

The following summer I went to the Gaiety, Manchester, to play in *Wild Heather,* a play by Dorothy Brandon. I lived alone in a bed-sitting-room in Lloyd Street, and was mothered by Mrs. Wood, my landlady. She waited up every night for me and brought me my supper on a tray. It was usually Heinz baked beans, or welsh rabbit, or something equally delicious, and she used to sit on the edge of a large feather bed and gossip with me while I ate it. It was a bright room with a permanently crooked Venetian blind veiled demurely by white lace curtains. There was an incandescent gas bracket with the mantle broken at the end, which shed an acid yellow glare over everything and almost succeeding in taking the colour out of the eiderdown. There was a 'fire-screen-ornament' in the grate made of crinkled paper, and on the mantelpiece several photographs of Mrs. Wood's sister as Sindbad the Sailor in tights leaning against a log of wood. The bathroom was down one flight of stairs and contained a fierce geyser which blew up occasionally, and once completely destroyed the 'fringe' of a well-known character actress.

Edyth Goodall was the leading lady in *Wild Heather*, and Helen Haye and Lyn Harding were also in it. It was a strong social drama in which everyone seemed miscast. I played Helen Haye's son, and drifted in and out until the end of the second act, when I drifted out for good, which left me free to go and watch the variety bills at the Palace and Hippodrome. During the second week of the run I went to the Palace every night to see Clara Evelyn and Ivy St. Helier playing and singing at two grand pianos placed back to back. I tackled them both one day in the Midland Hotel, and was invited to tea in their sitting-room where I immediately played them some songs I had written. Miss St. Helier gave me a wise little lecture on the value of 'authority' in a piano entertainer; she also showed me some good striking chords to play as introduction to almost any song. I profited a lot from that afternoon.

During the last of our three weeks' run two important events occurred. The first was the appearance at the stage door one evening of a dark enthusiastic American who said his name was Gilbert Miller, and that he had come especially from London to see my performance, as Charles Hawtrey had suggested me for a part in the new Haddon Chambers comedy *The Saving Grace*, which they were producing jointly at the Garrick. He asked me to supper at the Midland, and I was flattered and amazed that anyone so important should be so human and unmanagerial. He told me that he had feared that I should look too young for the part, and that as there was only a cast of seven, including Hawtrey himself, it was necessary for everyone to be absolutely first-rate, if not actually a star. I aged visibly in manner and deportment and became almost off-hand in my efforts not to appear too youthful, but he assured me that he thought me good and that I would certainly be engaged, whereupon I was too dazed to be more than

[63]

mildly astonished when he suddenly asked me quite seriously whether I would care for Marie Lohr to play opposite me. By that time I should only have given a languid nod if he had told me that Ellen Terry was going to play my baby sister.

We chatted on, and he told me several plots of plays that his father, Henry Miller, had produced in New York. He told them in detail and with tremendous vivacity, occasionally rearranging the knives and forks and plates to illustrate the more dramatic passages; at one moment he actually sprang up from his chair and shouted: 'Never, never, never!' loudly, much to the dismay of the head waiter. Finally he left me in order to catch the midnight train back to London and as I was far too inflated to contemplate the squalor of the last tram, I grandly renounced it and took a taxi all the way to Lloyd Street.

The second important event of that week was the beginning of a friendship which has lasted hilariously until now, and shows every indication of enduring through any worlds which may lie beyond us, always providing that those worlds be as redundant of theatrical jokes and humours as this one is. I stepped off a tram outside the Midland Hotel on my way to play a matinée and met Bobbie Andrews and Ivor Novello. I had not seen Bobbie since we were boy actors in the dear old romantic days of Savoy parties and teas in Lyons's Corner House. He was now definitely grown-up, as well he might be, having advanced reluctantly into his early twenties, although I must admit that his years sat but lightly upon him. He introduced me to Ivor, and we stood there chatting while I tried to adjust my mind to the shock. My illusion of this romantic handsome youth who had composed 'Keep the Home Fires Burning' drooped and died and lay in the gutter between the tram-lines and the curb. The reason for this was that I had caught him in a completely 'off' moment. He was not sitting at a grand piano. He was not in naval uniform. The eager Galahad expression which distinguished every photograph of him was lacking. His face was yellow, and he had omitted to shave owing to a morning rehearsal. He was wearing an odd overcoat with an astrakhan collar and a degraded brown hat, and if he had suddenly produced a violin from somewhere and played the 'Barcarole' from *The Tales of Hoffmann,* I should have given him threepence from sheer pity.

They walked along to the stage door of the Gaiety with me, and Ivor asked me to come over to the Prince's Theatre when I had finished my performance to see the last act of his musical comedy *Arlette,* which was playing there before opening in London. I remember very little about *Arlette* except the score, which was charming. Winifred Barnes was in it and Joseph Coyne and the plot was Ruritanian.

Afterwards we had tea in Ivor's rooms at the Midland, and he shaved and changed into a dinner-jacket for a company supper party. I envied thoroughly everything about him. His looks, his personality, his assured position, his dinner clothes, his bedroom and bath, and above all, the supper party. I pictured him sipping champagne and laughing gaily, warm in the conviction that he was adored by everybody at the table. I envied the easy intimacy with which he referred to Winifred Barnes as 'Betty' and Joseph Coyne (my hero of *The Quaker Girl*) as 'Joe.' I don't think honestly that there was any meanness in my envy. I didn't begrudge him his glamorous life, nobody who knew Ivor for five minutes could ever begrudge him anything. I just felt suddenly conscious of the long way I had to go before I could break into the magic atmosphere in which he moved and breathed with such nonchalance. In bed that night in my combined room I devoured minced haddock on toast with a certain distaste. A sense of frustration oppressed me. Here was I, seventeen years old, bursting with remarkable talent, a witty and delightful companion, with an interesting if not actually good-looking face and an excellent figure, just wasting time, treading water, not getting anywhere. My forthcoming engagement in *The Saving Grace* was of course comforting, but an unknown young actor in an all-star cast would not stand much chance of sending the critics into hyperboles of praise. I admit that for a little while I did toy with the vision of an unforeseen ovation on the first night at the Garrick with Hawtrey and Marie Lohr and Ellis Jeffries pushing me in front of them and imploring me to make a speech, but common sense robbed this dream of any conviction, and I looked at the photograph Ivor had given me, propped up against Sindbad on the mantelpiece, with a lowering admiration not far removed from hatred.

To know theatrical stars by their Christian names seemed to me then to be the apex of achievement. So far I had very few to my credit. Madge (Titheradge), Debbi (Cicely Debenham), Cicely and Jack (Courtneidge and Hulbert), Peggy (Edyth Goodall), and Mary (Mary Glynne). With Pauline Chase I had never got further than Miss Chase, let alone 'Polly.' This appeared to be rather a meagre list, and I resolved to embellish it as soon as possible. I dropped off to sleep in the midst of an ecstatic dream-supper-party in which Gladys (Cooper), Elsie (Janis) and Irene (Vanbrugh) were all saying: 'We must get Noel to sing us something.'

(22)

The Saving Grace was a gentle, witty, and delightful comedy, and it is a source of great pride to me that I had the good fortune to play in it. The cast were: Charles Hawtrey, Ellis Jeffries, Emily Brooke (not Marie Lohr), May Blayney, A. E. George, Mary Jerrold and myself. We opened at the Gaiety, Manchester, which I had left only a fortnight before, and on the opening night Hawtrey made a speech mentioning each member of the company and finishing up with a brief biographical sketch of me. He told how I had played for him on and off since I was a little boy of eleven, and that the public had better watch me carefully in the future as I was undoubtedly going to be a good actor. The audience applauded and he led me forward and shook hands with me, and I fear that I cried a little, but imperceptibly.

My part was reasonably large, and I was really quite good in it, owing to the kindness and care of Hawtrey's direction. He took endless trouble with me. I was nervous and scared at rehearsals and painfully aware that I was actually too young for the part. All this I endeavoured to conceal under a manner of uppish assurance which couldn't have deceived him because he was never impatient, and taught me during those two short weeks many technical points of comedy acting which I use to this day. The play opened at the Garrick after Manchester and was an immediate success, despite the fact that the times were unhappy, and all optimism appeared to be fading into a dreary suspicion that the war was permanent and eternal. For several weeks we had a series of air raids. Hawtrey used to stop the first act by advancing to the footlights to tell the audience that the warning had been given, and that if those present who wished to take shelter would kindly leave as quietly as possible, the play would proceed. Whereupon, a few usually shuffled out and we continued, with forced brightness, to prove that even actors could be brave in the face of danger. The full fury of the raids invariably occurred during my love scene with Emily Brooke; this irritated us considerably. The banging of the anti-aircraft guns and the reverberations from bombs falling, not only robbed us of the attention of the audience, but destroyed any subtle 'nuances' we might attempt in the scene, for in order that any of the words might be heard at all we had to bellow like bulls. On several occasions small pieces of shrapnel fell through the roof over the stage and tinkled on the thin canvas ceiling immediately above our heads.

Meanwhile, drastic changes had taken place in my family life. Mother, growing weary of the purposeless, poverty-stricken gentility of existence in a maisonette at Clapham Common, suddenly revolted and determined to do something about it. She had a series of consultations with my Aunt Ida who had been successfully running a lodging-house in Ebury Street for several years, and decided that she would do the same thing. The tenants of 111, Ebury Street, which was almost opposite to my aunt's house, wished to sell the remainder of their lease with all the furniture and what was ironically termed 'the goodwill of the business' thrown in. After a lot of discussion about inventories and instalments, and a series of scenes enacted in the home in alternate moods of gloomy foreboding and the rosiest enthusiasm, until finally Mother took the plunge, signed several incomprehensible legal documents, and we moved in *en bloc,* Auntie Vida included. There was quite a lot of additional argument over this as Auntie Vida had been nourishing a secret desire to live by herself in some sad building for dead naval officers' daughters in Wimbledon. Poor old Auntie Borby had died the previous year, the house at Lee-on-the-Solent had long been given up, and she was completely alone except for us. We jumped on the Wimbledon idea firmly, suspecting misplaced martyrdom, so she came with us and was allotted a minute bedroom under the roof next to mine.

Number 111 was a tall house with an austere personality and passably good furniture. There was a wooden room built out at the back known as the 'bungalow' which we inhabited together with our dining-room table and chairs, the walnut davenport, the Organo piano (which imitated an organ when anyone pressed its extra pedal), an old and much beloved sofa with its intestines coming out, and a lot of family photographs; also many of Grandfather's pictures, and his sword and dirk hung horizontally on the wall with a faded photograph of Uncle Ran, as a boy, on one side of them, and me as a mushroom on the other.

We had two servants to begin with, and nearly our full complement of lodgers, most of whom had stayed on after the house had changed hands. Mother worked like a slave, cooking meals, rushing up and down the high steep stairs, organising, dealing with tradesmen, income-tax collectors, rate collectors, and in later years occasionally brokers' men. Payne's pianos had evaporated into an inconclusive mist of failure and Father had no work to do, so he contented himself with making model yachts for his own amusement. They were beautiful yachts and, I believe, structurally accurate in every detail, and he sailed them backwards and forwards across the Clapham Common pond, and the Battersea Park pond, and the Round Pond, and the Serpentine, while Mother discharged servants, engaged window-cleaners, found out how to make aspic jelly from Mrs. Beeton, and anxiously added up Eric's Manor House school expenses.

We soon discovered that two servants were too expensive and so we had to make do with one, which meant a lot of housework for Mother in addition to the cooking. The lodgers were amiable and frequently serenely inconsiderate. They left every once in a while, and grave apprehension reigned in the bungalow, until the empty rooms were occupied again. Mother became more or less inured to the drudgery, but her spirit drooped a little and she looked unbearably tired.

The Saving Grace ran for several months, and I began to be recognised a little bit for the first time in my life. Occasionally I noticed people nudging one another when I passed in the street, and once a strange woman spoke to me in a bus and said that she thought I gave ever such a good performance. In addition to being in a distinguished success with a distinguished cast, I had a dressing-room to myself for the first time, which, I think, pleased me more than anything.

I had a dresser called Terry, whom I shared with A. E. George, and I gave tea-parties on matinée days. Stoj generally came and Aishie Pharall, a big girl with a fox-terrier, who had been on tour with her. After we had been running a little while Mr. Camplin Smith, the stage manager, took it upon himself to use my precious dressing-room in which to interview stray applicants for small parts and understudies. He did this while I was on the stage without saying anything about it to me. One day I came up after the second act and discovered Stoj and Aishie waiting on the stairs, having been refused admittance, whereupon, swollen with the importance of my position, I lost my temper and behaved very badly. I went straight to Mr. Hawtrey's room and refused to go on in the last act. Hawtrey listened patiently to my incoherent tirade, sent for Camplin Smith, and told him he was never to use my room again without my permission, and then told me gently and firmly that if I gave myself airs and talked such nonsense I should not be given the chance of going on in the last act, nor indeed in any act, as I should be immediately sacked and never be allowed to appear in a company of his again. After that he hit me quite hard on the behind and sent me up to my tea-party.

I suppose if I had been with any other management, this appalling impertinence would have done for me completely, but

Hawtrey knew a whole lot of things that other managers never even suspected. He knew how to bring out young talent without storming and bullying. He knew how to conduct the most irritating rehearsals without sacrificing one atom of his dignity or authority. He also knew that very youthful actors were frequently victimised by their own frustrated conceits, and that to deal harshly with them might crush down their small confidence and suffocate any genuine talent they might have. He had humour and kindliness, and a sure expert knowledge of the theatre, and he managed, without apparent effort, to be much beloved. It is one of my lasting regrets that he died before I had time to justify a little his faith in me.

PART TWO

MY CAREER in the British Army was brief and inglorious. In 1914 and 1915, when the first patriotic call to arms had sounded, I had been too young even to wish to respond. I was too concentrated on my own struggles and ambitions to be able to view the war as anything but an inevitable background. Air raids, darkened streets, familiar names in the casualty lists, concerts for the wounded, food rations, coupons, and the universal smear of khaki over everything were so much part of everyday life that any other conditions seemed impossible to visualise.

In January 1918 I was examined by a medical board and informed that my slight T.B. tendency of three years ago would prevent me from being passed fit for active service and would also debar me from entering any of the Officers' Training Corps, but that I would be called up for some kind of service in due course, and was to hold myself in readiness. This was almost as great a relief to me as it was to Mother. The spirit of sacrifice, the conviction of speedy victory, and even the sense of national pride had faded in the minds of most people into a cheerless resignation. Four futile years had robbed even bravery of its glamour, and the far greater gallantry of courage in the face of anti-climax was too remote for dejected civilians to grasp. It was certainly too abstract an ideal to inspire a self-centred young actor. I remained in a state of relief tinged with uneasiness until the end of the run of *The Saving Grace,* and was rehearsing a meaty dramatic part in a play by Miss Hazel May, when a horrible little grey card fluttered through the letter-box of 111, Ebury Street, summoning me immediately to a medical board at the Camberwell Swimming Baths. I sent a telegram to Mr. Ayliff, who was producing the play, and set off in the tram for Camberwell. At the end of several hours of beastliness during which I stood about naked on cold floors and was pinched and prodded by brusque doctors, I was told to dress myself, given an identification card, and ordered to line up with a group of about fifty men in various stages of physical and mental decay. Presently a sergeant took charge of us and marched us untidily to Whitehall, where we were shut up in a stuffy hut overlooking the park for about two hours while lots of papers were signed. This over, the sergeant again took us in charge and we marched up Whitehall, along the Strand and over Waterloo Bridge to Waterloo Station. I kept my head averted in case any of my friends should see me on their way out from their matinées at the Adelphi and the Vaudeville. We entrained at Waterloo and finally arrived at Hounslow where we marched to the barracks and were put into one hut, all fifty of us, and dealt out slices of bread and margarine, cups of greasy cocoa, and three blankets each for the night. There was a slight scene while we were undressing because the man next to me was found to be covered with sores. After a good deal of argument he was led away protesting, and I was generously offered one of his blankets extra, which, although shivering with cold, I thought it wiser to refuse.

The next morning we were given uniforms and boots and porridge and paraded in front of an irritable officer with a wart over one eye. We were also made to swill our mouths out with some bright pink disinfectant and wash our teeth over a long trough. By this time my despair had given place to a still, determined rage. I contemplated, alternatively, fainting suddenly in the middle of the barrack square, or making a wild dash for the gates, but my common sense told me that neither of these dramatic gestures would do me any good at all, and that the only thing was to keep my head and think out some more subtle means of escape. I had made up my mind definitely that in no circumstances whatever would I spend another night in that hut. At eleven o'clock, after we had done some perfunctory drill and been shown how to put on our puttees properly, we were given half an hour's rest. I waited until all the others were sitting around in the hut and smoking and cursing, and then I went boldly up to the sergeant and asked if I could speak to him privately for a moment. He led me outside, whereupon I pressed a ten-shilling note into his hand and asked him to lead me to the commanding officer. He told me to wait for ten minutes and disappeared. Presently he came back and took me across the square and passed me on to another sergeant, who in turn took me into an office where two clerks were sitting at typewriters. Here I waited until the commanding officer arrived. He looked me up and down searchingly and asked me what was the matter. I told him that I had been called up the day before without any preliminary warning, and without any time to settle up my private affairs, and that it was essential for me to have a day's leave in order to straighten things out. Finally, after a certain amount of questioning, he said I could have the rest of the day off providing I reported back at nine o'clock P.M. A railway pass was made out for me and within an hour I was sitting in the train wearing a uniform that was far too small, and a hat that was far too big.

I went straight home, and after an hysterical reunion with Mother, who greeted me with as much fervour as if I had spent four years in the front line, I changed into my own clothes and set off in a taxi. I had a hastily composed list in my pocket of everyone I knew who might conceivably be influential enough to help me. The list numbered two generals, two colonels, and a captain; with grim persistence I saw them all, and not one of them could offer me the faintest hope. If I had come to them before, they said, it would have been quite easy, but as things were, it was too late and the only thing for me to do was to resign myself to the inevitable. The last on my list was a captain in the Air Force whom I had met casually at one or two parties. He was as affable and kindly as the others and equally hopeless, except that he gave me a note to a friend of his, Lieutenant Boughey at the War Office. I arrived at the War Office just as everybody was leaving. Someone told me that Lieutenant Boughey had gone five minutes before, then a small corporal interfered and said that he had not gone and was still in his office. I was led into his room, and I must have looked pretty exhausted for he offered me a drink at once and told me to sit down and take it easy. I explained my troubles to him as briefly and calmly as I could, and within ten minutes he had telephoned the commanding officer at Hounslow and informed him in a sharp official voice that there had been a disgraceful muddle over N. Coward, who was perfectly fit and had no earthly right to be in a Labour corps, and that his civilian clothes were to be sent home immediately, together with any papers there were concerning him. After this we had another drink and discussed Lord Kitchener, the war, the theatre, and my immediate future in the army. Lieutenant Boughey said that he could get me into the Artists' Rifles O.T.C., and that he would arrange for me to have a couple of weeks' leave before joining up. I thanked him as coherently as I could and went home, marvelling that a busy man at the end of a long day's work should take such trouble to help an insignificant stranger. I never saw him again, and a few months later I heard a rumour that he had been killed.

(2)

In due course my papers arrived from the Artists' Rifles, and I was sent down with a batch of about twenty recruits to the training camp at Gidea Park in Essex. It was only a little way from London, and we were allowed leave every other week-end. A sergeant-major lectured us all briskly at the outset and explained that as we were now soldiers of the King, our only thoughts henceforward must be of our country and our regiment. He commanded us to turn our minds from all trivial sentimentalities such as homes and sweethearts, and wives and mothers, and concentrate upon becoming fearless, hard-bitten fighters. This little homily depressed me, and I noted with a certain wan satisfaction that it also appeared to sadden my companions. When it was over, a group of us walked dismally into the town of Romford, our duties being finished for the day. We all tried hard to march along in an upright soldierly manner but the military spirit was as yet young in us. My puttees kept on coming undone, and I dropped my cane seventeen times.

The other men in my company (Company C) were pleasant. The food wasn't good, but on the other hand it wasn't bad. The routine was hard but not callous, and those weeks should by rights have done me a lot of good. Unfortunately, however, I couldn't adapt myself to these new circumstances. It wasn't that I didn't try. I did. I made tremendous efforts, but it was no use. My stage life had ill-prepared me for any discipline other than that of the theatre, and that discipline is peculiar to itself. In almost any branch of the theatre it is individuality that counts. In the army it is exactly the opposite. You are drilled and trained and lectured as a unit, one of thousands. I did my best and learnt a lot of things. I learnt how to fold blankets into a sort of bag and how to sleep inside it. I learnt how to polish buttons, how to roll and unroll puttees, how to carry a short cane, how to salute, and also how to stab sacks of straw accurately with a bayonet under the sharp eye of a bloodthirsty corporal with a highly developed sense of drama, who lashed our imaginations to the requisite pitch of fury by shouting: 'They're bellies, they're bellies, they're all German bellies!' The one thing I never learnt was to accept it all tranquilly. The sergeant-major's words had not sunk deep enough. I couldn't wipe my mind clean of Mother and home. I twisted about miserably inside my blankets at night wondering whether Miss Daubeney was still inhabiting the third floor, and whether the drawing-room suite was still vacant, and how Mother was managing to pay Eric's school expenses without the help of my weekly salary. I was tortured with the thought that I was wasting time. The needs of my King and Country seemed unimportant compared with the vital necessity of forging ahead with my own career. It was a matter of pressing urgency to me that I should become rich and successful as soon as possible. Soon enough in fact to be able to get Mother out of that damned kitchen for ever. All this, I fully realise, was reprehensible. There were millions of young men with far graver responsibilities than mine who were sacrificing their lives daily, and there were millions of mothers in far more tragic circumstances; but these reflections were powerless to jerk my spirit free of myself and my own personal problems, and as it is my object in this book to be as truthful as I can, I must confess that I was resentful and rebellious and profoundly wretched. Oddly enough, the thought of going to the front didn't worry me particularly. To begin with, the prospect was far away in the future, after months of training as a cadet and as an officer. In addition to this, the fact that I had been graded B 2 instead of A 1 by the various medical boards made the chance of any actual fighting even more remote. My unhappiness was concerned with the immediate present and cowardice had honestly no part in it. Soon the unfamiliarly hard routine coupled with my inward miseries began to affect me physically. I developed cracking headaches and was unable to sleep. I bought a bottle of aspirin in Romford, but it was only effective for a little while. It was ridiculous to hope for quiet in a hut with thirty men in it, and the noise every night before 'lights out' seemed to cut through my head like a saw. I used to twist string round my finger until it cut me, to prevent myself from giving way to nerves and yelling the place down.

*　　　*　　　*　　　*　　　*

One morning, a few weeks after I had been in the camp, we were all doubling back from musketry drill along the ribbed wooden paths that ran between the different huts. I caught my foot in one of the slats and fell heavily, striking my head against one of the stakes by the side of the path. I gather that I had concussion because my memory of the next three days is almost completely blank, although I dimly remember Ivor's *Arlette* score running incessantly through my mind. This was accounted for a long while afterwards when someone told me that while I was lying on the corporal's bed in Hut 10 waiting for the arrival of the doctor, the regimental band was practising next door. I can only fix accurately upon two moments of consciousness. One, in the camp hospital, when I woke to the surprising vision of the company commander sitting on my bed, with his face, which was long and amiable with a moustache on it, seeming to weave up and down close to mine. I believe he asked me a lot of questions, but I forget what they were or whether or not I answered any of them satisfactorily. The only other clear moment in those strange hours was the sudden realisation that I was being conveyed rapidly backwards in bed, and that there was an orderly in khaki reading a book against a background of swiftly moving hedges. I awoke finally in the emergency ward of the First London General Hospital, with Mother bending over me and explaining tearfully that I had been unconscious for three days and nights.

(3)

I remained in the First London General Hospital for six weeks, in a large ward with about twenty other inmates, most of whom were shell-shock cases. I was examined by several different doctors, thoroughly, casually, suspiciously, and kindly. None of them seemed to know what was the matter with me. Some of them fired searching questions at me; abrupt and irrelevant questions obviously calculated to catch me out in the event of the whole thing being a hoax. Their suspicions were pretty adequately disproved by my temperature chart which resembled an outline of the Rocky Mountains drawn by a drunken child. They traced back my medical history and cross-examined Mother, who finally gratified them by remembering that I had been knocked down by a bicycle at the age of five. This apparently accounted for everything, and we all settled ourselves to wait until the brain tumour showed further signs of life. It didn't, and I convalesced gradually. My headaches became less frequent and less violent. My temperature returned to normal, and after a couple of weeks I was able to sleep at night without the aid of either aspirin or bromide. Mother visited me every day and brought me books and fruit, although where she found the money to pay for them I shall never know. I conceived a passion for the works of two authors, Sheila Kaye-Smith and G. B. Stern, and I wrote them both long letters of admiration to which they replied promptly. A considerable correspondence ensued, and when we ultimately met we discovered that we were already old friends.

During my really convalescent, out-of-bed period, when I wore hospital blue and helped to carry meals to the bedridden and sweep out the ward, I met, in the Y.M.C.A. hut which was attached to the hospital, a young New Zealander named Geoffrey Holdsworth. He endeared himself to me by sitting wide-eyed by the rickety upright piano and imploring me to play him the 'Lilac Domino' waltz. This paved the way to mutual confidences, and he took me down to the kitchens to introduce me to a friend of his who was one of the cooks; thereafter, by means of various sly devices, Geoffrey and I were always given the slightly better quality food reserved for the officers. He also showed me a broken place in the wall at the end of the grounds by which it was possible to escape after the morning duties were finished, which was generally about eleven, and not return until roll call at six. This was a dangerous proceeding but exciting. We were only actually allowed out for one afternoon a week from two until five, but with the aid of the broken wall and a convenient tree we enjoyed many hours of extra freedom. The initial steps were the most perilous—a casual walk along the path, then a swift glance all round, and a sudden dart into the shrubbery. Once over the wall there was only the brief agony of a nonchalant stroll to the tram stop, which was the worst of all really, because the desire to run whenever a sergeant or an officer appeared had to be sternly crushed down. There was always the dread of being accosted and asked to show a 'pass.' However, I weathered all the dangers and was never caught.

Upon arrival at Ebury Street I bathed and changed, and set out for the West End, an actor once more, wearing coloured shirts and ties and silk socks, with shoes that felt strangely light after the heavy army boots, and a heart that felt lighter still. I saw a lot of Ivor and Bobbie and Gladys Gunn (now Gladys Henson), and one day Ivor gave me a dress-circle seat for the opening matinée of his new revue at the Vaudeville, in which Beatrice Lillie was the leading lady, and Gertrude Lawrence was understudying her. In his flat there was a delicious atmosphere of slight quarrels and gossiping. Everyone drank a lot of tea and discussed what Charlot had said and what Fay (Compton) had said and how Eddie (Marsh) thought it was marvellous anyway. This would have to be changed and that would certainly have to be changed. The whole conversation swirled around all the topics I loved best, occasionally enhanced, but never interrupted, by peculiar noises from the next room in which Mme. Novello Davies gave interminable singing lessons to small Welsh women in grey clothes.

(4)

I repaid Geoffrey Holdsworth's good offices by changing the course of his life. I lent him G. B. Stern's books and also showed him some of her letters, whereupon he immediately wrote to her himself and a few months later married her. As they are now divorced, I will deny myself the pleasure of romantic digression and disassociate myself firmly from the whole affair.

On my discharge from the hospital I was given a week's leave before returning to camp. This I spent in Devonshire with Stoj and her fiancé, Lyndon Tyson. He was tall and docile, and much in love with her; otherwise I am sure he would have objected to my presence during what was undoubtedly a sort of pre-nuptial honeymoon. It was a peaceful and pleasant week enlivened by only one serious row; caused by Lyndon meeting Stoj and me face to face on the hotel landing as we issued forth blandly from the bathroom together. It took several hours of threefold hysteria and many tears and recriminations to erase the unworthy suspicions from his mind, but by tea-time everything was rosy again, and we all sat on the bench and talked about life intellectually and without resentment.

When I arrived back at the camp I was put on 'Light Duties', which consisted of polishing practically everything, and helping to clean out the latrines. This was far from enjoyable; but I had more leisure than before, and spent most of it sitting in the canteen drinking cups of strong tea and eating odd messes of bright pink jelly with whipped cream on top, which the local lady workers behind the bar arranged daintily in glass dishes.

I persevered wearily with my 'Light Duties' and tried, without much success, to keep my mind from dwelling too much upon the utter futility of the situation. I felt physically well enough for about three-quarters of every day, and then suddenly, unreasonably, and without warning, a cloud of black melancholia would envelop me, draining all colour and vitality from everything and changing the friendly noises of the canteen into a nerve-racking din from which I fled to the church hut. This, although gloomy, was at least empty and still. I lashed myself with accusations of hysteria and self-pity, aware that I was a poor weakling, a spineless creature of no integrity, unable to cope with anything more formidable than a row of footlights and a Saturday-night audience. These emotional orgies usually passed after an hour or so and I crept back, ashamed, to Hut 10, and scuffled into my blankets as unobtrusively as possible, in the hope that no one would comment upon my red-rimmed eyes.

After a few weeks my headaches began to recur, but not very badly; at least, not badly enough to prevent me from applying for an afternoon's leave to attend the Theatrical Garden Party. Up to now I had helped Vane Featherstone every year with her 'Jarley's Wax-works', and it had always been a day of ecstasy for me, hobnobbing with the stars on the more or less equal terms dictated by Charity. The company commander, with a slightly ironical smile, granted my request and I endured the next few days in a fever of anxiety in case anything should occur to prevent me from going. My anxiety was well-founded. The morning before the day of the garden party I woke with such a violent headache that I was incapable of standing up. The doctor came into the hut to examine me and I was carted off to the camp hospital. Later on in the day I was examined by two other doctors, and the next morning at eleven o'clock I was put in an ambulance and driven to the General Military Hospital at Colchester. It was a beautiful sunny day, fashioned by God for morning suits and silk hats and white gloves and flowered chiffons. I pictured the gay crowds at the Botanical Gardens, old ladies from the suburbs in black taffeta, character actresses of small standing in large feather boas, eminent male stars with button-holes and cravats, and Gladys Cooper smiling immaculately, wearing shell pink and wheeling a barrow. I smelt the little 'Jarley's Wax-works' tent, hot canvas and trampled grass and tea, and knew wretchedly that I should never see any of it again, that the doctors at the First London General Hospital had been right about there being a tumour on my brain, and that I was lost for ever in frustration, misery, and pain.

(5)

My first night in the Colchester Hospital was spent in a general ward. My head was bad and I couldn't sleep. The night nurse refused to give me aspirin because she said that I had not yet been diagnosed, so I twisted and turned and stared at the shadows the night lamp made upon the ceiling, wondering whether they would operate on my brain in the morning, and, if so, whether they would use a hammer and a chisel as I heard they did in mastoid operations. I also wondered whether there would be time for Mother to get to Colchester for my death and whether I should be conscious or unconscious when she arrived.

They didn't operate on me in the morning. They thought of something far better, which was to move me straightway into an epileptic ward in the annex. They also omitted to tell me that it was an epileptic ward, probably not wishing to deprive me of the full flavour of surprise, when the patient opposite to me proceeded to have several fits one after another before I had been in the place half an hour.

An epileptic fit is not a pleasant sight at the best of times, and as

[83]

there were twelve epileptics in the ward and the moment one started they all started, my condition of acute neurasthenia showed no noticeable signs of improvement for the first week or so. As I remained there for two months I naturally became inured, and, later on, even managed to be quite helpful to the nurses. I acquired the technique of squeezing the patients' tongues back into place by a deft pressure on the throat. I learnt how to hold their arms in a certain position to prevent their springing off the bed and out of the window, and I also learnt not to mind being flecked with their foam and saliva. I had a few bad moments at first, when I realised that not a single one of them suspected that he was epileptic. The minute anyone finished having a fit he generally went to sleep and woke up with no memory of it whatever. Most of them seemed rather bewildered at being there at all. The thought that I might be having fits myself all the time without knowing it was horrible, and when I questioned the nurses I wasn't quite able to believe their kindly denials, so I kept myself wide awake for twenty-four hours and checked off every ten minutes in an exercise book. I did this twice a week for the first three weeks. The strain of keeping awake all night long was awful, but the relief of finding every ten minutes safely marked was well worth it.

The rounds were made every morning by a lady doctor of bird-like appearance. She was brusque, efficient and quite idiotic. Once a week she was accompanied by the medical officer in charge of the whole annex, and on these occasions her brusquerie became almost frantic. She yapped and poked and prodded and flounced from bed to bed, giving shrill orders to the nurses and snapping her teeth together like castanets.

Nobody seemed to consider it worth while to attempt to diagnose my case with any degree of thoroughness, and so there I remained through July and August, passing the time in bed by writing a bad novel, and reading a little and walking a little on the common whenever I could get a 'pass' for the afternoon. Sidney Lomer had a house in Colchester and I used to have tea with him sometimes. One day General (Splash) Ashmore, whom I had

known when I was in *The Saving Grace,* made an official visit to
the hospital. We all stood to attention when he clanked into the
ward with some doctors and A.D.C.s in attendance, and he sent
my stock up considerably by chatting to me for about ten minutes.
Fortunately the dignity of the occasion was unimpaired by anybody having a fit, although a short while after he had left, a boy
called Barnet, in the next bed to mine had seven straight off, doubtless from sheer excitement.

Eventually the head medical officer called me into his office and
told me that I was to go before the next medical board which
occurred in a week's time, and that he had recommended me for
complete discharge from the army. He said, reasonably, that my
value as a soldier of the King amounted to a total loss, and that the
sooner I got out of it the better for all concerned. I was stupefied
with surprise and relief, but I retained enough sense not to give
way to it too much. I believe I even managed to look a little
wistful, which either deceived or amused him, for he patted me on
the back and dismissed me amiably.

I went before the medical board after six days of feverish anticipation of freedom, during which I had written hysterical letters
home and received correspondingly ecstatic ones back. My own
medical officer was not present at the board and the doctors who
were, after a cursory glance at me and my papers, marked me
back for full duty with the Artists' Rifles and dismissed me curtly
without argument.

I went back to the ward slowly, quite stunned, and trying to
adjust my mind to the full bitterness of disappointment. To have
been so near release, to have known so definitely that the futile
wasteful months were at last over, and now, by the order of a few
strange doctors who had glanced casually through my papers and
knew nothing of my circumstances, to be sent back to the beginning again seemed too crushing a blow to realise.

I sat on my bed and opened a book, trying while I was staring
at the pages, to phrase in my mind a telegram to Mother, a
telegram that would explain the truth adequately, without up-
setting her too much. While I was occupied with this, the head

sister came in and, noting from my expression that something was wrong, called me outside and asked me what had happened. Under her sympathetic eye I managed to explain my doom more or less coherently. She thought for a moment or two and then, with surprising professional brusqueness, told me that I looked seedy and that I was to go to bed immediately for a week until the head doctor came back from his holiday; she also added stonily that it might be necessary to put me on a diet. With this she left me and I went to bed and wrote out a telegram to Mother saying that there had been a slight delay, but that she wasn't to worry as everything would be all right.

The head doctor returned from his holiday a day earlier than he was expected, and was astonished and angry to find me still littering up the ward. He interviewed me briefly in his office, and said that the medical board had behaved like bloody fools, and that not only would I be discharged within a week, but that he would see to it that I got a year's pension. Three days after this I was passed rapidly through another medical board and was signed finally out of the British Army. I still had to wait for a few days while the papers went through, but this I didn't mind in the least, as I was nominally free and could wander about the town and go to the pictures providing I was back every night by nine o'clock.

The day before my actual discharge I was escorted up to London by a sergeant, who took me to the Pensions Office where I submitted to a good deal of questioning and was finally conceded a pension of seven shillings and sixpence a week for a term of six months. When all this was over we had a couple of hours to spare before catching the train back to Colchester, so I took the sergeant to Ebury Street and we had tea in the bungalow. Mother sent Auntie Vida round the corner to get a coffee cake at Barret and Pomeroy's and the whole occasion passed off delightfully. The sergeant, under Father's tutelage, experimented with the Organo piano and expressed great enthusiasm for Grandfather's pictures. Mother suggested that he might like a peep at my press-cutting book but I squashed this hurriedly, fearing that the early photographs of me in tights as Prince Mussel might sully a hitherto successful afternoon.

The next morning, wearing a navy-blue suit and carrying a kitbag, I said good-bye to the epileptics and the nurses and my beloved head sister, and settled myself in a third-class carriage of the London train in a state of indescribable happiness. The fact that the train passed through Gidea Park and Romford gave an extra fillip to my joy. Somewhere between these two grim stations I observed a long line of Artists' Rifles tramping along the dusty road, but the train was travelling too quickly for me to be able to distinguish any familiar faces. At Liverpool Street I took a taxi and drove through the city streets. It was twelve noon, in the full tide of traffic, and the hot August sun beat down upon taxis and trucks and drays and red friendly buses. It also beat down with kindly impartiality upon the Gaiety, the Vaudeville, the Savoy, and the Adelphi theatres and I pictured, as I passed them, the cool pre-matinée gloom of their interiors. Cleaners swishing dust sheets from the boxes and dress-circles, understudies meandering about their stages under a working light, clutching scripts and mumbling inaudibly with an occasional sharp interruption from the stage manager at the prompt table, a genial hum of vacuum cleaners from the front of the house, and strong shafts of alien sunlight striking down from open doors, and from the flies on to forlorn detached pieces of scenery; backings and flats against white-washed walls, unfinished staircases and shorn fragments of balustrade waiting about untidily to be set in act one symmetry by the staff at two o'clock.

I almost wept with sentimental love for it all; it seemed that æons had passed since I had been part of it. I reflected then, without a shadow of embarrassment, upon my unworthy performance as a soldier. There was no room in my heart for anything but thankfulness that I was free again to shape my life as I wanted.

PART THREE

My FIRST STEP after my discharge from the Army was to look for an engagement. I sauntered into all the agents' offices and announced that I was free. I informed every management, verbally and by letter, that I was theirs for the asking, and discovered that although I had played a leading part in *The Saving Grace,* not one of them seemed to care. I appeared at crowded auditions wearing an immaculate suit and an air of amused condescension which deceived nobody and merely succeeded in irritating the other aspirants. I had written a number of light songs during the past years, and I sang them repeatedly, accompanying myself on the piano. There was a sentimental ballad, 'Tamarisk Town,' and a bright point number, 'Forbidden Fruit,' which I think is worthy of record as it was the first complete lyric I ever wrote. The perceptive reader will, I am sure, detect, even in this very youthful effort, that unfortunate taint of worldly cynicism which, I am so frequently told, degrades much of my later work.

> *'Every Peach, out of reach, is attractive*
> *'Cos it's just a little bit too high,*
> *And you'll find that every man*
> *Will try to pluck it if he can*
> *As he passes by.*

> *'For the brute loves the fruit that's forbidden*
> *And I'll bet you half-a-crown*
> *He'll appreciate the flavour of it much much more*
> *If he has to climb a bit to shake it down.'*

I can only suppose that this cold-blooded realism was too much for the managers, because they neither made any offers for me nor for the song. I remember on one occasion Beatrice Lillie incurred the grave displeasure of Andre Charlot by bringing me in to sing for him before an afternoon rehearsal. He informed her afterwards that he would not have his valuable time wasted by trivial young composers who played the piano badly and sang worse and that never, in any circumstances, was she to do such a thing again.

In all theatrical experience I know of nothing more dispiriting than an average audition. A bleak denuded stage only illuminated by one or two glaring working lights. A weary accompanist at a rickety upright piano. In the second or third row of the stalls, with the dim auditorium stretching behind them, sit a small group of people upon whom your livelihood depends, who mutter constantly to each other and whose faces, on the rare occasions that they are turned towards the stage, register such forbidding boredom that gay words stick in the gullet, and voice tones, so resonant and musical in the bathroom, issue forth in strangulated squeaks. An additional horror is the awareness that the sides of the stage are packed with implacable ambition. Every watching eye is steely with determination, marking with satisfaction each nervous shudder and each false note. The inexperienced, of course, suffer the most. They usually embark upon some lengthy song or aria and are stricken into bewildered silence half-way through by a sharp 'Thank you' from the stalls, and an abrupt cessation of all sound from the piano, after which, trembling, they give their names and addresses to the stage manager and go away, tortured by the knowledge that their top B flat, for which they had been conserving all their vocal energy, has not been heard at all. The wise ones sing only one refrain, sometimes only the last part of it if it happens to be over-long. Dancers have a very bad time as a rule, unless they bring their own accompanists, for in the hands of the lady provided by the management their carefully rehearsed tempos change inexorably from fast to slow and from slow to fast, heedless of their scurryings and gaspings and muttered supplications.

For most auditions ordinary day clothes are worn, embellished usually with borrowed finery. I believe that a white fox fur belonging to Beryl Norman was actually identified in the course of one month on nineteen different people. There are always a few, however, who put on fancy costumes and make up elaborately. Panniers, crinolines, insecure home-made bustles, and the inevitable pierrot suits with depressed tulle ruffles. Dancing girls used to wear imaginative 'practice dress' but this in later years has gradually discarded its bows and frills and shrunk to nothing more or less than a plain one-piece swimming suit.

My own audition apparel was usually a navy-blue suit with a coloured shirt, tie, socks, and handkerchief to match. I had not learned then that an exact duplication of colours ill becomes the well-dressed man. My bearing was a blend of assurance and professional vivacity; the fact that my bowels were as water I hope was not apparent to anybody. I used to walk on to the stage, bow politely in the direction of the stalls and say 'Good morning', sometimes, owing to nerves, a trifle more loudly than I had intended. Then, having banished the accompanist with a lordly gesture, I sat down at the piano on a stool that was invariably either too low or too high, and rattled off a few authoritative introductory chords, inwardly appalled by the tone and quality of the piano, but preserving an air of insouciance. I then swivelled round sharply, announced my song, and started it before anyone had time to stop me. My voice was small but my diction clear, assisted by a violent interplay of facial expressions. My rendition of a song in those days was a model of exhaustive technique. Sustained pauses, gay laughs, knowing looks. All the paraphernalia of Harry Fragson and Margaret Cooper and Tom Clare. Frequently, if the dreaded 'Thank you' came in the middle of a verse, I pretended not to hear it and continued with only a faint quickening of tempo until either a second and louder 'Thank you' stopped me, or I was allowed to finish.

One day Grossmith and Laurillard held a big audition at the Shaftesbury Theatre. They were planning the production of an American musical comedy called *Oh Boy,* with music by Jerome

Kern. I received one of the usual audition cards, and arrived at the theatre in good time to force my way in front of those who had got there before me. When I had finally achieved the stage and the piano, and was half-way through my song, I noticed that Grossmith and Laurillard and all their myrmidons in the stalls were so immersed in conversation that not one of them was looking at me. I stopped dead and waited until their voices had died into silence. Then, with what I hoped was icy dignity, I said that I saw no point in wasting my time singing to them if they continued to waste their time not listening to me. There was a horrified gasp from those waiting at the side of the stage, and the stage manager nervously rustled a lot of papers. Then George Grossmith, whose manners have always been a long way above reproach, walked down to the orchestra rail and invited me gently to start my song again from the beginning. When I had finished, they asked me to come down into the stalls, where, after a few preliminary courtesies had been exchanged, I was engaged at a salary of twelve pounds a week. The actual part I was to play would be decided upon later, but in the meantime I could rest assured that my remarkable talents should have full scope.

(2)

Rehearsals for *Oh Boy* were not scheduled to begin for a few weeks, so I wrote to G. B. Stern, who was staying at St. Merryn, in Cornwall, with the Dawson-Scott family, and suggested that now was the moment for our long-deferred meeting. She replied immediately that Mrs. Dawson-Scott would be delighted to lodge me for a fortnight, which, I discovered later, was a slight over-statement, and that it would be a friendly gesture on my part to offer two pounds a week for my bed and board. This seemed a perfectly satisfactory arrangement and so I set forth for Cornwall, having sent a telegram on my way to the station, a blithe, cheerful, and apparently quite fatal telegram: 'Arriving Padstow five-thirty. Tall and divinely handsome in grey.' I was met at

Padstow by a strange man with a cart, and as we drove along the sandy roads, I listened to the surf thundering on the beach a mile or so away, and noted, with familiar pleasure, the Cornish shapes and sounds and smells. It was a glorious summer evening, and I was extremely happy. My future was assured. A good twelve-pound-a-week job in a musical comedy, which would certainly run a year. A chance to captivate London audiences for all time with my irresistible singing and dancing. Two weeks of sunshine and bathing and picnics and brilliant literary conversation. G. B. Stern and the kindly devil-may-care Dawson-Scotts entranced with my company and responding joyously to my witty sallies. All the gods were smiling at me without a trace of irony, and there seemed to be nothing to cloud my contentment.

These anticipations were, as usual, too good to be true. That holiday, although far from dull, was an established failure from the outset. G. B. Stern herself justified and surpassed my mental picture of her, and we were friends immediately, but the Dawson-Scotts, the kindly devil-may-care Dawson-Scotts, were a bad let down, for not only did they dislike me on sight, but they had worked up a definite distaste for me long before I arrived. I was theatrical to begin with, and it was inevitable that I would be luxury-loving, unable to swim or climb rocks, unappreciative of the country, and very affected in my speech. On to this elaborate pyramid of prejudice my telegram fluttered, my odious, conceited telegram: 'Arriving Padstow five-thirty. Tall and divinely handsome in grey.'

Mrs. Dawson-Scott, a writer of 'strong' books which reeked of earth, and sea-wrack, and primitive childbirth, and hot, sweet breasts, had had, I suspected, little time to cultivate social grace. She wore a red tea-gown and no shoes or stockings, and, as far as I was concerned, a remarkably forbidding expression. Her family dutifully followed her example and my first evening with them was far from cosy. I remember, during supper, when I suggested that they should call me 'Noel', being painfully rebuffed by the reply, 'I think, Mr. Coward, we would rather wait a little.'

Marjorie, the daughter, softened a little towards me later on in the week and we had an abortive heart-to-heart talk during a 'spratting' expedition in the moonlight. This melting might be explained by the fact that I was quite adept at plunging the curved knife into the wet sand as the waves receded and, in spite of my theatrical decadence, managed to catch more sprats than any of them. She informed me with compelling frankness, as we walked along the shore, that the whole family hated me, to which I replied, with equal candour, that the hatred was entirely mutual, and that I wouldn't have stayed a day with them had it not been for Peter (G. B. Stern), and that I had paid my two pounds a week in advance.

The elder son, Christopher, was less actively unpleasant to me, his only efforts to discomfit me consisting of sharp cries of 'Bet you can't do this', followed by a flying leap on to a slippery rock, or something equally valorous. These manly exhibitions ceased when, in addition to cutting his knee quite badly, he discovered that I was unimpressed.

The younger son, Toby, was the nicest of the lot, and actually showed traces of a sense of humour.

Peter and I managed to get away by ourselves as much as possible, and these hours were peaceful and happy. We discussed plots for plays and novels. We dwelt untiringly upon the peculiarities of the Dawson-Scotts. We watched German submarines torpedoing cargo boats far out to sea, and wandered along the beach looking for pieces of wreckage, and wondering, fearfully, whether or not we should find any dead bodies.

Peter listened and nodded, and giggled appropriately, as we sat on the beach with our backs against a rock, and I enlarged, at great length, upon my ambitions as a playwright, composer, lyric writer, and novelist. Never once did she suggest that I seemed to be taking rather too much upon myself. Never once did she trot out the 'Jack of all trades master of none' bugbear, from which, even at that age, I had suffered a good deal. She recognised easily in me the familiar creative urge, and permitted my Ego to strut bravely before her.

My actual achievements up to date amounted to very little. I had written quite a lot, in spare moments, during the last few years. Plays, singly, and in collaboration with Stoj. Short stories, verses, and one meretricious full-length novel. I had also composed a good many songs, and written lyrics for some tunes of Max Darewski's and Doris Joel's.

I stayed for my full fortnight at St. Merryn, having no intention of denying myself Peter's company just because that imperceptive family failed to respond to my charms. As a matter of fact, after the first few days, they became much more agreeable and even, on one or two occasions, seemed disposed to be amused at my conversation, but these moments were too rare and ephemeral to form the basis of a lasting friendship. We met a few times during the following years, generally at the 'To-morrow' Club. I also dined with them once in Hampstead.

The introduction of celebrated names into autobiographies is a rule that I am too timorous to ignore, therefore I will put on record that, between the years 1917 and 1919, I knew G. B. Stern, Sheila Kaye-Smith, Charles Scott-Moncrieff, Fay Compton, Charles Hawtrey, Ivor Novello, Gertrude Lawrence and Beatrice Lillie. I was on pleasant, but not intimate, terms with Rebecca West, Hugh Walpole, W. Somerset Maugham, Yvonne Arnaud, H. G. Wells, Rose Macaulay, Olive Wadsley, Billie Carleton, Viola Tree, Ronald Colman, Madge Titheradge, Lady Carisbrooke, Lady Londesborough and Nellie Wallace. I could also nod at and be nodded to by Compton Mackenzie, Irene Vanbrugh, Violet Vanbrugh, Gladys Cooper, John Galsworthy, Gerald du Maurier, Nigel Playfair, E. F. Benson, John Lane, Elsie Janis, Maurice Chevalier and Lynn Fontanne. This last name was insignificant then and belonged to a scraggy, friendly girl with intelligent brown eyes and a raucous laugh. The above list must make it obvious to the meanest intelligence that I was progressing like wild-fire. The plans nurtured in my bed-sitting-room in Manchester were blooming and I could now use a considerable number of effective Christian names without fear of swift and crushing humiliation.

(3)

The day before the first rehearsal of *Oh Joy* (it had been re-named, doubtless because the arrogant Americanism of *Oh Boy* might stir the English public's stomach to revolt), I was stricken with a bad attack of influenza. This was a bitter blow to me, and for several days I lay feverishly visualising the thrills and excitements taking place without me. At last, very weak, but determined, I was allowed to get up and take a taxi to the theatre. My head felt light, and my legs wobbly, but I walked on to the stage as firmly as possible. The morning rehearsal was just about to begin, and the play was being directed by an American producer named Austin Hurgon, who, when I approached him, regarded me from a tremendously high altitude. I asked him if he had received my telegram explaining why I had not been able to attend before, and he said: 'What telegram?' I then told him my name and he said: 'Noel what?' Discouraged but persevering, I went on to explain that I had been engaged by Mr. Grossmith and Mr. Laurillard to play one of the principal parts. He said, with sarcasm, that he was very sorry to contradict me, but that the principal as well as the small parts had been filled ages ago, in addition to which he was regrettably forced to admit that he had never heard of me in his life. All this took place before the amused gaze of the entire company. I replied, with as much dignity as I could muster, that there was obviously some mistake, and that if he would kindly telephone the office, the muddle would be rectified. He retorted that he had no time to waste telephoning while he was rehearsing, and that I had probably been engaged for the chorus, which was rehearsing elsewhere. Trying hard to keep emotion out of my voice, I said that I had certainly not been engaged for the chorus. Whereupon he snatched up the chorus list from the prompt table, glanced through it, and triumphantly read out my name. This called forth a titter from the company, and I walked off the stage and out into the

street without another word. I went into a public-house in Shaftesbury Avenue, had a glass of neat brandy to pull me together, and
took a taxi to the Grossmith and Laurillard offices in Golden
Square, where I demanded to see Mr. Laurillard. After about
twenty minutes I was ushered into his room where my pent-up
emotions broke into a full-blooded fury. I think I must have
roared very loudly indeed, for he looked startled, and kept on
waving his hand in the air, apparently in an effort to dam the
spate of words pouring on to his head. After a while I calmed
down, and he expressed great sympathy and regret, admitting that
there had indeed been a mistake, as there was no part suitable for
me in *Oh Joy*. I opened my mouth to launch a fresh tirade, but he
silenced me with more soothing words, explaining that my performance in *The Saving Grace* had convinced him that I was far
too good a straight actor to waste my time in anything so trivial
as musical comedy, and that there was a good part for me in
Scandal, the new Cosmo Hamilton play, which was to be produced at the Strand Theatre in December with a superb cast headed
by Arthur Bourchier and Kyrle Bellew. This, although better than
nothing, was still not enough to compensate me for the miseries
of that morning, and I went unhappily home to bed, not particularly cheered by the reflection that I had ample time to recover
from my influenza, as the rehearsals for *Scandal* were not due to
begin for two whole months.

I occupied myself during those two months by starting another
novel. It was a lush work called *Cherry Pan,* dealing in a whimsical vein with the adventures of a daughter of Pan, who, born into
a modern world, contrived to be arch, and elfin, and altogether
nauseating, for nearly thirty thousand words. She finally petered
out, owing to lack of enthusiasm on my part, and lack of stamina
on hers.

(4)

The house in Ebury Street was, at this time, running comparatively smoothly. Our faithful standby, Miss Daubeney, was

still with us on the third floor. She was a niece of Lord Brassey, and had been known to sail on his yacht, a photograph of which adorned the mantelpiece in a silver frame. She was friendly and kind, and one of our temporary housemaids, in a transport of Irish enthusiasm, described her as being 'downright aristocratic.' On the ground floor 'dining-room suite' we had a Mr. and Mrs. Farina, the most charming of all our lodgers. I dined with them frequently, repressing a sense of guilt in eating the excellently cooked food that I knew Mother had been labouring over in the kitchen. Mrs. Farina evinced a kindly passion for being read to, and consequently had to listen, poor woman, to everything I had ever written. She was appreciative and only occasionally critical, and did me a power of good.

I managed to sell a few magazine stories here and there, and was once led by Stoj into the presence of a Miss Ethel Mannin, who was the editor or sub-editor of the *Blue Magazine.* I met her again many years afterwards at a literary dinner party given by Mr. George Doran; and was flattered to discover, upon reading her book, *Confessions and Impressions,* recently, that these two brief encounters had obviously constituted, in her mind, a delightful intimacy.

Through the influence of Max Darewski, I signed a three years' contract with his brother Herman, who at that time was the head of a music publishing firm in Charing Cross Road. The contract was for lyrics only, and I was to be paid fifty pounds the first year, seventy-five pounds the second year, and one hundred pounds the third year. I appeared dutifully every week or so, for the first few months, armed with verses, and ideas for songs. I waited many hours in the outer office, and sometimes even penetrated into the next-to-the-outer office, but seldom, if ever, clapped eyes on Herman Darewski, and nobody seemed at all interested in my lyrics. At the end of the first year I began to get a little anxious about the second instalment of seventy-five pounds. But I needn't have worried because it was paid to me without rancour, on the day specified. During the third year of my contract I was too busy with other affairs to go near the office until the last day, when I called to receive my cheque for a hundred pounds. Herman Darewski's third or fourth secretary handed it to me with a charming smile, and, after a brief exchange of social amenities, I had a cup of tea in the outer office and went home. Some while after this the Herman Darewski publishing firm went bust, a fact that has never altogether astonished me.

On Armistice Day I wandered about the streets during the morning and afternoon, and in the evening dined with Tony and Juanita Ganderillas, whom I had met originally at one of General Ashmore's musical parties. They were Chileans, wealthy, gay and kind. After dinner we drove in a dark-red Rolls-Royce through the Park and into Trafalgar Square, where we stuck, while hordes of screaming people climbed on to the roof of the car, the footboards and the radiator. We screamed with them, and shook hands with as many as we could, and I felt ignobly delighted, in this moment of national rejoicing, to be in a tail coat, a Rolls-Royce, and obviously aristocratic company. After a couple of hours in Trafalgar Square, we managed to get to the Savoy where everybody wore paper caps, and threw streamers, and drank champagne, and Delysia, in a glittering pink dress, stood on a table and sang the 'Marseillaise' over and over again to wild applause. It was a thrilling night, and I regret to say that the tragic significance of it was almost entirely lost upon me. I had not consciously suffered much from the war, apart from those unhappy months in training camps and hospitals. I had been a small boy of fourteen when it started, too young to realise what it was all about, and now that it was over, I could only perceive that life would probably be a good deal more enjoyable without it. I have noticed, just lately, a certain tendency among contemporary journalistic writers to class me with the generation that was 'ineradicably scarred by the war.' They have found, upon analysing my plays, a sense of profound disillusionment, a dreadful nerve-racked cynicism, obviously the heritage of those four black years, and I have searched myself carefully to discover any grounds for believing this dramatic implication to be true. I have found none. I was not in the least scarred by the war.

It was little more to me at the time than a dully oppressive background, and although I certainly acquired a few nasty scratches from the years immediately following it, the reasons for my warped disenchantment with life must be sought elsewhere.

(5)

My part in *Scandal* was small, and, as a character, nebulous. I made a brief appearance at the beginning of act two in a grey suit, and a still briefer appearance at the beginning of act three, dressed, I forget why, as Sir Walter Raleigh. The play was what's known as 'strong.' The 'big scene' took place in a bedroom, after all the smaller parts had gone home. Beatrice Hinchliffe (Kyrle Bellew), having tricked the strong and silent family friend (Arthur Bourchier) into a *mariage blanc,* suddenly discovered, on the wedding night, that she was deeply in love with him. This had the unfortunate effect of sending her into transports of coquetry. She bounced about on the nuptial bed, employing archness, defiance, tenderness, temper, and tears, until Arthur Bourchier, goaded to a frenzy of suppressed passion, lashed her, cringing, on to her silken pillows, with a virile and dramatic speech concluding with the terrifying words: 'If you and I were alone on a desert island I wouldn't . . .' etc., etc., with which he turned definitely on his heel and left her as the curtain fell. In the last act, which took place on a yacht, after a comic seasick cameo contributed by Gladys Ffolliot, everything was smoothed out satisfactorily, and everybody forgave everybody else. I never considered it a good play, but perhaps I was prejudiced by the fact that my part in it was so unimportant.

Arthur Bourchier and Kyrle Bellew were charming to me, and arranged for me to have a little dressing-room to myself. Norah Swinburne was sweet and friendly, and I loved Mary Robson dearly, from the first rehearsal onwards. Apart from these pleasant contacts, my stock was low in the company. I behaved badly, and was accused, justifiably, by Millie Hylton, of making hen noises whenever she came on to the stage. I was also heartily detested by Gladys Ffolliot, who had overheard me say to someone that her dog, Daphne, smelt like a drain. The truth of this statement in no way mitigated her rage, and she complained about me to the management whenever possible. Clare Greet lodged a few complaints, too, from time to time, but I think this was only out of loyalty to the others. The theatre was frequently divided into camps, for and against me. Mary Robson's dressing-room was my refuge, where the various skirmishes were discussed with considerable hilarity. Our laughter was sometimes over-loud, and went echoing down the passage to torment the ears of my enemies. Arthur Bourchier and Kyrle occasionally admonished me with some attempt at severity, but they were seldom able to keep going for long without a twinkle appearing in their eyes, and when their door had closed upon my unconvincingly downcast figure, I used to hear them snorting with laughter. Finally Arthur Bourchier called me very seriously into his room, and informed me that the management were going to give me my notice at the end of the week. He suggested, kindly, that it would be a good idea for me to anticipate this by writing them a letter of resignation, thereby saving myself the humiliation of being actually sacked. He said that he, personally, would be very sorry to lose me, as he considered me an excellent actor, but that in the future I must behave much better, and be particularly careful never to offend women in the theatre, especially the slightly older ones, as their dislike, once incurred, was implacable and very, very dangerous.

When I got home that night I spent a happy hour composing a letter to Grossmith and Laurillard. I explained, with dignity, that owing to the peculiar behaviour of the old ladies in the cast, I felt myself compelled to tender my resignation, and that I should be exceedingly obliged if they could see their way to accepting my fortnight's notice. I remained, theirs, very sincerely. They saw their way to accepting my fortnight's notice with unflattering clearness, and when I arrived at the theatre the next night, an envelope containing the salary due to me was handed to me by the stage-door keeper, and I was allowed only half an hour to collect my things from my dressing-room. This was a shock, but not a bad one. I was already steeled to losing my job, and two weeks one way or another didn't make much difference. I detected in this waspish gesture from the powers a certain lack of dignity, and although I should, by rights, have left the Strand Theatre for ever, burning with shame, and with my tail between my legs, my exit was actually a jaunty affair, untinged with sadness. I packed my things, said my good-byes to the Bourchiers and Mary and Norah, rattled blithely on all the old ladies' doors, and drove off in a taxi, feeling pleasantly free, and in the best of spirits.

During that engagement I formed a fixed resolution to go to America. Mary, who had played in New York several times, thrilled me by her descriptions of it. We had dinner in the grill room of the Waldorf on matinée days, and she enumerated, at great length, the delights of American theatre life. The theatres themselves were the acme of luxury. The acting was far and away superior to anything that would be seen in London. There were apparently two very attractive brothers called Shubert, who produced masses of plays every season with a lavish disregard for expense, and welcomed any English actor, however small, with enthusiasm. There was also a kindly old body named Al Woods, who produced the best melodramas in the world, outside of David Belasco, who was of course a species of divinity. In addition to these brilliant philanthropists, there was the Flat Iron Building, the Woolworth Building, which I visualised as a pyramid of scarlet and gold, rising to the clouds in tier upon tier of ten-cent magnificence, the Pennsylvania Station, Times Square, Central Park (on a grander scale than Hyde Park), the Hippodrome stage, which could support and display at least fifty elephants abreast, the Metropolitan Opera House, glittering with Astors and Belmonts and Vanderbilts, Wall Street, the Bronx Zoo, Coney Island, and, most exciting of all, Broadway by night. Broadway by night seemed to be my cup of tea entirely. Its splendours and its noise and its crowds haunted my imagination. Its gigantic sky-signs dazzled my dreams, flashing in a myriad lights, with unfailing regularity, the two words 'Noel Coward.'

Apart from the great American idea, I conceived a passably good plot for a play, and, as in those days conception was only removed from achievement by the actual time required for putting the words on paper, it was completed inside a week. It was entitled *The Last Trick* and was a melodrama in four acts. The first and second acts were quite amusing, the third act good, and the last act weak and amateurish. The plot hinged on the 'revenge' *motif* and wasn't particularly original, but the dialogue was effective, and showed a marked improvement on my other work. I took the play to Gilbert Miller, and he seemed to be impressed with it. He said that he was leaving for New York in a few weeks' time and would like to take it with him, and that he might possibly be able to arrange for it to be produced. I lunched with him a few days later, and he told me the plots of several plays that he had seen in Vienna, Berlin, Paris and Buda-Pesth. He also gave me some useful pieces of advice on the art of play-writing. He said, among other things, that although my dialogue was nearly always good, my construction was lousy. He said that someone had told his father, who in turn had told him, that the construction of a play was as important as the foundations of a house, whereas dialogue, however good, could only, at best, be considered as interior decoration. This, I recognised immediately, as being authentic wisdom. He said, on parting, that he was quite convinced that before long I would write a first-rate play, and that when I did, he would be only too delighted to produce it. He detained me for a few moments at the door by giving me an example of a really well-constructed scene. It was from the third act of a thrilling play he had recently attended in Stockholm.

Buoyed up by Gilbert Miller's encouragement, I wrote two bad plays and one better one. The first two are not worthy of discussion, but the third, *The Rat Trap,* was my first really serious attempt at psychological conflict. Even in the light of later experience, I can still see in it two well-written scenes. As a whole, of course, it was immature, but it was much steadier than anything I had done hitherto. The last act, as usual, went to pieces, but when I had finished it, I felt, for the first time with genuine conviction, that I could really write plays.

(6)

In the early spring of 1919 I went again to stay with Mrs. Cooper at Hambleton. I drove a car for the first time. I rode a horse for the first time, with no fear, but with little grace. I sang at village concerts, sometimes alone, sometimes with Mrs. Cooper's daughter, Phyllis. With her soprano I harmonised breathily, making up for my lack of volume with the maximum of expression. We sang 'Trot here, trot there' from *Veronique,* also 'The Swing Song' from the same score. The villagers applauded us lustily, their hands and hearts warmed by the knowledge that, although my voice might seem to be a trifle reedy, I was actually, in manner and fact, a *bona fide* professional, accustomed to charming vaster multitudes from the vaster stages of the best London theatres.

Small memories are the most insistent, and I like to catch again, for a moment, the feel of the sharp spring air as we drove home at night after a concert, the smell of the wood fire in the library where we discussed, over hot soup and sandwiches, the triumphs of the evening. All the warm, comfortable ingredients of country-house life were there, the very unfamiliarity of the atmosphere enhancing its charm for me, and I felt happily aloof from the squabblings of angry old character actresses. This, I reflected, quite wrongly, was my rightful sphere, and I would go upstairs to bed, undress, and brush my teeth, still, until sleep closed down upon me, accurate in my performance of a country gentleman.

It must not be imagined that Mrs. Cooper was my only contact with the shires. She was the first, but by no means the last. She, it is true, St. Peter'd me into that bleak, horse-infested paradise, but once inside, I fended for myself. Other country houses opened welcoming doors to me. Some were larger and grander than Hambleton. Some were smaller and more exclusively concerned with the chase. None, however, was so individually agreeable, and I returned to the mattresses in front of the fire, the faded peach-coloured brocade curtains, and the brass hot-water cans, with a sense of relief, a familiar home-sweet-home contentment.

Witham-on-the-Hill was one of my pleasanter excursions. It was a lovely old house, richly ordered, and belonging to the Keld Fenwicks. I was invited there, oddly enough, for a 'shoot', I forget now what exactly was being shot, but it was probably duck. At least twenty people were staying in the house, and some of them wore velvet smoking jackets in the evening, and there were two very large greyhounds, which fortunately took a fancy to me. The food was delicious, and I found several volumes of Marie Antoinette's secret memoirs in the library, which I read luxuriously, during the day, while the 'shoot' was at its height. The evenings might have been a trifle dull for me if I had not been so enchanted with the authenticity of the atmosphere. The setting and the dialogue were perfect, the character performances superb, and there seemed to be, only every now and then, a suspicion of over-acting among the smaller parts.

The London managers during that year continued to disregard me, and I continued to write plays and magazine stories, occasionally selling some of the latter, and making enough money here and there to keep myself in clothes and help out with the house.

Now that I considered myself definitely 'set' as a writer, the horror of being out of an engagement was less dreadful. I could be my own master, and work alone, beholden to nobody. My plays were steadily achieving more 'body' and consistence. I flung aside all bastard whimsies and concentrated on realism. No pert elf or faun dared even to peep round a tree at me in 1919. Pan and Pierrot retired, disgruntled, into oblivion as far as I was concerned, and, I am glad to say, have remained there until this day. My mind, not unnaturally, jumped over-far in the opposite direction. I dealt, almost exclusively, with the most lurid types; tarts, pimps, sinister courtesans, and cynical adulterers whirled across my pages in great profusion. This phase finally passed, owing to a withering lack of response from magazine editors, but it was all useful and I don't regret any of it.

Some new friends appeared. One of these was Betty Chester. Her real name was Grundtvig, and she lived with her mother and father in Chester Square.

Lorn Macnaughtan was a constant visitor at their house. She was tall and fair, with good hands and a nice speaking voice. She had been to school with Betty, and accepted a certain amount of Grundtvig patronage with slyly humorous grace. As she has been my personal secretary and close friend for nearly fifteen years, I find it difficult to describe her as I saw her then, for the first time. She seemed unremarkable in manner and personality, but there was authority in her quietness which was probably the heritage of many ancient, kilted Macnaughtans, who, in the long past, had stumped dourly over their Scottish estates. It was puzzling to try to reconcile her obvious distinction with the fact that she was, at the moment, in the chorus at the Empire, as she appeared to have no attributes whatever for that particular sphere. Her feet were large and her figure unvoluptuous; she could neither dance nor sing, and her movements were never especially graceful. She was slightly self-conscious, and her pale, clear complexion seldom conceded to wantonness more than an occasional dab of powder. When I knew her better, I discovered that her stage career was as surprising to herself as to everybody else. She had managed to get chorus and understudy jobs, sometimes through influence, sometimes through grim determination, because, the Macnaughtan splendour having faded into a small house in Wellington Square, it was essential for her to make enough money to live on.

All this accounted for the strange flashes of chorus-girl jargon which sprang from Lorn's lips bawdily, at the most unexpected moments, and frequently shattered the small, tightly encased propriety of Mr. Grundtvig.

By this time I had moved down from my tiny top attic in III,

Ebury Street to a more nobly proportioned room on the floor next to the top. In this, I was able to give occasional tea-parties, with the social elements tastefully mixed. Gertie Lawrence used to come, bringing with her various haughty young Guards officers who sat about, puzzled by the theatrical conversation, but securely wrapped in regimental poise. Mrs. Cooper came, too, and wailed agreeably at Stoj and Lyndon, and Peter and Sheila and Betty and Lorn. Every now and then I thoughtlessly chose the day of our housemaid's afternoon out, and was embarrassed to see Father waltzing into the room with the tea-tray. Everyone immediately rose to say 'How do you do?' and shake hands, to which he couldn't possibly respond until somebody relieved him of the tea-things. I glossed over those slight contretemps with, what I hoped, was easy Bohemian geniality, and tried not to intercept the ironic glances that any strangers present exchanged with each other.

One day a young man called Stewart Forster appeared. He was a lieutenant in the Coldstream Guards, with a deceptively guileless personality, and a timid, butter-coloured moustache, which, with the passing of time, I regret to say, has become large and quite red. Then, however, it was innocuous and faintly apologetic, as though it knew perfectly well that it had no right to be there at all, and wouldn't be, but for the exigencies of military etiquette.

Stewart asked me, on leaving, if I would care to dine with him on guard at St. James's Palace the following week. I accepted with alacrity and regretted that I had no decorations other than my army discharge medal with which to adorn the occasion. I hadn't even a tail coat. I didn't mention this, but hired one from Moss Brothers the day before I was due to appear at the Palace.

I arrived on the stroke of eight o'clock, and was conducted to the mess by an austere corporal. The traditional pomp of the atmosphere felt chilly at first, but there was an underlying glamour in it which thawed me presently, and, with the aid of a glass of extremely dry sherry, I expanded sufficiently to make a joke about my tail coat, which no eye, however well schooled in good manners, could possibly regard in anything but a comic light. Moss

Brothers had certainly let me down badly. The sleeves had a Pagliacci fullness, and the tails rebounded from my calves as I walked.

At about eleven o'clock Stewart imposed upon himself a gigantic bearskin, which looked as though it might slip down and extinguish him entirely at the slightest sharp movement. He also buckled on his sword, and clanked out into the courtyard, where I heard his voice barking shrilly to the accompaniment of shuffling feet. When he came back I had one more glass of port, said my good-byes, and left, no longer oppressed by military tradition, but quite definitely part of it.

I walked home, down the Mall and past Buckingham Palace, much elated by my evening, and reflecting that uniform was undoubtedly very becoming to Englishmen, and that white-gloved orderlies, tawny port, a polished, shiny table decorated with silver regimental trophies, warm red-shaded lights, and large oil paintings of Their Majesties, all combined to impart to the most ordinary conversation an indescribable and imperishable charm.

(7)

In August 1919 I played Ralph in *The Knight of the Burning Pestle* at the Birmingham Repertory Theatre.

For me, there was a quality of fantasy about the whole engagement. Nigel Playfair directed the production with a touching fidelity to Elizabethan atmosphere. No curtain. No footlights. A circular stage, fringed with uneasy gallants, who sat on stools, and smoked clay pipes. There was a musicians' gallery high up on a rostrum at the back, containing a few local fiddlers, their upper parts correctly be-ruffed and be-wigged, and their lower parts more comfortably encased in their ordinary Birmingham trousers. Sometimes they forgot to leave off their pince-nez, and were flurried into doing so by urgent hisses from the conscientious gallants. I was not very good as Ralph, owing to a total lack of understanding of the play. It was my first and only experience of Elizabethan comedy and, being unable to detect any great humour on it, I played that poor apprentice with a stubborn Mayfair distinction, which threw the whole thing out of key. This was largely Nigel Playfair's fault. He directed with more elfishness than authority, and cheered the rehearsals with many little jokes, which, although vastly appreciated by Betty Chester and me, were not actually helpful to our performances. Betty played The Citizen's Wife with youth, charm and great vivacity, which, considering that she was supposed to be a bawdy matron of about forty-five, was hardly appropriate.

The Knight of the Burning Pestle could not be considered a really progressive step in my career as an actor. I had mouthed and postured my way through it with little conviction and no sense of period. I was unaware of this, however, and, even if I had realised it, I doubt whether I should have cared very much, because, in course of those three short weeks, Fortune favoured me with such a violent and unexpected slap on the back, that not only Birmingham, but the whole world, seemed to be transformed. The people in the streets, hitherto rather dingy-looking, with grim, manufacturing faces, suddenly changed into happy, smiling creatures, stepping lightly over pavements, no longer grey, and wearing gay colours. Not so much as one drop of rain fell for at least three days. And even my landlady, Mrs. Hunter, a woman of sad regrets if ever there was one, seemed to forget for a spell her Bright's disease, and melt into cheerfulness. All this on account of one brief cablegram from Gilbert Miller in New York informing me in lilting, business-like terms, that Al Woods wished to pay five hundred dollars for a year's option on my play *The Last Trick*.

Five hundred dollars, after calculations in Betty's dressing-room, resolved itself into the still fantastic, but more understandable sum of one hundred pounds.

I remember rushing to the Queen's Hotel in full make-up, between the first and second acts of the matinée, sending an enthusiastic reply from the hall porter's desk, and, on my way back to the theatre, buying a very large bottle of toilet water at Boots Cash Chemists.

When I returned to London, the five hundred dollars was duly paid me, in pounds, by Gilbert Miller's secretary, and within a few days another cable arrived, this time saying that Al Woods would like to buy the play outright for a further fifteen hundred dollars, as it was necessary for it to be rewritten by a more technically expert playwright than myself.

Never having received more than a few guineas for anything I had ever written, this windfall was a shock which even my self-confidence was unable to meet calmly. I couldn't believe that there wasn't some mistake, some sinister catch in it, until Mother and I had been to a bank in the City and actually watched, with glistening eyes, the money sliding over the counter to us. Even the fact that at the moment I happened to be suffering from a degrading boil on the end of my nose failed to depress the occasion.

I burst forth rapidly into several new suits, paid a large part of our over-due quarterly instalment on the Ebury Street house, and bought a second-hand grand piano at Harrods, which contributed richness and joy to my room, and considerable pain to the lodgers immediately above and below it.

I glanced back happily upon recent penury, over which the haze of distance already seemed to be shimmering (a fancy which later proved to be distinctly premature), and walked on winged feet along Bedford Street, St. Martin's Lane, Garrick Street, Charing Cross Road, Wardour Street, Green Street, Coventry Street and Shaftesbury Avenue, crossing myself devoutly outside theatrical agents' offices, and finishing up daily with an expensive lunch at the Ivy.

The Ivy had been a generous friend to me in the past, allowing me many meals, when it knew perfectly well that the chances of their being paid for were slender. And so now, sheathed in sudden prosperity, it seemed only fitting that I should eat there until I burst.

I went to many parties in my new tail suit, savouring to the full the sensation of being well-dressed for the first time. The days of twirling anxiously before Moss Brothers' looking-glasses were over. No more hitching of the arm-pits to prevent sleeves from enveloping the hands altogether. No more bracing of out-grown trousers to their lowest, with the consciousness that the slightest movement of the arms would display a mortifying expanse of shirt between waistcoat and flies. All that belonged to the past. Now I could dance and dine securely, feeling smart, and *soigné,* and very, very smooth.

When relying upon my own funds, I chose a suitably under-standing partner such as Gertie Lawrence, or Meggie Albanesi, and we would dine frugally, and go to Murray's, or Rector's, or the Savoy, where it was possible to slip in by the Embankment entrance without a ticket.

When invited, I patronised the Grafton Galleries, the Ritz, Ciro's, and, on one occasion, even Claridge's.

Michael Arlen was also just beginning to blossom about this time. We used to wave languidly to each other across dance floors, shedding our worldliness later, in obscure corners. He was very dapper, and his Hawes and Curtis backless waistcoats aroused envy in me, which I soon placated, by ordering some for myself, but his exquisite pearl and platinum watch chain was beyond competition, and all I could do was to admire it bravely, and hope, in my heart, that perhaps it was just a little bit ostentatious.

(8)

When Gilbert Miller returned to London, he asked me to go to see him in his office, where he continued his lecture on play con-struction where he had left off several months before.

He described to me the plots of *La Tosca, Fedora, The Easiest Way,* and *Within the Law,* which, incidentally, I had seen three times. He then went on to say that he himself had a good idea for a light comedy, but that he would like me to write it, preferably with Charles Hawtrey in mind, and that, if I did it well enough, he would produce it in London during the following spring.

I was then, as I am now, extremely chary of the thought of writing anything based upon somebody else's idea, but I persevered, and within the next few weeks, manufactured an amiable little play entitled (by Gilbert Miller) *I'll Leave It to You.*

The dialogue, on the whole, was amusing, and unpretentious, and the construction was not bad, but it was too mild and unassuming to be able to awake any really resounding echoes in the hearts of the great public, and although I was naturally entranced with it, Gilbert was not quite as enthusiastic as I had hoped he would be.

He suggested several alterations, some of which I agreed to, and all of which I made, and after a series of discussions, he departed for America again, having promised me that on his return he would arrange for a try-out production at the Gaiety Theatre, Manchester, in April. I had to content myself with this, and the reflection that although six months was a long time to wait, I had at least had the sense to write a part in the play for myself, in which I should undoubtedly, when the moment came, score an overwhelming personal triumph.

(9)

In January I went to Paris with Stewart Forster, according to a plan formulated during the summer at Rumwood, Stewart's home in Kent. We stayed at the Ritz for the first night, and at a small hotel in the Rue Caumartin for the rest of the week.

As it was the first time that we had, either of us, been out of England, our behaviour was entirely true to form.

We sipped apéritifs outside the Café de la Paix, visited the Louvre, Napoleon's Tomb, Notre Dame, Versailles, the Moulin Rouge, and the Folies Bergères.

We dined at Prunier's and the Café de Paris, and danced endlessly round the cabarets of Montmartre with metallic tarts, who persisted in mistaking us for Americans.

We even quarrelled mildly over a young lady from Cincinnati, who drove us about in her car, accepted floral offerings, and flirted with us magnificently, never for one instant deviating from that fine line of conduct which separates racy conversation from staunch moral integrity. This we recognised as a racial peculiarity, and were duly impressed by it, if a trifle irritated.

We met a Russian prince, *soi-disant,* who owned a racing car which looked like a red pepper, and a French mistress who looked like all the pictures of flaming adventuresses in the world rolled into one, but who, on closer acquaintance, turned out to be dull and deeply sentimental.

It was an enjoyable week, and we absorbed the sights and sounds and smells of Paris thoroughly and satisfactorily, and when we left, sadly, to return to England, we possessed a certain 'manner' which had not been apparent before. Our vocabularies also were the richer by several French phrases, and three complete sentences, two of which were unrepeatable.

In February Mrs. Cooper invited me to go to Alassio with her for a fortnight, and so for the first time I slept in a wagon-lit, experienced the thrilling, damp coldness of a frontier station at two o'clock in the morning, and whirled through Switzerland and down on to the Lombardy plains with my nose buttoned against the railway carriage window. In Alassio we stayed at the Grand Hotel, and breakfasted daily on a balcony overlooking dusty palm trees, and glittering blue sea. Behind the hotel there were plaster houses in pale colours, olive groves, cypresses, lush curtains of wistaria and bougainvillea, and serried ranks of snowcapped mountains.

I have returned there since, more experienced in travel, having seen higher mountains, richer foliage, and bluer seas, and realised that Alassio is really nothing out of the ordinary, that there are hundreds of other little towns nestling in the shadow of the Alpes Maritimes, with just the same coloured houses and twisted streets, and just the same palm trees, and fishing boats, and pungent smells. But that was the first time, the first thrill of discovery, the first proof I had ever had that hot sunshine was anywhere possible in February.

Upon arriving back in London, I discovered that Gilbert Miller was not returning after all, and had put the producing of *I'll Leave It to You* in the hands of Robert Oswald, the general manager of the Gaiety, Manchester. Stanley Bell was to direct the play, and the cast chosen included Kate Cutler, Farren Soutar, Muriel Pope, Stella Jesse, Douglas Jefferies, Lois Stuart, Moya Nugent, Esmé Wynne (Stoj), and myself.

The first night in Manchester was tremendously exciting. The play went well all through and, at the end, the audience cheered, and Kate pushed me forward to make a speech. I was feeling far too emotional to be able to relinquish her hand, and so I stood there, clutching it, and experiencing the curious sensation of success. There was I, and there was an audience applauding and cheering, and as I advanced a step, the applause and the cheers swelled louder and then died away into complete silence. I made quite a nice little speech. It was boyish and modest, and had been carefully rehearsed alone in my digs beforehand. I had seen too many authors hauled on to the stage on first nights, trembling and confused, with goggling eyes, to make the mistake of being caught unprepared.

When it was all over and I went out of the stage door, there was a large crowd of gallery girls waiting on the pavement, and I signed their autograph books with a flourish and enjoyed myself deeply.

Towards the end of our first week in Manchester Mrs. Charles Hawtrey and Mrs. Gilbert Miller came down from London to see the play. I was very nervous, and Kate and Stanley and I prayed ardently that there would be a good audience, and no hitches in the performance. Contrary to what generally happens on those occasions, there was a good audience, and the performance was smoother and better than it had ever been, and when, at the end, I had to make my speech in response to the cheers, I was visualising clearly an immediate production at the St. James's Theatre, with Hawtrey playing Uncle Daniel. The faces of Mrs. Hawtrey and Mrs. Miller, when Stanley Bell ushered them into my dressing-room afterwards, were sadly disillusioning. They both stood there, shaking their heads slowly and tenderly, like china mandarins. They were both filled and brimming over with sympathy, as though they had just been present at the greatest theatrical catastrophe of modern times. They both kissed me, said that they were afraid the play wouldn't have a chance in London, and that they would have to cable to Gilbert immediately to say what they honestly and truly thought. Upon this, I lost my temper inwardly, but fortunately not outwardly, and said that I was sorry that they were so disappointed in the play, but that luckily the audiences we had played to didn't seem to be quite so hard to please. I then added, with firmness and a touch of hysterical bravado, that whether Gilbert Miller and Charles Hawtrey were interested, or whether they weren't, the play would definitely be produced in London within the next few months! Upon which, they both wobbled their heads again, and went out.

When they had gone Stanley took me to supper at the Midland and did his best to cheer me up, but without much success. With both Hawtrey and Gilbert Miller ruled out, our chances of London production were small. However, I drove back to Lloyd Street, grimly determined that *I'll Leave It to You* was not going to peter out of existence with only three weeks in Manchester to its credit.

(10)

I'll Leave It to You opened in London at the New Theatre on July 21st, 1920, two and a half months after its try-out in Manchester. It was presented by Mary Moore (Lady Wyndham) with the same cast, excepting Farren Soutar, who had been replaced by Holman Clarke. The first night was a roaring success, and I made another boyish speech. Lots of my friends were there including Bobbie and Ivor, neither of whom came round to see me afterwards, which hurt me bitterly. When I eventually tackled them about this, Ivor replied that the play, in the intervals of irritating him excessively, had bored him stiff. So that was that.

The critics were mostly very enthusiastic, and said a lot about it having been a great night, and that a new playwright had been discovered, etc., but unfortunately their praise was not potent enough to lure audiences to the New Theatre for more than five weeks, so the run ended rather miserably, the last week being rendered still gloomier by Lady Wyndham, who, with adamant economy, insisted that our lighting should be cut down to half.

However, I sold the amateur rights to Samuel French for a comfortable sum, and feeling much the better for my brief encouragement, both financially and spiritually, set to work with renewed vigour on a play called *Barriers Down,* which was awful.

In November Nigel Playfair decided to produce *The Knight of the Burning Pestle* at the Kingsway Theatre, so we rehearsed it all over again, and finally opened, to tepid enthusiasm.

Mrs. Patrick Campbell came one night in a box, and great excitement reigned behind the scenes. This excitement waned towards the end of the play, when it was discovered that she had been sound asleep since the beginning of the first act. I sent her an outraged message through a mutual friend, and the next night there she was again, in the same box, but far from sleepy. She wore long white gloves, and applauded wildly every time I stepped on to the stage. Elsie Janis and Mrs. Janis brought a party to a matinée one day, prompted by sheer courtesy and kindness to me, and they sat, from the beginning to the end, bored and bewildered beyond relief, but infinitely polite. Many years later Elsie told me what they had really thought of the show, all of which goes to prove that Americans have very beautiful manners.

Just before Christmas I developed suddenly a temperature of a hundred and two. The doctor forbade me to play, but, imbued with that misguided 'old-trouper' bravery, I insisted, with the result that I gave sixteen members of the company mumps. Nigel himself played my part for a little, but even his fine performance couldn't contend against the bad business and the mumps, so the play closed, and I signed a contract to appear in Gilbert Miller's production of an American comedy, *Polly with a Past,* at the St. James's Theatre. Rehearsals were not to start until February, so I had a few weeks free for a holiday.

I bought myself a second-class ticket to Rapallo, and stayed there for two days at the Casino Hotel. Then, as I knew no one at all, and couldn't speak a word of Italian, my independent spirit wilted a trifle, and I beat a hasty retreat to Alassio, where I knew Mrs. Cooper was staying. She was delighted to see me, and once more I settled myself into the Grand Hotel.

After I had been there a few days I was asked to sing at a concert at the English Club. The concert was bad, and the piano dreadful, but I sang several songs with lofty professional arrogance, only slightly deflated by a smartly dressed young woman in the front row, who appeared to be fighting an attack of convulsive giggles with singular lack of success. I remember frowning at her coldly several times, but this only seemed to send her into fresh paroxysms. When I met her afterwards with Mrs. Cooper, she had regained control and was very poised indeed. Her name was Gladys Calthrop. I asked her what there was about my singing that had made her laugh so much, and, after a few evasions, she explained that it wasn't my singing exactly, but that I had looked funny.

It is strange how many really important moments in life slip by in the procession, unnoted, and devoid of prescience. No guardian angel whacks a sharp triangle in the brain, and the heavens remain commonplace. It is not my intention in this book to delve deeply into personal relationships, but as Gladys Calthrop has been so intimately concerned with all my best work, and so intrinsically part of my failures and successes, I feel that a small, retrospective fanfare is not entirely out of place. In appearance she was less attractive then than she is now. Her eyes and figure were good. Her brain was alert, and her sense of humour keen, though somewhat impaired by a slight bias towards highbrow Bohemianism.

The remaining few days of my stay in Alassio we passed almost entirely together. We went for walks. We went for drives. We sat on the beach, in olive groves, and on terraces overhanging the sea. We discussed vehemently Life, Love, Art, Marriage, Suicide and Religion. We went to a *festa* at the Combattente Club, and left politely with the English contingent, returning later, when foreign

constraint had fled, to enjoy ourselves. It was this *festa* that supplied the basis for my ill-fated play *Sirocco*. There was much
tawdry glamour to it, contributed by sweet champagne, an electric
piano, paper streamers, and the usual paraphernalia of Latin carni-
val.

(11)

Polly with a Past opened at the St. James's Theatre on March
2nd. It was an American farce which had had a big success in New
York, where the name part had been created by Ina Claire. In
London Polly was played by Edna Best, who was good, but appeared too adolescent in the latter part of the play when she was
supposed to be a dashing French adventuress. Donald Calthrop
was the leading man, and the rest of the cast consisted of Aubrey
Smith, Helen Haye, Alice Moffat, Claude Rains, Arthur Hather-
ton, Edith Evans, Henry Kendall and me. Donald Calthrop and
Harry Kendall had the two best men parts, and, as in *Charley's
Aunt,* I was the 'feed.' By the end of the run, however, I was em-
broidering and overacting to such an extent that they had to fight
like steers to get their lines over at all.

During this run another life-long friend made his appearance:
Jeffrey Amherst, or, rather Jeffrey Holmesdale, as he was then.
His father was the Earl Amherst, and he, Jeffrey, held the rank
of captain in the Coldstream Guards. He was small and fair, and
his gallant military record seemed slightly incongruous, until
you had known him a little. He was gay and a trifle strained, and
there was a certain quality of secrecy in him, entirely unfurtive,
but stronger than mere reserve. It was as though he knew many
things too closely, and was consequently over-wary. I dined with
him several times, 'on guard' and at home with his family. I
watched him twinkling and giggling through several noisy theatrical parties, but it took a long while for even me to begin to know
him.

Polly with a Past bored me early in its run, but I was working
hard outside the theatre. Songs, sketches, and plays were bursting

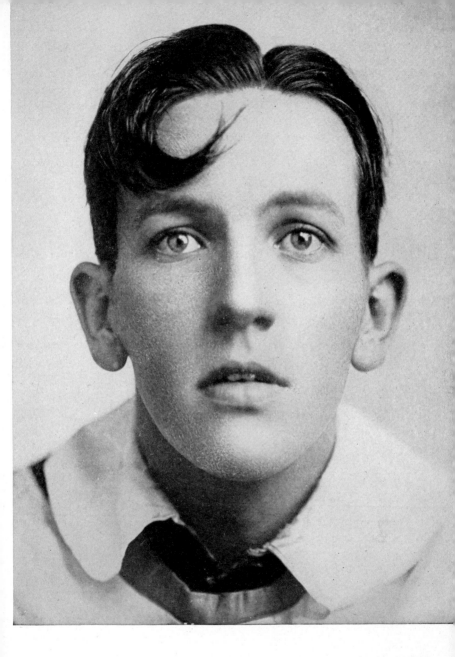

As Ralph
in THE KNIGHT OF THE BURNING PESTLE
Kingsway Theatre, 1920

With STOJ in
I'll Leave It To Y
New Theatre, 1920

out of me far too quickly, and without nearly enough critical discrimination. My best effort during that period was a comedy in three acts, *The Young Idea,* which was primarily inspired by Shaw's *You Never Can Tell.* Dolly and Phillip being my original prototypes for Sholto and Gerda, I felt rather guilty of plagiarism, however inept, and when the play was finished, J. E. Vedrenne kindly sent it to Shaw, to find out whether or not he had any objections. A short while afterwards I received my script back from Shaw, scribbled all over with alterations and suggestions, and accompanied by a long letter, which, to my lasting regret, I was idiotic enough to lose. However, the gist of it was that I showed every indication of becoming a good playwright, providing that I never again in my life read another word that he, Shaw, had ever written. It was, as might be expected, a brilliant letter, and I took its advice only half-heartedly. But there was more than brilliance in the trouble that that great man had taken in going minutely over the work of a comparatively unknown young writer.

(12)

The re-birth of my determination to go to America occurred at one of Ivor's supper parties, and was caused, I think, by the presence of Jeanne Eagels who had just made a big success in New York, in a play called *Daddies.* She talked vividly of the American theatre and I felt instinctively that she was a fine actress, and was thrilled to think that there were many others like her just on the other side of the ocean. In this I was wrong. Of all the actresses I have ever seen, there has never been one quite like Jeanne Eagels.

Ivor's parties, in those days, were great fun. In later years they seem to have become a trifle staid and less spontaneous, but perhaps the fault lies with me, perhaps I have grown blasé, and the thrill of star-gazing has turned sour and curdled. At any rate, at that time a party at The Flat was a signal for general rejoicing. The Flat sat, and still sits, on the very top of the Strand Theatre, and in order to reach it, a perilous ascent was made in a small, self-worked lift. Ivor's guests crushed themselves timorously together in this frightening little box, someone pulled a rope, there was a sharp grinding noise, a scream from some less hardy member of the party; then, swaying and rattling, the box ascended. Upon reaching the top, it would hit the roof with a crash and, more often than not, creak all the way down again.

Many people preferred to toil up seven long flights of stairs rather than face the lift, but I was one of the braver spirits, on one occasion actually making six complete journeys before I could induce it to stop.

The big room of the flat had a raised dais running across one end. Upon this there were sometimes two, at other times no, grand pianos, sometimes a gramophone, and nearly always Viola Tree. The high spots of the parties were reached in this room. Charades were performed, people did stunts, Olga Lynn sang, and Fay Compton immediately did an imitation of Olga Lynn singing. Visiting musicians were subtly lured to the piano. Native musicians rushed to it. Rival leading ladies had verbal scuffles. Divorced couples hobnobbed with each other, and with each other's co-respondents. Bitter enemies met face to face, and either swept majestically from the room, or stayed to ruffle Ivor's hair.

Jeffrey Holmesdale added an extra fillip to my American dream by telling me that he was sailing for New York at the end of May, to represent his father at some sort of centenary festival at Amherst College in Massachusetts. It seemed improbable at the moment that there could be the least chance of my going with him. *Polly with a Past* was still playing to good business, I had a run-of-the-play contract, and in addition there was the ever-present money difficulty. True, things were going better in Ebury Street, I had been earning a good salary for quite a long while, and had a certain amount in the bank, but not nearly enough to pay my return fare to America. I could, I suppose, have taken a passage on some little freight boat, but I was determined to make my first arrival as stylish as possible. I had heard a good deal about the American reverence for success, and on the strength of having had one play produced in London and having played several important parts, I felt that it would be bad policy to creep in, unannounced, by the tradesmen's entrance.

I brooded over all this for several weeks, and finally, by borrowing here and there and selling two songs to Ned Lathom, who didn't want them in the least and only bought them out of charity, I scraped together a hundred pounds, which was enough for my fare one way, on the Aquitania, with a little over for expenses.

The next step was to obtain permission from Gilbert Miller to leave the cast of *Polly* which I did, a few weeks before it closed, and at the end of May 1921 Jeffrey and I set sail on the first of our many journeys together.

PART FOUR

To have embarked for America with a bundle of manuscripts, a one-way ticket, and only seventeen pounds to spare was, I suppose, rather foolhardy, and when the Aquitania had left Cherbourg a few miles astern, fears twittered in my stomach like birds in a paper bag, and I reflected that from almost every point of view I was a fool. Admittedly, my faith in my own talents remained unwavering, but it did seem unduly optimistic to suppose that the Americans would be perceptive enough to see me immediately in the same light in which I saw myself. In this, I was perfectly right. They didn't.

However, the weather was warm, the sea calm, and I should have Jeffrey to lean on for three weeks at least, so I snapped out of my despondency and sent a cheerful radio to Mother.

I appeared at the ship's concert, supporting the chief steward who sang 'Mandalay', a wizened buck-and-wing dancer from the second class, and a big woman in black satin, who played the fiddle, the piano, the xylophone, and, for an encore, the cornet.

New York rose out of the sea to greet us. It was a breathless June morning, and wads of cotton-wool smoke lay motionless among the high towers. The Statue of Liberty seemed insignificant but the harbour was glorious. There will always be a stinging enchantment for me in this arrival. Even now, when I know it so well in every aspect, my heart jumps a little. Then it was entirely new to me. We slid gently past Battery Park, still green with early summer, the skyscrapers moved gracefully aside to show still further vistas, and, a long way below us, platoons of straw hats passed by on ferry-boats. As we drew near the dock, several fussy little tugs came out to meet us and finally, after tremendous efforts, succeeded in coaxing and nuzzling us alongside.

We were met by Naps Alington, Gabrielle Enthoven, Cecile Sartoris and Teddie Gerard. I knew Teddie and Naps, but had never met the other two, and was naturally unaware at the moment that I was destined to live with them for several months. Jeffrey and I went, first of all, to the Algonquin, which I had heard was a comfortable, theatrical, and reasonable hotel. It was all that and more, and in later years I have grown to love it dearly. But then, in a violent heat-wave, it seemed airless and stuffy, and so, after the first night there, we moved: Jeffrey to share Nap's flat in Eighth Street, and I to the Brevoort, at the lower end of Fifth Avenue.

That first evening in New York is clear in my memory. I refused to dine with Teddie and Naps and Jeffrey, because I wanted to go to a theatre. And so I promised to rejoin them all afterwards, and went off by myself. I sauntered down Broadway alone, gazing up at the sky-signs, being bumped into, pushed, and shoved by the endless, slow-moving crowds on the sidewalks. The sky was not yet quite dark and the million lights flamed against it, changing it from rich blue to deep purple. It was grander than Mary Robson had described, and more sharply beautiful than I could ever have imagined—a slightly tawdry beauty, detached, impersonal, and a little scarifying.

I walked up and down several side streets, looking at the pictures outside the theatres, and, finally deciding upon one, went into the Klaw Theatre. The play was *Nice People* by Rachel Crothers, starring Francine Larrimore, and including among the smaller parts Tallulah Bankhead and Katherine Cornell. I thought the production and acting good, and the play poor, but what interested me most was the tempo. Bred in the tradition of gentle English comedy with its inevitable maids, butlers, flower vases, and tea-tables, it took me a good ten minutes of the first act to understand what anyone was saying. They all seemed to be talking at once. Presently I began to disentangle the threads, and learnt my first lesson in American acting, which was the technique of realising, first, which lines in the script are superfluous, and second, knowing when, and how, to throw them away.

After the play I took a taxi down to Teddie's house in Washington Square where I found the party in exceedingly full swing. From out of the haze of chatter, piano playing, and cigarette smoke, I managed to extricate a dark, attractive woman, whose eyes slanted upwards at the corners, and who seemed unable to carry on a connected conversation in one language for more than three minutes. This was Poldowski, or, to give her her nonprofessional name, Lady Dean-Paul. She had left her husband and children in England, and had come to America for much the same reason that I had: an urgent determination to make money.

Apart from her, the party bewildered me, and after a little while I crept away from it, and went back to the Algonquin, overtired and deflated after all the excitements of the day.

The first week in New York was great fun until the novelty had evaporated slightly and my spare cash had evaporated entirely. We did everything we should have done. We went up the Woolworth Building. We gaped appropriately at the majesty of the Pennsylvania and Grand Central stations. We battled our way along Wall Street during the rush hour. We went to Coney Island on a Sunday night, and were jolted and rattled and bumped at a terrific speed through pitch-black tunnels, over canvas mountains, disembarking, green in the face, to consume 'hot dogs' and nonalcoholic beer. We learnt to distinguish between 'expresses' and 'locals' in the subway. We went to Harlem, and drifted from cabaret to cabaret, jigging to alien rhythms, and listening to strange wailings and screechings, until our feet ached, our ears buzzed, and our eyes blinked, in the cool dawn.

We went to the New Amsterdam Theatre to see Marilyn Miller in *Sally,* and came away cheerfully enchanted. We went to the Globe Theatre to see the Ziegfeld Follies, and watched the famous, much-advertised beauties languidly boring themselves and the audience with their too-perfect figures, their total lack of expression. In the same show there was, fortunately, Fannie Brice, to revive our interest in the theatre. She sang 'Second-Hand Rose' with that particular brand of sentimentality sacred to Jewish-American comediennes. We even went, as the guests of Averill Harriman, to watch the scions of the rich play polo.

Apart from these excursions, I delivered the three letters of introduction that I had secured before leaving England. They were addressed to Al Woods, David Belasco and Charles Dillingham respectively. Al Woods was friendly, and told me that *The Last Trick* had been re-written several times, by several different people, but that he feared nothing could ever be done with it. He also said he was going to Europe for a month or so, and that when he returned he would be delighted to read anything that I had to show him.

Charles Dillingham was away (I think in Colorado), but his manager, Fred Latham, was very amiable and let me go and talk to him in his office on many different occasions. He gave me a lot of kind advice about writing plays, and said that he was going away for a month or so, as he badly needed a holiday.

David Belasco was impressive, and wore a purple silk dressing-gown. He also told me a great deal about play-writing, emphasising his words with striking gestures and seeming, every now and then, to digress a little from the subject in hand. I tentatively suggested that he might be interested in reading one of my scripts, and he agreed that nothing would delight him more except for the unfortunate fact that, owing to doctor's orders, he was compelled to go away for a month or so.

These three stimulating contacts emboldened me to move from the small room that I was occupying at the Brevoort, to a much smaller one, practically in the eaves.

(2)

A little while before leaving England I had written, in collaboration with Lorn Macnaughtan, a short book of burlesque historical memoirs entitled *A Withered Nosegay*. Lorn did the illustrations and the book was published by Christophers. Some of it was funny, and the basic idea was good, but it was written with too much zest and personal enjoyment, and, consequently, fell a long way short of success. Burlesque at any time is dangerous ground and for young and inexperienced writers usually disastrous. In this particular book there was a lot that was crude and careless, and I have often regretted that the idea didn't come to me a little later, when I should have been more aware of its pitfalls and better equipped to grapple with it.

However, I took it with me to America and sold several of the separate parts of it to *Vanity Fair*. This happened only a few weeks after my arrival, and, although the payment was small, it was encouraging.

After Jeffrey had gone back to England, Gabrielle Enthoven and Cecile Sartoris offered me a room in their studio in Washington Square. They said that when I sold a play, or made some money somehow, I could pay rent, but until then I was to be their guest. They were neither of them in the least well off and this was a blessed gesture of sheer charity. I accepted and moved in immediately, grateful not only for their kindness, but for their company.

The studio was small, with white-washed walls and dark, polished furniture. Occasionally, in the evenings, we went out to the pictures, but usually we stayed at home and dined quietly in pyjamas. Candles flickered in sconces on the walls whenever there was enough breeze, and we drank red wine from the little Italian grocer's round the corner.

Irene Dean-Paul and Cecile sometimes made a little money by giving 'Verlaine' recitals in the homes of the wealthy. Irene had set, exquisitely, many of the poems to music, and sang them in her husky, attractive 'musician's voice.'

Cecile recited in a rhythmic monotone, her mouth twisted a little at one corner, and her eyes, apparently far away, gazing on enchanted woods and white moons.

There were frequently quarrels, smoothed over ultimately by Gabrielle's tact. Irene flew into rages easily, and delivered vitriolic tirades against American houses, American culture, and American hostesses in particular. On one occasion, after she and Cecile had trailed all the way to Boston to give a recital, she took exception to something that had been said about *l'heure exquise,* and tearing the hard-earned cheque into little pieces, flung them dramatically in the hostess's face. Repercussions of this scene occurred at intervals for many weeks afterwards.

Irene lived in a flat in West 70th Street. It was several flights up, and panelled in sickly pitch-pine. She had a grim but tender-hearted maid, from whom she was perpetually borrowing and who lived, silently, in the back somewhere and never seemed to go out farther than the delicatessen at the corner of the street.

Sometimes, when things looked especially black, we dolled ourselves up to the nines, she in an elaborate evening dress, and me in a dinner jacket, and went to the Ritz roof, or Delmonico's to dine and dance. The dining, according to a prearranged plan, consisted of my ordering some light dish, and Irene feeling suddenly ill and being unable to eat a morsel. Later, when the waiter had left us, she would plunge a fork on to my plate, and we would eat hungrily to the last scrap. Occasionally, if we were in luck, some more or less rich acquaintance appeared and took us on to a night-club. When this occurred we at once demanded vast ham sandwiches, and considered the evening definitely a success.

One day when, as usual, we were at low ebb, Irene received an invitation to go and stay the week-end with a Mrs. Magee in Mount Kisco, and asked me to go with her. It was a beautiful house and a nice house-party, and we refused to allow the fact that we hadn't enough money to tip the servants to detract one whit from our enjoyment, which was wise of us because, as it turned out, I happened to play rummy on the Sunday night, and made six dollars fifty.

We returned, smoothed out by luxury, and feeling much better.

With all her lightness, humour and infectious high spirits, Irene was a tragic figure. Her integrity as an artist was fine and uncompromising, too uncompromising to be satisfied with small success, and somehow not quite steel enough, not sufficiently swaddled in egotism to shield her from the irritation of failure.

Not that her work was ever a failure, far from it. Her music has a strength and sincerity beyond the reach, I think, of contemporary criticism. Her failure lay within herself, in her abrupt pride, and sudden sharp intolerance, and her inability, when in certain moods, to accept the small change of friendship, even from those whom she knew loved her deeply. All this, I believe, she realised clearly at times, but she happened to be a genuine victim of that much over-worked phrase 'artistic temperament', and suffered accordingly. Her friends also suffered accordingly but, in my opinion, were well repaid by the privilege of knowing her.

(3)

At the beginning of August Cecile and Gabrielle both went away, leaving me in charge of the studio and in command of a strange Negress called Gertrude, who appeared for an hour or so every morning and ambled lethargically about with a broom. Her clothes were garish, oddly shaped, and a detached stay-busk reared itself up from the small of her back like a crane.

This, actually, was a bad period for me. I was penniless and very lonely. The few people that I knew in New York were away, it being midsummer. Even Irene forsook me for a while. I saw Teddie Gerard occasionally, and Naps, but they were both, although friendly, occupied with their own affairs.

Every theatrical manager in America seemed to have vanished completely, nearly all the theatres were closed, and several of the manuscripts I had brought with me had been consigned to some secret vault by the Theatre Guild, from which it was impossible to extricate them, or even hear news of how they were faring.

I acquired many of the stock habits of the forlorn and poverty-stricken, such as tramping the streets, contemplating daring robberies, and sitting on park benches. Unfortunately, owing to my carefully conserved wardrobe, I was invariably asked for money by my brother paupers, and was once addressed as 'sir' by an obviously prosperous Chinaman. Battery Park was really the nicest place to sit, but it was a long walk from Washington Square. Here, however, I found the company more varied and picturesque than in Central Park, also there was the sea to look at, and it was cooler. Sentimentally, of course, it had its drawbacks, because there were nearly always ships sailing away to England, and I had to avert my eyes and do a little honest, manly fist-clenching and shoulder-squaring.

I used to get packets of bacon, on credit, from the Italian grocer just near the studio, and cook it sparingly in the kitchenette. Luckily the weather was far too hot for me to want to eat very much. The kitchenette became suffocating quickly, and so I found it more comfortable, when actually frying, to be stark naked. This aroused the moral indignation of a cop, who had been observing me from the other side of the street, and he came and banged loudly on the door. I put on a dressing-gown, and ran downstairs with the bacon fork still in my hand and upon opening the door received the full force of his rage, which evaporated quickly when I asked him if he would care for a little red wine. He came up into the studio and polished off three glasses. I offered him some bacon, which he refused, but at parting he kindly lent me his revolver because, he said, it was a dangerous neighbourhood, and living there as I was, completely alone, *anything* might happen. When he had gone, I lay awake for most of the night restraining the impulse to shoot at every shadow cast by the street lamp on to the white studio wall.

Later on in the month things began to look up a bit. I sold *A Withered Nosegay* to Boni and Liveright, and got a small advance for it. I made some new friends. Horace Liveright himself, Beatrice and George Kaufman, Blythe Daly and Tallulah Bankhead. I also spent a pleasant evening in a cafeteria with an old friend, Ronald Colman, who had just opened in a play that was a flop, and was discouraged and unhappy. We cheered each other by formulating brave ambitions. He was determined to get to the coast to try his luck in pictures, and I was equally determined not to leave America until I had had a play accepted.

On the strength of this mutual stimulus, I started immediately to write *Sirocco* with Eva Le Gallienne and Joseph Schildkraut in mind for the leading parts. They were at that moment playing in Molnar's *Liliom*. I finished it quickly, and had no particular cause to regret it until several years later.

Florence Magee invited me to Mount Kisco a number of times, and I went, gratefully, whenever I had enough for the fare. Laurette Taylor and Hartley Manners returned to town from the country with Dwight and Marguerite, Laurette's children by her first marriage, and settled themselves into an odd demi-Gothic edifice on Riverside Drive. This house possessed one enormous room below stairs, with an open fireplace, much tortured woodwork, and stained-glass windows, and, upstairs, many small rooms on different levels, varying in décor from Laurette's gilt and be-laced bedroom and a formal mahoganied dining-room, to the correct and rather heavy-handed virility of Hartley's study, with its sports trophies, pipe-racks, and sturdy writing-table.

Hartley was a charming man, but his spirit seemed to be shut up permanently inside a sort of 'iron virgin' of moral principles. This, as far as I was concerned, made any lengthy conversations difficult. I had to tread lightly, and in the few literary discussions that we had, I soon learned not to allow enthusiasm to carry me too far, and to hop aside, nimbly, from any anti-social, anti-religious, or remotely sexual allusion. Laurette, on the other hand, was frequently blunt to the point of embarrassment. She was naïve, intolerant, lovable, and entirely devoid of tact. Her humour was quick as lightning, and she could pounce from a great height with all the swift accuracy of a pelican diving into the sea, seldom failing to spear some poor, wriggling fish, and disquieting considerably the other fish present. Her taste in dress was poor, and her loveliness triumphed over many inopportune bows and ostrich feathers, but her taste as an actress was unassailable.

On Sunday evenings up on Riverside Drive we had cold supper and played games, often rather acrimonious games, owing to Laurette's abrupt disapproval of any guest (whether invited by Hartley, Marguerite, Dwight or herself) who turned out to be self-conscious, nervous, or unable to act an adverb or an historical personage with proper abandon. There were also, very often, shrill arguments concerning rules. These were waged entirely among the family, and frequently ended in all four of them leaving the room and retiring upstairs, where, later on, they might be discovered, by any guest bold enough to go in search of them, amicably drinking tea in the kitchen.

It was inevitable that someone should eventually utilise portions of this eccentricity in a play, and I am only grateful to Fate that no guest of the Hartley Manners thought of writing *Hay Fever* before I did.

Lynn Fontanne returned from Chicago, where she had been playing a trial run of *Dulcy,* her first star part, written especially for her by George Kaufman and Marc Connelly. Her career in America had hitherto been devoted almost entirely to supporting Laurette in various plays of Hartley's. On the strength of her comedy performance in one of these, *Dulcy* was created, and proved to be a decisive triumph for her. As yet, however, there were still two months to endure before New York production, and she was a prey to the usual nervous forebodings, her moods alternating between hysterical gaiety and the most intense melancholy.

She and Alfred Lunt were, to put it mildly, 'courting' at the moment, and lived in a theatrical lodging-house somewhere in the West Seventies, known as 'Dr. Rounds'.' Any actor, however vagrant, was welcome at Dr. Rounds'. The food was good, and the house comfortably untidy and Dr. Rounds herself quite remarkable. She had greyish hair and shrewd, wary eyes, which sized you up accurately on sight, and she would occasionally relate gruesomely medical stories from out of the mysterious limbo of her early years. There was also in the house, in addition to Barry Baxter and the other lodgers, a maid-of-all-work, *café au lait* in colour and correctly true to type in action, who crooned incessantly in and out of all the rooms, and bashed dust-pans and tin pails joyously against the banisters.

From these shabby, congenial rooms, we projected ourselves into future eminence. We discussed, the three of us, over deli-

With
GERTRUDE LAWRENCE
in London Calling
Duke of York's Theatre, 1923

With the chorus in LONDON CALLING
Duke of York's Theatre, 1923

catessen potato salad and dill pickles, our most secret dreams of success. Lynn and Alfred were to be married. That was the first plan. Then they were to become definitely idols of the public. That was the second plan. Then, all this being successfully accomplished, they were to act exclusively together. This was the third plan. It remained for me to supply the fourth, which was that when all three of us had become stars of sufficient magnitude to be able to count upon an individual following irrespective of each other, then, poised serenely upon that enviable plane of achievement, we would meet and act triumphantly together.

After these prophetic orgies we often found it necessary to bring ourselves down to earth by taking brisk walks to the corner of the street and back, or going to the pictures. Once Lynn and I even sank so low as to make a charabanc trip to Chinatown.

In the meanwhile, we all had a long way to go and there was the immediate terror of the first night of *Dulcy* looming nearer and nearer. When the actual moment arrived, Alfred and I left Lynn in her dressing-room (to employ the hour and a half before the curtain rose by making-up, and dressing, and being methodically sick), and paced miserably up and down the street. We drifted in and out of soda-fountains, consuming endless Coca Colas and frosted chocolates, and behaving generally like anxious fathers expecting twins. Presently we watched, in panic, cars and taxis beginning to arrive at the theatre, and so we went in, and, clamping ourselves to our seats in the back row of the stalls, steeled ourselves to talk casually and wave and nod to acquaintances.

From the moment that Lynn flounced on in the first act, wearing a smart black velvet gown and appearing to be completely in command of herself and the play, we knew that everything was going to be all right, as indeed it was, and by the time the applause had died away after the second act we discovered that not only were we no longer pinching each other black and blue, but that we were quite relaxed and actually enjoying ourselves.

Soon after this I struck a bad patch again and, when I could really bear it no longer, I summoned up courage to go and borrow twenty dollars from Lynn. This courage was entirely my own concern and nothing whatever to do with Lynn. I knew that she would willingly give me anything that I asked for. But of all the many borrowings I have had to do in my time, I think I loathed that one the most. It wasn't humiliated pride that oppressed me, nor yet any false shame of my bad circumstances, all these things were too clearly understood among us, but somehow, in spite of my grey suit, blue shirt and tie, and brightly shined shoes, I felt vaguely bedraggled, as though my spirit hadn't been pressed properly and was shabby and creased.

I arrived at the theatre too soon, a long while before the end of the matinée, and walked up and down the alley until I could tell, by the sound of applause, that the curtain had fallen. Of course, a troop of people came round to see Lynn, and I had to wait for several more years until they left. I finally had to interrupt Lynn in the middle of a detailed description of a new bit of business she had inserted in the second act, and pop the question, almost crossly, at her. She said: 'Darling, of course, don't be so silly,' delved in her bag, and handed me the money without deviating at all from what she was saying. The next morning I received a letter from Jim Whigham, the editor of the *Metropolitan Magazine,* asking me to lunch with him at the Brook Club. He had been staying at Mount Kisco with the Magees, and had read while there a copy of *I'll Leave It to You,* which I had sent to Florence, as a sort of bread and butter gesture, after my first visit. He said, in course of lunch, that if I would consider turning it into a short story he would pay me five hundred dollars for it. I nearly choked, but managed to say, casually enough, that I would try, and the rest of the meal passed in a sort of haze which was rather a pity really, as I had not had the chance of eating such good food for a long time.

I reflected gleefully, on the way home, that for five hundred dollars I would gladly consider turning *War and Peace* into a music-hall sketch.

The result of all this was that, within three days, Lynn was paid back, swooning with surprise. The Italian grocer was paid back for two months of long-since consumed eggs and bacon. Gertrude received, with her usual lethargy, six weeks' arrears of wages. And I was able to send forty pounds home to Mother, to compensate for the loss of Mrs. Herriot, who had inconsiderately abandoned our drawing-room suite early in June in favour of the grave.

(4)

With the beginning of the autumn season New York became cooler in temperature and much hotter in theatrical activity. Broadway awoke from its summer sleep, and the first batch of 'fall productions' opened and closed in all directions. Homburgs took the place of straw hats, and coinciding with the return of all the managers to town, came the return of all my manuscripts. I was delighted to see them again, and read them through with keen pleasure, particularly *The Young Idea,* which, like *I'll Leave It to You,* I turned into a short story and sold to the *Metropolitan* for a further five hundred dollars.

I felt now much more secure financially, which was just as well, as I had a letter from Cecile in Bar Harbour saying that she and Gabrielle were not coming back to the studio at all and were, in fact, going to give it up for good. Upon receipt of this I moved out immediately, and went back to the Brevoort.

I was rather glad to be in an hotel again, especially as I had the satisfaction of knowing that I should be able to pay my bill quite regularly every week for some time to come. The studio had, of course, been a godsend to me, but I had passed too many miserable days in it, and been too lonely there, to feel any deep regret at leaving it. Also, during the last few weeks, several unfortunate things had occurred. To begin with, my laundryman, a fat, jolly little Chinaman, had been murdered in a street fight on the next block, which depressed me, as his Monday morning visits were benign and friendly. Then, I arrived home late one night to discover that the downstairs passage window and the Yale lock on the door had both been broken, and although nothing inside had been touched, I felt, even with my carefully unloaded revolver, a little insecure. Finally, and worst of all, I had a plague of bedbugs. These (having played in the pottery towns) were not entirely strangers to me, but as, in America, the oranges, apples, bananas, and buildings are far bigger than anywhere else in the world, so it is with their bedbugs. I awoke one night to find the walls, the bed, and myself covered with flat, slow-moving trouser buttons, which bit savagely, and, when squashed, smelt overpoweringly of almonds. I spent the hours until dawn shuddering in the kitchen, with all the lights on.

The next day, apart from a few corpses, there wasn't a sign of them, and the fumigators, when they arrived, expressed rather scornful scepticism, saying that I must have exaggerated as the walls and the ceiling and the floor showed no indications, and that there wasn't anywhere else they could possibly have come from. Nevertheless, upon my insisting, they fumigated the whole place and, in course of their labours, discovered several hundred hale and hearty bugs living cosily inside a tapestry picture of the Virgin Mary.

The various managers, although unenthusiastic about my plays, were most hospitable, asking me to lunch at the Astor, urging me to adapt sure-fire successes from the Hungarian, and sending me tickets for first nights. Even the remote Mr. Belasco crashed through with a balcony seat for his revival of *The Easiest Way* with Frances Starr. This was interesting as she gave a fine performance, and even though the play did appear to be a trifle dated, it was first-rate melodrama beautifully lit and directed. In the interval between the second and third acts, I contrived, by a casual word, to creep into the heart of Alexander Woollcott. The word was 'vexing.' I said, without any particularly witty intent, that I had found the performance of one of the actors in the play very vexing, whereupon the warm September night was instantly shattered by strange cluckings and gurglings and sharp, shrill wails of pleasure. I was unused to abandoned displays from eminent critics, as a matter of fact I was unused to eminent critics, and I regarded this capering figure on the sidewalk with astonishment. Later on

I became accustomed to such outbursts, finding, to my occasional dismay, that they worked both ways. Alexander Woollcott, in a rage, has all the tenderness and restraint of a newly caged cobra, and, when striking, much the same admirable precision. He has written, during the last ten years, a good deal about me in various newspapers and magazines. He has, in criticism, brought me to the dust and raised me on to high pedestals, usually giving a sly, rococo twist to the pedestals. He has, in biographical sketches, sacrificed, without pang of conscience, many of my nobler characteristics to pertinent witticisms. He has coaxed, relentlessly, many hundreds of dollars out of me at backgammon and Russian bank, and been loudly and urgently clamorous for payment.

In 1928, when I was playing with Beatrice Lillie in *This Year of Grace,* he objected bitterly to my performance of a song, 'A Room with a View.' And as a final inducement to me to relinquish it to my understudy, he appeared one night in a stage box with a party, each member of which buried his and her face in a newspaper the moment I began to sing. All these gestures and many others of a like devilishness have, oddly enough, merely served to cement even more strongly my fondness for him, and there he sits, and will probably continue to sit for ever, firmly ensconced in my affections, wearing a dreadful old green dressing-gown, playing to me all the Gilbert and Sullivan records that he knows I hate, and ordering me shrilly from the house whenever I win one point from him at any game of chance.

For the moment, however, we must leave him in September 1921, whooping outside the Lyceum Theatre, and turn to more austere encounters. Such, for instance, as my meeting with another critic at another first night, Mr. George Jean Nathan. Him I found deeply impressive, if somewhat studied in manner, and even if I had known then how much time and ink he was going to waste in the future in roasting the pants off me, I should still have been unable to help liking the little man.

A little later on came the first really important opening of the season. This was an all-star production of *The Circle* by Somerset Maugham. Estelle Winwood, John Drew and Mrs. Leslie Carter played the parts originally created in London by Fay Compton, Allan Aynesworth and Lottie Venne. The night was particularly englamoured by the fact that it was the return of Mrs. Carter to the stage after many years' absence.

I realised, after she had been on the stage for a little while, how superb she must have been in her flamboyant Zazas and Du Barrys of earlier years. I could visualise her clearly, through the brilliant web of Maugham's dialogue, posturing dramatically through bravura scenes, with scarlet hair piled high and her voluptuous figure dripping with Belasco jewels, but here, with sharp modern wit to express, she seemed strained and ill at ease. The most tawny lionesses wilt in captivity, and I couldn't help feeling that Mrs. Carter was wilting considerably behind the polite bars of social comedy.

Lester Donahue appeared suddenly out of the gloom at the back of the stalls and reminded me that we had met in London, and that he had given me seats for his piano recital at the Æolian Hall. I remembered it with enthusiasm, not only because he had played beautifully that afternoon, but because I was delighted to see his pink, cherubic little face again.

A few days later he moved over from wherever he was and came to the Brevoort. This was nice for me because he had a piano in his room which I used frequently.

We went to a lot of parties together, at one of which we found a childhood friend of his, Peggy Wood. Unfortunately she was not playing in anything at the moment, and so I was unable to judge for myself whether or not Lester's ecstatic descriptions of her work were justified until nearly ten years later, when she walked with such exquisite distinction through the shiny double doors in the first act of *Bitter Sweet*.

With Lester also I saw Fred and Adele Astaire for the first time, in a musical comedy called *The Love Letter*. I hadn't realised before then that such rhythm and taste in dancing were possible.

Every Thursday and Saturday there were midnight performances of *Shuffle Along*, which was playing somewhere up in the

West Sixties. This was, I believe, one of the first entirely coloured revues.

Throughout the whole jumble of songs and sketches and dances there darted the swift, vivid genius of Florence Mills, at one moment moving like a streak of quicksilver, the next still against some gaudily painted back-drop, nothing animated about her at all, except her wide smile and the little pulse in her throat, throbbing like a bird while she sang:

> 'Love will find a way
> Tho' skies now are grey,
> Love like ours can never be ruled,
> Cupid's not fooled that way . . .'

When she died a few years ago, many thousands of people followed her to the cemetery. Most of Broadway, and all of Harlem. And when the service was over and the hymns had been sung, there was no more music until, just as the small coffin was being lowered into the grave, a sudden burst of singing rose to the skies, saluting her passing with the song that she had made so famous: 'Bye-bye, Blackbird.'

(5)

On the last day of October I sailed for home on the S.S. Cedric, one of the smaller White Star ships.

I stood on deck until the skyline had disappeared into the rain, and retired to my cabin in which I remained, prostrate with sea-sickness, for three days. When I ultimately emerged, still faintly green, the sea was calmer and the sun was shining, and I was able to sit wanly in a deck chair nibbling, every now and then, a little cold beef and baked potato and allowing the events of the past five months to pass in stately review before my mind's eye, over the more unpleasant of which glamour was already beginning to settle.

I re-lived, with slight dramatic overtones, many hours of despair. I saw a brave, tragic youth trudging through the hot streets to his accustomed bench in Battery Park, friendless and alone, gazing out over the sea to where Green England lay, and sharing, perhaps, a crust with some kindly Negro.

I saw the same gallant figure attired in deep evening dress attending the smartest first nights, with not even a nickel in his trouser pocket to pay his subway fare home. I also saw him, cowering naked in the kitchen, beset on all sides by voracious bedbugs.

I sorted my new friends with genuine pleasure. Lynn and Alfred, Alec Woollcott, Lester, Cecile and Gabrielle, Florence Magee, Irene, Laurette, Beatrice and George Kaufman, the Astaires, the countless others, all of whom had been charming to me, and all of whom I knew I should be enchanted to see again at any time, anywhere.

In addition to these there were some, who for some reason or other, possibly from sheer modesty, failed to appear in my memory while I was writing the preceding pages. Perhaps they felt that by shuffling late into their places they might interfere with the flow of my narrative. However, two at least were important to me, and if the others persist in lurking in the shadows that's their look-out. The two to be specified are Hoytie Wiborg and Gladys Barbour.

I stayed with Hoytie at Easthampton, where we ate good food, played bad tennis, argued on intellectual subjects, rode the surf on a large rubber mattress, and, on one occasion, nearly drowned.

Hoytie dabbled passionately in the Arts. She talked of Picasso, Van Gogh, Scriabin and Stravinsky. She lectured me austerely upon my own talents, intimating with great firmness that if I continued along my present lines, writing lyrics, sketches, plays and music, etc., that no good could ever possibly result from it. Facile versatility, she prophesied, would lead me surely to a dilettante's grave, and that if I must go on writing so much, and so quickly, at least I must give up imagining for one moment that I had the least talent for music. This, she said, she really knew about, and that as I could neither read it, nor write it, and as my execution on the piano was only erratic in the right hand and non-existent in the left, the sooner I eliminated the whole idea from my bag of tricks the better.

Years later, on the first night of *Bitter Sweet,* remembering this conversation, I smiled at her from my box with a slight gleam of triumph in my eye, but she only shook her head gloomily, as though her worst forebodings had been incontrovertibly proven.

Gladys Barbour was chalk to Hoytie's cheese. She was small and fair, whereas Hoytie was tall and dark. She preferred dancing to Picasso, and Gershwin to Stravinsky. She shared in common with Hoytie a generous heart and an infinite capacity for taking trouble to help people she liked and, incidentally, was responsible, through the kind offices of her husband, for the comfortable free cabin on the Cedric which I was now occupying. One night in New York, during a party at some night-club, she suddenly presented me with a mascot which was nothing more or less than a twenty-dollar gold piece. I am certain to this day that she gave it to me entirely because she knew I was broke, but, sentimental to the last, I refrained for two whole weeks from changing it, and when finally I could resist the temptation no longer, I found that it had been stolen by one of the bell-boys at the Brevoort. Altogether, I looked back tenderly across the sea to Gladys Barbour.

The S.S. Cedric was a small boat, compared with its enormous sisters, the Majestic and the Olympic, but it was comfortable enough. It was also old, and slow, and wallowed through the sea like a fat swimmer, past her prime, doing a perpetual breast stroke.

There were not many people on board. But among the few was one of definite interest, Dr. Marie Stopes. She had, appropriately, the eyes of a fanatic, but the rest of her was dim, excepting her conversation. This was surprisingly vivid, and almost exclusively concerned with the theatre. Naturally this was a comfort to me, and we discussed plays for hours in a small rustic tea-room aft of the promenade deck.

We docked at Liverpool in snow and sleet, and I went ashore.

hugging to myself the excitement of a surprise arrival. I couldn't resist sending Mother a telegram from Lime Street Station, and I spent the interminable five-hour journey in the train, imagining her face when she opened it and noted where it had been handed in.

The home-coming was entirely successful, and unspoiled by anti-climax. The bungalow was *en fête*. There were one or two new lodgers peering out of the windows, and a new and very young housemaid, who stood first on one leg and then on the other, and giggled loudly throughout the first flurry of reunion. Mother was flushed and hilarious, but I noticed a certain strain under her joy, and my heart sank a little, but rebounded again almost immediately with the realisation that whatever might be happening behind the scenes in that beastly house, we were at least all together again.

In so far as the complete success of my New York adventure was concerned, I felt a trifle dubious. Financially speaking it had obviously been a failure, as I had returned with only seven pounds more than when I had landed five months before. However, I had seen a lot, experienced a lot, and learned a lot. I knew New York thoroughly, better actually than I have ever known it since. The subway, the elevated, cheap cafeterias, park benches, and loneliness have been no part of my later visits. But I felt, even then, certain small regrets.

To be poor in your own country is bad enough, and to be poor among strangers should, by rights, be very much worse. But, somewhat to my surprise, I realised that in my case it had not been worse at all. I remembered the Chinese laundryman, Gertrude, the Italian grocer, and the Irish cop. I remembered conversations in buses, and cinemas, and soda fountains. I remembered the beauty of New York at night, viewed, not from a smart penthouse on Park Avenue, but from a crowded seat in Washington Square. And it seemed in spite of its hardness and irritating, noisy efficiency, a great and exciting place.

PART FIVE

In REVIEWING THE PAST, it is difficult to check off accurately, which, among the millions of small incidents, adventures, pleasures and pains, have been essential to the development of character, or, at any rate, interesting enough in themselves to be worth describing.

When this book is finished, corrected, revised and lying snugly bound in the publisher's office, I feel sure that many unrecorded events will arise to mock and torment me. Many people, also. Already, I find that there are several that I have left out. Among these, oddly enough, some of considerable importance. Grace Forster for instance, Stewart's mother. She should have made her entrance a long way back, swishing across shady lawns and night-clubs, wrapped in gallant vanity, and smelling slyly of amber.

Farther back still, a hunt ball at Oakham seems to have been mislaid somehow. To this I was taken by Lady Londesborough, and was deeply, although not too rapturously, impressed by it. I remember a lot of pink coats, and much deafening gaiety. I also remember a bad band and a worse floor and, more pleasantly, Burgersh, now Lord Westmorland, whose face, doubtless out of deference to the Cottesmore, seemed pinker than the pinkest coat present, and whose charm, even through the loudest din, remained inviolate.

Among other unrelated things floating in my memory, I can see clearly a man being run over by a bus just opposite the National Gallery; a Mercedes car, belonging to a gentleman called Harry Hart, which seldom got farther than Maidenhead;

and a home-made turban of Joyce Barbour's fashioned saucily in 1916 from a bandana handkerchief.

The year of 1922 began for me in a welter of financial embarrassment. The hows, whys, and wherefores would make dull reading, enough that there were borrowings, mortgages on my beloved piano, pawnshops, black moments of distress, brokers' men, and, worst of all, days when even Mother's invincible spirit came near to being broken.

Nobody seemed to be interested in my plays. Nobody seemed anxious to offer me parts at even reasonable salaries. Every now and then I managed to sell a short story or a song, and once I got a hundred pounds for grinding out an adaptation of a French play for Dennis Eadie. Altogether, it was a gloomy and depressing period.

In former days, of course, I could probably have gone out on tour or procured a small job in London, but now having played two or three leading parts, and actually appeared in my own play in the West End, I was in the awkward situation of being too well known to be able to accept little jobs, and not well-known enough to be able to command big ones.

Every morning Mother used to come and sit on my bed while I had my breakfast. This was the one hour in the day that she allowed herself to relax, and I could always tell by her face, the moment it appeared round the door, if anything awful had happened. There was a certain artificial chirpiness about her on bad days, manufactured out of a determination not to let me see that she was worried, which generally broke down before I had finished my first cup of coffee.

We were getting more and more deeply into debt, and even with the house full, which it wasn't, the income from it was not sufficient to meet the quarterly instalments, the rent, the taxes, the electric light bills, and the living expenses of Father, Mother, Auntie Vida, Eric and me.

What worried me most was the dread that Mother would suddenly break completely and become seriously ill. Her heart was not strong, and the strain of the last few years had been appalling.

This I was determined to avert at all costs, even if the brokers took possession of the house and we were all flung into the street.

I went to see Ned Lathom, knowing how kind and generous he was, and also knowing how many hundreds of people had already sponged upon him, and asked him flatly, without preliminaries, to lend me two hundred pounds. He refused almost sharply, and he added that he would willingly give me two hundred pounds, but that never, in any circumstances, would he lend money to anybody ever again, it was too dangerous a commodity, he said, to pass between friends.

I have a lot of gratitude in my heart, towards many people, but it is too special and private an emotion to spill into print. There are hundreds of ways of describing unkindness and meanness and little cruelties. A sly dig at the right moment can work wonders. But just try to write of generosity. Try to frame in words an unrelated, motiveless gesture of sheer kindness and you are lost. The warmth behind the phrases dissipates before they reach the paper, and there they lie, under your hand, sneering up at you, coldly effusive and dead as mutton.

At any rate, with Ned's cheque in my pocket, the sun shone, temporarily, with all its might. About a hundred and fifty of the two hundred pounds went immediately to various creditors. The remaining fifty I held on to, because I had a plan in mind, which, after a discussion with Gladys Calthrop, I sprang on Mother, suddenly, and clinched before she had time to argue.

The plan was that Father was to take charge of the house, and that I was to find a little cottage in the country somewhere, where she could rest completely, for several months, and where I could come for week-ends, and write. She at once made a pyramid of small difficulties which I swept grandly away. There wasn't much conviction behind them anyhow, and a few days later Gladys and I went to Dymchurch, where Athene Seyler had lent me her cottage for a fortnight, and from this we set forth daily in search of a small, inexpensive house for Mother.

Dymchurch in March was bleak, windy, cold and full of charm. We bicycled and walked for days over the marshes, with Fred,

Gladys's brown spaniel, padding along behind us, and plunging in and out of the dykes. We zigzagged backwards and forwards between Ham Street and Ivychurch, Appledore and New Romney. We climbed up on to Aldington Knoll and looked at the cliffs of France glinting in the sun across the steely grey channel. We found some early primroses and a lame sea-gull, which bit us fiercely, and messed, with the utmost abandon, all over the cottage. We went systematically through every available habitation within a radius of twenty-five miles, and finally found a small and tender one, nestling up against a public-house in the village of St. Mary's in the Marsh. It had four rooms, outside sanitation, a rental of ten shillings a week, and a superb view from the upper windows of unlimited sheep.

Mother seemed to be quite pleased with it, and so we moved in, and very soon the sea and the sky and the marshes began to work a little homely Kentish magic. There was nothing to do but read and write, and make expeditions into Dymchurch or New Romney to get provisions, and a lot of the tiredness was smoothed away from Mother's face within the first few weeks.

I bought a black mongrel at the Battersea Dogs' Home, and conveyed him, radiant in a new collar, to New Romney station, where Mother met us and fell in love with him at once. He was very young and spindly in the legs, and he promptly had a violent attack of distemper, which kept him hovering between life and death for seven weeks. However, nursing him provided an occupation for Mother during the days I had to spend in London.

There were a few neighbours for her to talk to. Mrs. Hinds, the owner of the inn next door, Mr. and Mrs. Cook, the vicar and his wife, Miss Hammond, the local schoolteacher. There were also the Bodys, who owned much of the property round about, and, not very far off, at Jesson, none other than E. Nesbit, who lived with her husband, and a gentle friend, in a series of spacious huts.

I called on her very soon, and found her as firm, as nice, and as humorous as her books had led me to expect. The skipper, her husband, was a grand old man, who loved her and guarded her devotedly through her last, rather sad years.

The friend, Miss Hill, was a wispy creature, with an air of vague detachment, which inspired Athene Seyler to christen her irreverently, 'The Green Hill Far Away.'

During that spring I spent most of my time at St. Mary's. The churchyard just across the road was a peaceful place in which to work, and it was there, propped up against a family tombstone, that I wrote *The Queen Was in the Parlour*. Nothing could be further removed from that play than the surroundings in which I wrote it. Its passionate love scenes and Ruritanian splendours emerged from my mind to the gentle cawing of rooks, and the bleating of new-born lambs. When I raised my eyes from a palace courtyard, lit by the flare of torches and brimming with revolutionaries, I saw the marshes stretching to the dark line of the sea wall, broken every now and then by dumpy little Martello towers, and, slightly inland on the right, a cluster of trees and houses and a square church tower—the village of New Romney.

On long summer evenings Mother and I used to ride up to Aldington Knoll on our bicycles, and wait there in the growing dusk, until the thin line of sea, four miles away, faded and disappeared in the white mist rising from the dykes, and then, looking down over the darkening country spreading all the way from Folkestone to Hastings, we would see lamps twinkling in cottage windows, bats swooping down from the high trees, and the lighthouses flashing all along the coast.

It would have been cheering, had we known then, that the land just below us would belong to us one day. That the farm-house, the five poplars, the thick woods, and lush fields stretching down to the Military Canal would all be ours to do with as we liked. But even as it was, without clairvoyance and future certainties, those evenings were lovely enough, and we pedalled home happily through the dark, our bicycle lamps making wobbling shadows across the roads, feeling that, after all, money troubles, rate collectors, and brokers' men, didn't matter so very much, as long as we had a water-tight, ten-shilling-a-week roof over our heads.

(2)

In June Robert Courtneidge took up an option on *The Young Idea,* to produce it in the early autumn for a six weeks' trial run in the provinces. This was an obvious change of fortune, and we set about casting it right away. I firmly, and very much against Courtneidge's will, insisted upon playing Sholto myself. I explained patiently, and at length, that as I had taken the trouble to write the part specially for myself, it would be both illogical and foolish to allow anyone else to get so much as a smell of it. Courtneidge's argument was that I was too old for it, that my personality was too sophisticated, and that in his opinion it would be much more effective played by someone with a more cherubic cast of countenance and a more naïve charm. What he really meant, of course, was that I was not a good enough actor for it. However he finally gave in with as good grace as possible, and we went to work on the other parts.

I had written Gerda for Edna Best, but, owing to some other contract, she was unobtainable, and so Ann Trevor was engaged. Kate Cutler, of course, was to be Jennifer. This also had been especially written for her, and of my other old *I'll Leave it to You* friends, Muriel Pope was cast for Cicely. The rest were Herbert Marshall, Clive Currie, Naomi Jacob, Phyllis Black, Molly Maitland (then Mrs. Herbert Marshall), Ambrose Manning and Martin Lewis, who was later replaced by Leslie Banks.

Rehearsals were to begin in August, and so I had nearly two months in which to enjoy myself, relieved, for the first time for a long while, of the horrible foreboding that I was never, never going to get work again as long as I lived.

Father, much to his own and everyone else's surprise, was not only running the house successfully, but deriving, on the whole, a great deal of personal gratification from it. Always naturally gregarious, he had a grand time talking to the lodgers and hopping in and out of their rooms with breakfast trays. Apparently he was more sociable than Mother, and not only achieved extreme popularity inside the house, but outside as well. All the tradesmen in the vicinity welcomed his morning appearance with the dog (an obsequious Pomeranian), and even the window-cleaner was accorded fortnightly a brief but intimate chat. May Weaver, the now not so new housemaid who had been present on my return from the States, relaxed into delirious gaiety with Mother's restraining influence removed. She scampered madly up and down stairs singing shrilly, and never, except very, very late in the afternoon, dreamt of wearing a cap, a small gesture to refinement upon which Mother had obdurately insisted.

(3)

A short while after the contract for *The Young Idea* had been signed, I was invited by Lady Colefax to Oxford, where she had taken a house for a week, to entertain a party of young people for the Bullingdon dance. I knew her then only slightly, but we have been friends ever since.

Those few days were smooth and affable, and bathed in a gentle summer peace alien to me, and yet somehow vaguely familiar, which puzzled me at first, until I realised that my sense of having seen it all before was entirely due to the books I had read.

It was all there. All the paraphernalia of the eager young novelists, and touchingly accurate in detail.

There were the shady cloisters with the sun tracing Gothic patterns across the worn paving-stones. There were the rooks cawing in the high elms, the rich, over-laden rose gardens, the green velvet lawns, and the whacks and thuds of cricket bats and tennis rackets sounding gently from the other side of yew hedges.

There, beneath aged sycamores, were spread tea-tables, cushions, wicker chairs, 'Curate's Comforts,' and large bowls of strawberries and cream, the latter to be devoured by the returning game players who were so much, much more suitably attired for the country than I. Their shirts and flannels were yellow and well used, against which mine seemed too newly white, too immaculately moulded from musical comedy. Their socks, thick and carelessly wrinkled round their ankles, so unlike mine of too-thin silk caught up by intricate suspenders.

Their conversation, too, struck a traditional note in my ears. I seemed to know what they were going to say long before they said it. I sensed in their fledgeling jokes and light unsubtle badinage a certain quality of youthfulness that I had never known. And although I was the same age, if not younger than many of them, I felt suddenly old, over-experienced and quite definitely out of the picture.

This was not exactly an unhappy sensation. I had then, as always, no wish to change places with anyone in the world. But I felt a slight strain, as though I were playing in a scene for which I had not been sufficiently rehearsed. This evaporated soon after the first day and after I had grown to know them all a little, but I noted carefully many points, without envy or disdain or wistfulness, but merely with a keen eye on future performances.

On the night of the Bullingdon dance itself, the whole atmosphere suddenly shivered and jangled into awareness of a very unfamiliar personality indeed. The elms shuddered a little when a large car drew up at the door and disgorged, amid raucous laughter, the bouncing, Michelin figure of Elsa Maxwell. She was accompanied, sedately, by Mrs. Toulmin, fair and brittle and impressively *mondaine,* with her Chanel clothes, and sleek contented dressing-case. Elsa beside her looked as incongruous as a large brindle bull-dog out walking with a white Persian cat. She at once proceeded to whistle through that house like a cyclone, strumming the piano, laughing, talking, and striking the rose-white youth present into a coma of dumb bewilderment.

I loved her at once. I loved her round friendly face, with its little shrewd eyes darting about like animated currants in a Bath bun. I loved her high spirits and her loud infectious laugh. It was before the days when she became the Queen of Paris, and curdled her own personality with too much *crème de la crème*. In 1922 she was still a roystering buccaneer, and with all her boastfulness and noise and shrill assertiveness, intelligent and immensely lovable.

Why she suddenly appeared at Oxford that evening I shall never know. If I felt a little out of it in so fresh and young an atmosphere, Elsa must have felt like a visitor from another planet.

To write the true story of Elsa's life would be worth doing, but unfortunately quite impossible, for the simple reason that the details of it, the real mysteries and struggles and adventures, are untraceable. The only authority for data would be Elsa herself, but to appeal to her would be worse than useless. Not that she wouldn't be willing and happy to supply information, not that she wouldn't be perfectly delighted to pour treasure-troves of anecdotes and incidents and startling experiences, glittering jingling heaps of them, into the lap of anyone sympathetically disposed to listen. She is nothing if not generous in everything, a magnificent egotist into the bargain, and loves few things better than talking about herself.

But unhappily for the author engaged in these tantalising researches, one of the principal gifts that the wise Californian fairies brought to Elsa's christening was an untrammelled and peculiarly vivid imagination. This provides a complete world for her, colouring to excess, not only the things she has done, and does, but creating for her with equal reality the things she never has done and never will do.

At the height of her Paris fame Cole Porter inscribed the following little song for her, which she pounded joyously out of most of the pianos on the Continent:

> '*I met a friend of mine a week or two ago*
> *And he was all togged out.*
> *I said, "Excuse me, but I'd really like to know*
> *What this is all about.*
> *You're over-dressed, you're absurd!"*
> *He answered, "Haven't you heard?*

' "I'm dining with Elsa, with Elsa, supreme.
I'm going to meet Princesses
Wearing 'Coco Chanel' dresses
Going wild over strawberries and cream,
I've got Bromo Seltzer
To take when dinner ends
For I'm dining with Elsa
And her ninety-nine most intimate friends!" '

After the Bullingdon dance she departed for London, but not before she had invited me to a party the following Tuesday.

The Oxford house-party seemed a trifle flattened after she had left, a hazy indecisiveness hung about it, as though it were just coming to after an anæsthetic. But by the next day it had regained its normal composure, and proceeded pleasantly, with various diversions, to the end of the week.

(4)

Elsa's party was great fun with social and Bohemian graces tactfully mixed.

Dorothy Fellows-Gordon—'Dickie,' a life-long friend of Elsa's—was there, tall, nice-looking, with jet-black hair and a lovely singing voice. Later on in the evening when I was sitting talking to her in a corner, Elsa came over and joined us, and after they had both exchanged significant raised-eyebrow looks, Elsa said that they had a little proposition to make to me and that on no account was I to be offended. I couldn't imagine what on earth she was driving at, and so I laughed nervously and said that I was never offended at anything. Then she explained that she and Dickie were going for two weeks to Venice, and wanted me to go with them as their guest. She added, as a palliative to my wounded honour, that they would feel far more comfortable with a man to look after them and that I would really be doing them a great favor if I would consent.

[158]

I saw through this in a minute. I knew perfectly well that they didn't in the least need anyone to look after them, but were only trying to gloss over for me the unmentionable horror of having my expenses paid by two defenceless women. But it was sweet and sympathetic of them, and they did it beautifully. Obviously I accepted with enthusiasm and a few days later travelled over to Paris to join them.

None of us had ever been to Venice before, and the first sight of it, as we walked down the station steps into a gondola, sent us all off into a clamour of excitement. Elsa led, of course. Propped up against a cushion in the back seat she let forth a stream of enthusiasm into the gathering dusk. Superlatives flew through the air, ricochetting off mouldering palazzos and plopping into the water, as we swept under dark little bridges, swirled round sharp corners, and finally debouched on to the Grand Canal.

We were lucky that first evening. The air was clear and pure. A 'Serenata' passed close by us on its way to the lagoon, already lit with coloured lanterns and crammed to the gunwales with stout little tenors wearing white shirts and coloured sashes. One of them was tuning a guitar, another strummed absently on a small portable piano. Our gondoliers gave sharp atmospheric cries, and the sun set considerately as we arrived at the hotel, plunging the whole scene into a misty Turneresque beauty that robbed even Elsa of further adjectives.

That was certainly a glamorous fortnight. The loveliness of Venice alone would have been enough. The strange decayed magic of old palaces rising out of green canals, the dim archways, the remote misty lagoons stretching away behind the town towards Mestre. The brilliance and warm colour of the piazza in the evenings, a military band playing chirrupy selections from Verdi, gay crowds of people passing endlessly up and down through the arcades.

All this would have enraptured a far less impressionable mind than mine, and I could have returned home happily with such memories. More happily, perhaps, without the very different memories of the Lido and the myriads of feuds and scandals and small social rumpuses which took place there daily.

I found a few new friends—Muriel Draper, with plastered straw-coloured hair and full scarlet lips; Blanche Barrymore, with farouche Byronic locks flowing in the breeze and long billowing cloaks. And Mrs. Spears, a small attractive woman with deep sleepy eyes and a rather nervous smile, who said that she had completed a novel which was to be published soon, and was to be called *Jane—Our Stranger*. She omitted to tell me that her pen name was Mary Borden and so I visualised a light, slightly jejeune little book written to pass the time, and dealing, probably amateurishly, with the adventures of some winsome housemaid.

When I finally left Venice in order to get back to London for rehearsals of *The Young Idea,* Dickie and Elsa stayed behind for an extra week. They insisted, however, upon giving me my ticket and seeing me off at the station. I hung out of the window for a long while watching Elsa's little bobbing figure growing smaller and smaller until it seemed to dissolve into the grey platform, and reflecting that the life of a gigolo, unimpaired by amatory obligations, could undoubtedly be very delightful indeed.

(5)

We rehearsed *The Young Idea* in hot, smelly rehearsal rooms, and later in cool empty theatres. I felt as nervous at first, as if I had never acted before. Robert Courtneidge, although milder than in the old days, could still be scarifying, and I had the uncomfortable conviction all the time that he still disapproved of my playing the part. It was typical of his generosity, however, to take me aside a few days before we opened and tell me that he had been entirely wrong and that I was giving an excellent performance. Actually I believe that his kindness overstepped the truth. Perhaps I may have been better than he thought I was going to be, but I was a long way from giving a really good performance. There was certainly an improvement in my acting since *I'll*

Leave it to You, but I was still forcing points too much and giving knowing grimaces when delivering comedy lines. I had not learned then not to superimpose upon witty dialogue the top-heavy burden of personal mannerisms. In this instance, of course, I was both author and actor, and the former suffered considerably from the antics and over-emphasis of the latter.

The play opened at Bristol. The notices and business were both good, and we settled down complacently for a pleasant little tour.

On returning to London I had a long talk with Courtneidge, who said that although there was no immediate chance of getting a theatre, it might be possible to find a suitable one after Christmas when the pantomime and fairy-play rush was over. And so, faced with November fogs and at least two months of idleness, I decided on another little excursion to foreign parts.

Ned Lathom, I knew, was in Davos recovering from his first bout of T.B. I also knew that he had only his sister Barbara with him, and that they both would be probably pleased to see me, so I sent him a telegram and waited hopefully for the reply. It was comfortingly enthusiastic, so after buying a few sweaters, thick socks and breeches, off I went; second-class on the trains, but first-class on the boat, arriving the next day, my eyes dazzled by leagues of white snow in strong sunlight and my ears pleasantly humming in the high altitude to the jingling of sleigh-bells.

Ned looked better, but he still had coughing fits from time to time. He managed, as usual, to be amazingly luxurious and had surrounded himself with books, cushions and large rich sweets which, I am sure, were bad for him.

I stayed there for three weeks with Barbara and him alone before anyone else arrived. The Christmas season had not yet begun, and the only other occupants of the hotel were T.B. patients, all in various stages of the disease. It was a strange life, gay in the evenings, when everyone made an effort to dress, dine in the restaurant, and dance afterwards in the bar. During the days, of course, everybody had cures and treatments to undergo, and the whole hotel seemed dead and empty. At night, however, it regularly awoke. The gambling machine in the bar tinkled merrily, the band played, and there was the sound of corks popping and noisy conversation in many languages. Only very occasionally would someone slip away from the fun to flit upstairs, coughing, almost furtively, into a stained handkerchief.

Those evenings, with their noise and music and gaiety, were slightly macabre, but somehow not depressing. It was as though they were unrelated to ordinary existence—a few detached hours of pleasure, floating between life and death, untouchable by the sadness of either. The knowledge that practically everybody present, themselves included, would probably be dead within a year or so was, I suppose, tucked away behind the laughter of most of the people there, but it was in no way apparent. There seemed to be no strain in the air, no eager snatching at flying moments. Perhaps the disease itself carried with it a compensating illusion that ultimate cure was certain, that all the slow tedious intricate process of dying was nothing more than an interlude of small discomfort.

Ned, who had always been badly stage-struck, had financed Charlot's last revue *A to Z,* and still appeared to be avid for punishment. He made me play to him all the songs I had written, and when he realised that there were enough comparatively good ones to make up a score, he wired to Charlot commanding him to come out immediately. I was thrilled at the thought of doing a whole revue, but scared that Charlot, when he arrived, might not be quite as eager and appreciative as Ned. However, when he did arrive in due course he was expansive and benign, and a series of cigar-laden conferences ensued, during which *London Calling* was born.

I worked on sketches in the mornings, waking early when the clouds were still veiling the mountains, submitted them to Ned and Charlot in the afternoons, and within the space of a few days the whole plan of the show was roughly laid out. It was to be produced the following autumn, with Gertrude Lawrence, Maisie Gay, a comedian as yet undecided, and myself.

Charlot took me aside and told me that he would be unable to pay me more than fifteen pounds a week, as I was inexperienced in revue work, but that as I was bound to make a great deal of money out of royalties I was not to worry about it. I didn't worry about it at the time as I was too occupied with the show as a whole, but later I gave it a certain amount of thought. Charlot went back to England, seemingly pleased with everything, and left Ned and Barbara and me in a ferment of excitement.

Christmas pounced on Davos and everything lit up. Trainloads of strange people arrived daily. A whole extra wing of the hotel was thrown open. The Kurhaus, down in the village, surprisingly produced a highly decorated bar and a jazz band. The whole place became, with abrupt thoroughness, a resort. Ned's Christmas guests, it is unnecessary to remark, were far and away the star turn of the hotel.

In order of appearance, rather than precedence, they consisted of: Clifton Webb, Mrs. Fred (Teddie) Thompson, Gladys Cooper, Dick Wyndham, Edward Molyneux, Bobbie Howard, Dickie Gordon, Elsa Maxwell and Maxine Elliott. From their advent onwards life was less peaceful but certainly more stimulating. We went on tailing parties, stringing out in a long line of sleds behind a large sleigh in which Elsa sat screaming like a banshee. We went on skating parties, Swedish Punch parties, and lugeing parties. In course of one of these, quite unintentionally, I got caught up in a time-test race, and, to my amazement, on reaching the bottom was presented with a small silver cup. Apparently I came down the two and a quarter miles in just under four minutes, not, let it be understood, because I had the least desire to do so, but because, owing to the whole run having been re-banked and iced since Barbara and I had been on it, I was completely unable to stop myself.

Gladys Cooper took a marked dislike to me, and we had several acrid tussles, notably at a lunch party at the Kurhaus, where she remarked in a tone of maddening superiority that it was ridiculous of me to go on writing plays that were never produced, and that why on earth I didn't collaborate with someone who really knew the job, she couldn't understand.

I replied that as Shaw, Barrie and Maugham didn't collaborate

I saw no reason why I should. Whereupon she laughed, not without reason, and said that she had never heard of such conceit in her life and that she might just as well compare herself to Duse or Bernhardt. I jumped in here quickly on cue and retorted that the difference was not quite as fantastic as that. After which the lunch continued amid slightly nervous hilarity.

Oddly enough, after this preliminary blood-letting, Gladys and I parted glowing with mutual affection, and the glow has strengthened through the years, with never so much as a breath of disharmony.

(6)

The Young Idea opened at the Savoy Theatre in February to even more enthusiasm than had greeted *I'll Leave it to You*.

The play proceeded smoothly and at the end I made my usual self-deprecatory speech with a modesty which was rapidly becoming metallic, but which had the desired effect of lashing the audience to further ecstasies, and when the curtain had fallen we all rejoiced appropriately, although my personal satisfaction was edged with wariness. I remembered the effusions of the first night of *I'll Leave it to You*—the kindly intentioned but over-optimistic voices which had dinned into my ears that it was 'marvellous' and 'divine' and would undoubtedly 'run a year', and decided, before giving way completely to triumph, to bide my time until I saw the returns on Saturday night. In this I turned out to be wise, for in spite of excellent press notices and a deluge of superlatives from my acquaintances, the play folded up at the end of eight weeks.

But although brief, where the company was concerned it was a happy run. There were, of course, a number of the usual rumours that business was steadily going up, or that we were to be transferred to a smaller and more intimate theatre, or that a friend of Muriel Pope's had heard from a friend of hers in Keith Prowse that the libraries were about to take up a big deal stretching right into May. But being on a royalty basis, I saw the returns every night and was able to watch, without illusion, the sinister little figures growing weekly smaller and smaller until ultimately, after a sad but sympathetic conversation with Courtneidge, the fatal fortnight's notice was pinned up on the board.

Nevertheless, *The Young Idea* was one more step achieved and several perquisites accrued from it. Among them the sale of the publication and amateur rights to Samuel French, and a letter of the most generous praise from Mr. Charles Blake Cochran.

A few days later I lunched with him at the Berkeley, and flushed with perfectly chosen wine and still more perfectly chosen words of encouragement. I don't remember any premonition sitting behind my chair and nudging me into realisation that this was the first of an endless procession of similar lunches that dotted through future years, that hundreds of restaurant tables, bottles of hock and 'entrecôtes minutes' were waiting for us. It only seemed an extremely pleasant hour, significant because I hoped that he might be persuaded to produce a play of mine one day.

Meanwhile, things were not going so badly. Mother had returned to Ebury Street from St. Mary's, happier and in better health than she had been for a long time. She occasionally snatched the reins of management from Father and after a salutary crack or two with the whip, handed them back again so that the house jogged along amicably enough, like a dreary old family coach with Auntie Vida as a diminutive postilion hopping down every now and then to open the door for the lodgers.

When *The Young Idea* closed I went off to join Gladys Calthrop and Mrs. Cooper at Cap Ferrat, where the latter had rented a villa. It was a nice villa and the view from it was charming, but its peace and plenty were somewhat soured for Gladys and me by the presence of a Dominican prior to whom Mrs. Cooper was devoted, but who took a bleak dislike to us on sight. We bore his disapproval for as long as we could, and then realising that our being there was not only making things uncomfortable for Mrs. Cooper and for him but for ourselves as well, we departed in a deluge of Riviera rain for Italy.

We had very little money but it was a gay excursion and in due course we returned to Mrs. Cooper and found to our horror that the prior was still there. But this time we outstayed him and the rest of the holiday was peaceful and without incident.

(7)

In May a one-act comedy that I had written a year before was produced by the London Grand Guignol at the Little Theatre. It was called *The Better Half,* and was wittily played by Auriol Lee. In spite of this it was received with apathy; I think, possibly, because it was a satire and too flippant in atmosphere after the full-blooded horrors that had gone before it. Nevertheless, it was quite well written and served the purpose, if only for a little, of keeping my name before the public. Meanwhile Ned was back from Davos, much improved in health and already beginning to dissipate the effects of his cure by giving the rich lunches, dinners and supper parties that he loved so much. With his return the preparations for the revue were resumed. The date was set, the title *London Calling* was set, and the cast was set, that is, with the notable exception of the leading juvenile. This state of affairs was brought about by my stubborn and unaccountable refusal to play it. At any rate, it seemed unaccountable to those who had not been present during my brief fifteen-pound-a-week discussion with Charlot at Davos.

It had been arranged at the conference that I was to share the writing of the book with Ronald Jeans and the composing of the music with Philip Braham. This, although disappointing to me at first, I finally accepted as being a wise decision, as to do a whole show might have proved too heavy a burden on my inexperience. Also, during the conferences I had been unable to avoid noticing the fat and satisfying salaries that were to be received by Gertie Lawrence, Tubby Edlin and Maisie Gay, and the vision of myself, as the fourth of the quartette, earning five pounds a week less than I had received in both *I'll Leave it to You* and *The Young Idea* seemed unattractive. In consequence, I announced (for which

[166]

may God forgive me) that to appear in a musical show would injure irreparably my prestige as a straight actor.

After little argument my decision was accepted, but having in my contract as author a clause to the effect that I was to be consulted as to cast, I was able to raise adequate objections to the name of every juvenile suggested, until ultimately, after many weeks' wear and tear, I allowed myself to be persuaded to change my mind.

This time my business conversation with Charlot was even briefer, but much more to the point, resulting in a salary of forty pounds a week and an additional clause permitting me to leave the cast at the end of six months if I wished.

Now I had ample time for misgivings. My dancing was rusty, but of course that could be remedied by hard practice. (My singing was rustier, and I feared could not be remedied by all the practice in the world.) However, I persuaded Fred Astaire, who was playing in *Stop Flirting,* to coach me privately, which he did with unending patience and not too frightful results.

Amid the hurly-burly of countless Charlot productions there had lived and breathed and strummed, for many years, a small sharp-eyed woman named Elsie April, whose mastery of musical technique was miraculous. She could transfer melody and harmony on to paper with the swiftness of an expert shorthand stenographer. Her physical endurance, too, was staggering. She could sit at the piano through the longest rehearsals, the most tedious auditions, seldom, if ever, playing a wrong note and only demanding for sustenance an occasional cup of tea.

When I had been working with her for some time I asked her why it was that she continued to lavish her musical talent and experience on the work of others and never composed anything herself. Her reply was evasive, 'Well, dear, I never seem to have any time.'

London Calling for me was certainly a gold-mine of future alliances, for in addition to Elsie there was Dan O'Neil, the assistant stage manager. Early on in rehearsals we all found ourselves relying upon him for everything. If any props were missing, it was Danny who restored them. If there was an untraceable draught, it was Danny who discovered a window open high up in the flies and closed it. If there was noise at the side during a quiet scene, it was Danny who silenced it. And, above all, when we were tired after rehearsing all day and most of the night, feeling discouraged and certain to the depths of our souls that the whole thing was going to be a failure, it was Danny who invariably cheered us.

The dress rehearsals of *London Calling* were hectic, and the general frenzy was in no way mitigated by the frequent appearances of Ned in the stalls, accompanied by a few gay but critical friends. True, he thoughtfully brought champagne and chocolates as a rule, but our insides were too twisted with nerves to be able to respond suitably to luxuries.

Gertie and I clutched each other in corners and listened morosely to 'Pa' Braham shouting staccato instructions to the orchestra, to Carrie Graham, the ballet mistress, haranguing the chorus girls, to Maisie Gay moaning that her material was the least funny that she had yet encountered in a long and varied career, to Edward Molyneux's quiet but deadly disapproval of the way the show girls were wearing his dresses, and to the show girls' equally deadly but less quiet disapproval of the dresses themselves. The only person who seemed to be completely peaceful and at ease was Charlot, who sat with Ned and his friends in the stalls and seldom raised his voice.

At last, however, we actually opened, oddly enough, with a matinée, according to an eccentric whim of Charlot's which, nevertheless, had a certain amount of common sense to it. He figured that as we were all tired, a matinée, which didn't matter very much, would tire us just so much more and ensure us playing the first night entirely on our nerves. In this he was perfectly right. We did. We flagellated ourselves into giving a remarkably slick and good performance.

The hits of the show were primarily Maisie's singing of 'What Love Means to Girls Like Me', and her performance of Hernia Whittlebot, my little burlesque on the Sitwells. Next in order of applause came Gertie singing 'Carrie', and the duet 'You Were Meant for Me', which she and I did together, with a dance arranged by Fred Astaire.

Gertie sang 'Parisian Pierrot' exquisitely, and Edward had made it one of the loveliest stage pictures I have ever seen. Then there was Maisie as a tired soubrette singing 'Life in the Old Girl Yet.'

The only complete and glorious failure of the whole show was my performance of a single number, 'Sentiment,' which had gone so well at the dress-rehearsal and been so enthusiastically applauded by the friendly company in the stalls, that I bounded on at the opening performance fully confident that I was going to bring the house down. It certainly wasn't from want of trying that I didn't. I was immaculately dressed in tails, with a silk hat and a cane. I sang every witty couplet with perfect diction and a wealth of implication which sent them winging out into the dark auditorium, where they fell wetly, like pennies into mud. After this, discouraged but not quite despairing, I executed an intricate dance, painstakingly sweated over by Fred Astaire, tapping, after-beating, whacking my cane on the stage, and finally exiting to a spatter of applause led, I suspected, by Mother and Gladys.

Unfortunately the number could not be taken out, owing to the running order of the revue, and so nightly the audience and I were forced to endure it.

The revue was a tremendous success, and the Press notices, although a bit pernickety and fault-finding, were excellent from the point of box office. They were almost unanimous over one thing, however, and that was that I should never have been allowed to appear in it.

During the first two weeks of the run I received, to my intense surprise, a cross letter from Osbert Sitwell. In fact, so angry was it, that I first of all imagined it to be a joke. However, it was far from being a joke, and shortly afterwards another letter arrived, even crosser than the first. To this day I am still a little puzzled as to why that light-hearted burlesque should have aroused him, his brother and his sister to such paroxysms of fury. But the fact remains that it did, and I believe still does.

Soon after *London Calling* was launched, Charlot became immersed in preparations for a revue which was to be produced in partnership with Archie Selwyn in New York. This was to be a conglomeration of all the best numbers and sketches from the Charlot shows of the last few years, and in it were to be starred Beatrice Lillie, Jack Buchanan and, much to my horror, Gertrude Lawrence. This obviously meant that she would be only able to stay in *London Calling* for, at most, three months, as the new company was to sail almost immediately after Christmas.

In addition to this serious loss, we soon learned that we were also to be deprived of Danny, Carrie Graham, and several of our best chorus and small-part girls. I could only hope that it was a comfort to Ned and the other wretched backers to feel that they still had Maisie Gay, Tubby Edlin, me, and the scenery.

On account of this strange managerial juggling with success, the show began to deteriorate after the first three months, and although it ran for almost a year, it continued to deteriorate by leaps and bounds under the burden of successive new editions.

When Gertie left, Joyce Barbour took her place, and Charlot sailed away to America with his troupe, leaving us completely to our own devices. We continued, however, playing to more or less adequate business until his return in February, when he decided to plan still another new edition.

This time the revue was almost entirely reconstructed. Tubby Edlin left, and A. W. Baskcomb was engaged. Teddie Gerard came in with a vague manner, and several diamond bracelets. I decided to leave the cast, too. My six months were up, in fact I had played almost seven, and I had a longing to go to America again.

It was considered by some people to be very foolish of me to chuck up a forty-pound-a-week job, merely to satisfy my mania for travel and change, but to me it wasn't foolish at all. It was the result of careful thought.

To remain hopping about in a revue for which all my spontaneous enthusiasm had died ages ago, only for the sake of the salary, seemed to be a static, over-cautious policy. I felt, sincerely enough, that my creative impulse was suffering from the monotony of eight performances a week, and although during the run I had managed to write two full-length plays, *Fallen Angels* and *The Vortex,* I was far from satisfied.

I was convinced that new experiences and inspirations and ideas were waiting for me, far away from the Duke of York's Theatre, Ebury Street, and the Ivy, and I felt that there was no time to waste, as the future was drawing near and I was already twenty-four.

(8)

I sailed for New York on the Olympic in February, enjoying to the full the contrast in circumstances between this and my first voyage on the Aquitania three years before. I had a comfortable cabin; took my meals in the Ritz restaurant; accepted small extra attentions from the ship's personnel as tributes to my fame which, although far from assured, had at least been enough to procure me a dignified pose for the White Star Line photographer at Waterloo, and an enquiry as to my American plans by the Press reporter at Southampton.

I had no premonition of what the year would bring. No seer had whispered that by the end of it I would be catapulted into real notoriety. I was pleased with the way things were going, and I had two hundred and fifty pounds to spend. Mother was well and happy; before leaving I had rented for her a cottage at Docken-field, near Farnham in Surrey. True, we had taken it rather impulsively in a thick January fog which, when the lease was signed, lifted to disclose several villas in the too-immediate vicinity. But still, it was country and cost only forty pounds a year.

I could look back cheerfully on the last six months and reflect with a certain irony how odd it was that my first two plays, *I'll Leave it to You* and *The Young Idea,* having been praised almost unanimously by the critics, had failed, whereas *London Calling,* which had received only scant appreciation from them, had been a big success. The houses had been packed at every performance for the first three months. Society, with jewels and sables and white shirt-fronts had come and come again, occasionally over-flowing in driblets through the pass door and trickling in and out of the dressing-rooms. I had observed the curious attitude of the *soi-disant* smart set towards a successful musical show, an attitude which is special and apart, and has nothing in common with that of ordinary straight play-goers. It is patronising, of course, to a certain degree, but not consciously nor disagreeably so; unaware of anything but the gay aspects of the performance and anxious to participate a little, at any rate to the extent of using Christian names and referring to 'Numbers' rather than 'Songs.' They have, these back-stage explorers, naturally no suspicion that it is a privi-lege for them to be there at all. They have paid for their seats, and like children at a circus, they find it enjoyable to feed the animals afterwards. As a new animal I received many surprising visitors in my cage and learned quickly to do the little tricks that were ex-pected of me.

London Calling had done a lot for me. For the first time I had experienced the thrill of hearing my own music played in res-taurants. Also for the first time I had had the pleasure of seeing my name in electric lights outside a theatre. True, Maisie's and Gertie's names were on the best side of the sign facing down St. Martin's Lane towards Trafalgar Square, while Tubby Edlin's and mine were visible only to pedestrians approaching from the direction of Seven Dials, but still there it was, 'Noel Coward' in gleaming pink bulbs, and never failed to please me every time I looked up at it, which was often.

Nineteen twenty-four appears so far away now, much farther than earlier years. My vision of myself at eight and twelve and sixteen is clear, but at twenty-four I seem shadowy. I know how I looked, of course. The stage photographs show me in neat over-waisted suits, in pyjamas and dressing-gowns, and one in fanciful Russian dress with boots and a fur hat. My face was plumper and less lined than it is now, and my figure was good but a bit weedy. Of what was going on inside me, however, there is no indication. There seems an emptiness somewhere, a blandness of expression in the eyes. There is little aggressiveness in the arranged smiles and no impatience apparent at all, and in this the cameras must have lied, for I have always been impatient. Nowadays there is more truth in my photographs. I hope there is more truth in me, too.

(9)

New York was still decorated with the remains of a blizzard as the Olympic steamed up the river. Everything was black and dirty grey; the New Jersey cliffs looked sinister, and white smoke from the ships lay heavily like clouds over the harbour. Nobody met me, which didn't matter, as I had had a wire from Jeffrey at quarantine saying that he was busy on a job (New York *World*), had seats for *Rain,* and would call for me at the Ritz. There was no disappointment anywhere that evening. Jeffrey arrived, we dined and went to *Rain*. Jeanne Eagels had got us the management's seats in the second row. From the moment that she made her first entrance in those bedraggled trashy clothes and spoke her first lines, I knew from the timbre of her tough voice and the sullen slouch of her body that we were going to see great acting, and I was right. After we had been back-stage to see Jeanne we went to the Algonquin, for old time's sake, and had supper. Jeffrey was now a full-fledged reporter on the *World* and had 'covered' a great deal of Life and Death in the raw. After his first spate was exhausted I managed tactfully to erase some of the bloodstains from his conversation and supper became more appetising.

I went home to the Ritz pleasantly tired and accepted the soft pink carpets, gold elevator doors, and the general sense of rich comfort almost as though it were all my usual background. Almost, but not quite. My small two-dollar-fifty room at the Brevoort was only two years away, still in sight and mind. I planned to revisit it soon, probably the next day. I meant to go to Washington Square, too, and sit on my old bench, jumping back for a little into loneliness and poverty, but this time with no sting of reality in it. The well-sprung mattress received me graciously, and I remember thinking just before I dropped off to sleep how sad it would be to have had Ritzes always and been denied the keen pleasure of earning them.

When I saw the bill at the end of the first week, however, I discovered that my grandeur had been both incautious and premature, and I moved hastily into Lester Donahue's flat in East 32nd Street and slept on a couch in the sitting-room. We had great fun in that little flat and gave several select cocktail parties, but I kept the Ritz as my address, feeling that as the gesture had been made it would be foolish to allow it to appear too short-lived.

The month passed swiftly with no miseries and anxieties to keep me awake at nights. It was a real holiday. I went to plays in the best seats. I experienced the mixed pain and pleasure of seeing Jack Buchanan bring the house down in the Charlot revue singing 'Sentiment', watching to see why he should succeed so triumphantly where I had failed, and finding at first no adequate reason, except perhaps that it was because he apparently made no effort at all. It wasn't until later that I acknowledged to myself in secret that the truth of the matter was that his whole technique was superior to mine.

It was thrilling to see the three of them, Gertie Lawrence, Beatrice Lillie and Jack Buchanan, hailed as great stars by the whole of New York. It invested them, for me, with a new glamour, as though I were discovering them, too, and had never seen them before in my life. The appreciation of American audiences certainly gave an extra fillip to their performances. There was a shine on all of them, a happy gratification bursting through. I could swear that they had none of them ever been so good before.

I spent a lot of time with Lynn and Alfred, who were now married and living in a comfortable greenish apartment on Lexington Avenue. Lynn was just finishing a successful run of a comedy called *In Love with Love*. She was gay and attractive in it, utterly different from Dulcy which had been a bleating, essentially comic characterisation. In *In Love with Love* she also began to be beautiful. There was a new fullness in her figure and her movements were smoother. She wore a pale-pink dress in one scene which gave a warm glow to her skin, and when I noticed how she used her eyes and hands I suspected Alfred of rehearsing her in sex appeal. I think happiness and security had a lot to do with it, too. I have never known two people so happy together as the Lunts. If their whole-hearted engrossment in each other occasionally makes them a trifle remote from other people, so much the better. They could never be remote from real friendship.

Alfred was playing in *Outward Bound*. It was the first time I had ever seen him on the stage, and when I visited him in his dressing-room afterwards he went through all his hoops. I know those hoops so well now, that I can hear the paper crackling in anticipation before he dives through the first one; but then it was a surprise to me, rather a painful surprise. I had been deeply moved by his performance and was still feeling wrought up. I explained this to him from my heart, but no gleam of pleasure came into his rolling tragic eyes. He mowed down my praise with bitter self-recrimination. I had, he said, been privileged to see him give far and away the worst performance of his career. He had over-played, over-emotionalised, and used every ham trick that had ever been invented. Nothing I said could convince him to the contrary. At supper afterwards I observed that Lynn was un-moved by his despair. She said: 'Never mind, darling, you gave a lovely performance last Thursday matinée,' and went on with her scrambled eggs.

It must not be imagined that Alfred's dressing-room miseries are unreal or affected. His wretchedness, for the moment, is com-pletely genuine, a nervous reaction from having tried too hard for perfection; an actor's disease from which we all suffer from time to time, although few can plumb the depths so whole-heartedly as he does.

In *Design for Living* we all three gave the worst performances of our careers every night together for months, and managed to be very good indeed.

I found the personality of New York completely changed by winter. The sun, although brilliant enough, was detached and without warmth. Freezing winds whipped round the corners, and the buildings took on a knife-edged sharpness, casting shadows that looked as though they had been cut out of black paper. Park Avenue and Fifth Avenue were of course immaculate, but in many of the streets snow was still piled up in dirty mounds on the sidewalks. The hotels, the houses, the theatres, and even the taxis were over-heated. The sensation of undressing in luxurious warmth, opening the window the last second before getting into bed, and feeling the icy fresh air swirling into the room was delicious. I could recall without regret the airless nights in Washington Square, and the dead oppressive days when the whole city shimmered in heat haze, and the sun drained all colour from everything, softening the asphalt pavements into squelching rubber sponges, and cooking up the well-known champagne air until it felt like hot soup in the lungs.

I found several new friends, and together with them and some of my older ones I whirled through parties and trips to Harlem, and week-ends in the country. There were the Janises, Eva Le Gallienne, Ethel Barrymore, the Kaufmans, Woollcott and many others. Among the new ones was Neysa McMein; beautiful, untidy, casual, and too difficult to know in a short month. I had actually met her during my first visit, and I think I found her rather tiresome. I was even more hasty in my judgments in those days than I am now, and as frequently inaccurate. I remembered having been taken to her studio a couple of times, where I had met a miscellaneous selection of models, journalists, actors and Vanderbilts, swimming round and in and out like rather puzzled fish in a dusty aquarium. Neysa paid little or no attention to anyone except when they arrived or left, when, with a sudden spurt of social conscience, she would ram a paint-brush into her mouth and shake hands with a kind of dishevelled politeness.

I was too inexperienced and edgy then to appreciate properly her unique talent for living, but I can salute it now.

It was at the Hartley Manners' house that I met Douglas Fairbanks and Mary Pickford. This was a big thrill, particularly as they were both charming to me. I discovered that we were sailing together on the Olympic, and my mind busied itself with secret plans to get to know them well. I was at that period a bad celebrity snob. Whether it was sheer undiluted snobbishness, or just part of my devouring ambition to become a celebrity myself I don't know; at any rate it was a strong passion and at least the memory of it has induced in me a quite admirable tolerance in my own dealings with lion hunters. There is, I think, a real pleasure in reflected glory. I enjoyed it then tremendously and I enjoy it still. There is a technique to it, too. My method was always a careless indifference, so studied and practised that it could leave no doubt whatever in anybody's mind as to my easy intimacy with the object of the crowd's admiration. Other methods also can be equally successful, such as boorish irritation which I have seen used by stronger types with excellent effect. A let's-get-away-from-these-damn-fools-as-quickly-as-possible expression, apparent only when the chances of getting away are slight. With Douglas and Mary in 1924 any acquaintance of theirs could be surfeited with reflected mass-worship very swiftly. They were unable to go in or out of restaurants or theatres or hotels without dense hordes of people clamouring round them. Indeed, on the day that the Olympic was due to sail, the White Star Line had the forethought to send special warnings to all the passengers advising them to be on board at least two hours early. We sailed at midnight and I remember standing on deck (with Mary and Douglas, of course) as the ship moved slowly out into the river, and watching that vast sea of faces staring up from the lighted dock; hundreds of rows of pallid discs with black smudges on them where mouths were hanging open. It was an exhilarating sight, and I felt myself proudly to be the focusing point of a myriad sharp envies.

Much the same sort of thing occurred when we arrived at Southampton. The dock was black with people; so was the customs house and the station platform. Some hardy spirits actually sprinted along by the side of the train when it left, until at last the quickening pace caused them to fall back breathless, but still waving their arms like clockwork puppets that are beginning to run down a little.

Richard and Jean Norton had also been on the ship, and had planned a party for the Fairbanks to meet the Prince of Wales a few nights after their arrival in London. When they invited me, too, my acceptance was so exquisitely casual that I am quite sure that it betrayed to them my obvious delight. However, I went and enjoyed it, although I must admit I suffered a little from strain afterwards. I remember that Douglas did a lot of conjuring tricks, a habit to which he was then and still is, a keen addict, and that the Prince of Wales threw me into a frenzy by asking me to play a tune that I couldn't remember. Apart from these minor disadvantages the evening went with a swing.

(10)

London seemed dim to me on my return. I had not been away long enough to have missed it. Apart from seeing the family, Gladys, and a few others, there was no thrill in my arrival. The weather was damp and the whole town looked sullen, as though it were cross about something. New York was hard and clear in my mind like a diamond, unsmudged as a memory by any sentimental glamour, but sharp with efficiency, strenuous ambition and achievement; in fact all the qualities that I felt were necessary to me at that time. I felt I knew London too well and had toiled in it too long, with no prospect of unexpected adventures or sudden surprises lurking round its gentle corners. It gave me a sense of frustration and a bad cold. I went to a few theatres and was irritated by both the actors and the audiences, the former lackadaisical and the latter apathetic. *London Calling* was still running, and there was an even worse air of dreariness over that. The company ambled through the show, the fade-outs and blackouts were untidy, and the smart Molyneux dresses looked as though they had been used to wrap up hot-water bottles. I talked to Charlot about pepping it up a bit, but he wasn't interested, his mind being obviously occupied with more important plans, and so I went down to our cottage in Dockenfield and gave myself

[178]

up to my cold. When this passed, my depression passed with it, and I wrote *Hay Fever*. The idea came to me suddenly in the garden, and I finished it in about three days, a fact which later on, when I had become news value, seemed to excite gossip-writers inordinately, although why the public should care whether a play takes three days or three years to write I shall never understand. Perhaps they don't. However, when I had finished it and had it neatly typed and bound up, I read it through and was rather unimpressed with it. This was an odd sensation for me, as in those days I was almost always enchanted with everything I wrote. I knew certain scenes were good, especially the breakfast scene in the last act, and the dialogue between the giggling flapper and the diplomat in the first act, but apart from these it seemed to me a little tedious. I think that the reason for this was that I was passing through a transition stage as a writer; my dialogue was becoming more natural and less elaborate, and I was beginning to concentrate more on the comedy values of situation rather than the comedy values of actual lines. I expect that when I read through *Hay Fever* that first time, I was subconsciously bemoaning its lack of snappy epigrams. At any rate, I thought well enough of it to consider it a good vehicle for Marie Tempest, and so I took it up to London to read it to her. Both she and Willie Graham-Browne were kind and courteous as usual, and listened with careful attention, but when I had finished they both agreed with me that it was too light and plotless and generally lacking in action, and so back I went to the country again and wrote *Easy Virtue*. On this I worked hard and thought it excellent. I fully realised its similarity of theme to *The Second Mrs. Tanqueray*, but the construction and characterisation on the whole seemed to me to be more mature and balanced than anything I had written up to date. The critics, later on, didn't agree with me, but by the time it came to their attention I was in too good a position to care. Meanwhile *The Vortex* and *Fallen Angels* were voyaging disconsolately in and out of most of the London managers' offices. H. M. Harwood at least displayed enough interest to say that he might consider producing *The Vortex* at the Ambassadors, providing that I did not play the part of Nicky myself, but as one of my principal objects in writing the play had been to give myself a first-rate opportunity for dramatic acting, I refused his offer.

I had a much more hopeful nibble from Gladys Cooper, who wanted to play *Fallen Angels* with Madge Titheradge. They were both enthusiastic, and I, of course, was delighted. However, it all fell through during the next few months, more or less painlessly. Gladys had contracts to fulfil, so had Madge. When Gladys was going to be free, Madge was tied up, and vice versa, until everybody's interest and excitement died wearily, and *Fallen Angels* joined *Hay Fever* in oblivion.

Life in the Dockenfield cottage was pleasant but cramped. There was Mother and Auntie Vida, occasionally Father or Eric, and Gladys and me. I forget now where we all slept, but I do remember that no nocturnal cough nor sneeze nor digestive rumble went up unnoticed by any of us. We had a gentle wistful girl to help with the housework. Her name was Iris, and she meandered through the days in a sort of anæmic dream, from which she occasionally awoke to catch the afternoon bus for Farnham. Gladys and I drove about the countryside in a fast red tin bath which I had bought at the motor show. We visited, every now and then, acquaintances in the neighbourhood, among them some rather pompous friends of Gladys's childhood. Their name escapes me at the moment, but they were over-grand, and their house was large and ugly. It was filled with silver teapots, family paintings, tennis racquets, young people in flannels, sporting and hunting prints, mackintoshes, golf clubs, tweed coats, pipe-racks, and huge truculent cakes. I still retain a certain bitterness towards them, knowing that they were of the type that would fawn upon me now, and remembering how distantly, insufferably polite they were to me then. Mrs. Whatever-her-name-was was quite palpably convinced to the depths of her Christian soul that Gladys and I were conducting a furtive, illicit honeymoon just a few miles away across the fields. No amount of references to Mother or Auntie Vida could budge her suspicions; I saw them in her eyes, eager and lascivious, as they flickered at us over the tea-table. We left, thankfully, as soon as we could, feeling thoroughly uncomfortable and almost expecting Mother to greet us blind drunk in a dirty kimono.

(11)

In July I had a letter from Ruby Melville inviting me to stay with her in Deauville. Money was getting low again, but as I had enough to pay my fare, with a little over for expenses, I decided to go. So many of my earlier days seem to have been spent in a state of extreme penury among the very rich; Deauville couldn't have been smarter or wealthier or more fashionable than it was that year, at the height of its damp summer season. Nor could I have chosen a more thoroughly unsuitable place for a holiday, considering that I had about thirty pounds in the bank and no definite contracts to look forward to. However, I enjoyed myself watching people lose thousands at baccarat, and inventing thrilling dreams in which I suddenly found a mille-franc plaque under somebody's chair, sat down immediately at the big table, and in the course of a few hours won a vast fortune amid an envious crowd of onlookers. The dreams varied in superficial detail, but the climax was always the same.

A polo-playing friend of Ruby's lent us ponies and we rode them daily up and down the sands, borrowed riding-breeches spoiling for me a little the dashing picture I made. 'Noel Coward enjoying a brisk morning canter on the beach at Deauville' seemed a nice caption for my mind's eye, but I suffered, when we dismounted for the morning apéritif, from the consciousness that my seat was sagging behind me like the elephant's child.

Sir James Dunn arrived one day on a yacht with Lady Queensberry (now Lady Dunn), his daughter Mona, Diana and Duff Cooper, and several others. Large dinners were given nightly in the Casino, and certain private social dramas among the party enlivened the hours until dawn. I felt that I was seeing a side of life which should by rights be glamorous to eyes unfamiliar with it; all the correct adjuncts were there. Champagne. Beautifullygowned women. High-powered gambling. Obsequious maîtres d'hôtel. Moonlit terraces. A perfectly arranged production with all the parts well cast according to type. I think, perhaps, that there must have been something wrong with the dialogue. The author must have had a common mind, because soon I became irritated and bored and wanted to go home. The leading lady, as far as I was concerned, was Ruby. She was good all through. Her wit saved the more tedious scenes and her performance was gallant to the last.

Jimmy Dunn took a sudden interest in me at about four o'clock one morning and informed me, to my immense surprise, that I was a genius! My astonishment was natural, owing to the fact that up till that moment he had paid no attention to me whatever. However, I concluded rightly that Ruby had been trying to do me a good turn on the side and that it was up to me to take advantage of it; so I interrupted him with no more than a routine smile of self-deprecation, while he went on to say that I' obviously had a great career ahead of me, and that as he had been given to understand that I was oppressed by money worries it would give him great pleasure to finance me for the next five years. I should like to say here that no one could have more personal charm than Jimmy Dunn, when he likes to turn it on. He can be gentle, kind, humorous and sympathetic all at the same moment, and before that little interview was over I believed that all my troubles were ended, and that all I had to do was to go back to England and write what I wanted to write in comfort, with the certain knowledge that on the first day of every month for the next five years, a cheque for a hundred pounds was going to drop into the letter-box.

The next day I felt a trifle damped when he practically cut me dead at lunch, but in the evening his enthusiasm was re-born and he asked me, charmingly, to sing to him and Irene Queensberry in the deserted dining-room of the Royal Hotel, which was where the only available piano happened to be. It was a strange setting. Piled-up tables, shuttered windows, a dust-sheet pushed half off the piano, and a few palms in pots looking, under the sharp electric light, as though they were going to be sick. I felt some-how that I was singing for my life. Jimmy Dunn's personality was strong, and I expect the atmosphere of the whole place had nurtured in me a reverence for riches which, even in my most poverty-stricken moments, I had not been aware of before. They talked animatedly during my songs but appeared to be quite carried away with appreciation at the finish and, when I went with them to the Casino and actually won forty-eight francs at boule, I felt that my star had definitely risen for good.

On my return to England, Gladys was the first person, and I think the last, to whom I broke my glorious news. It wasn't so much that she poured cold water on the idea; she submerged it in a sea of icy disapproval. She pointed out that having got so far in my career unaided, it was idiotic to lose faith in myself at a critical moment which, when analysed, was critical only because I happened to have a slight overdraft and no immediate prospects. I had been in far worse straits before and managed to come out unscathed, and that to contemplate tying myself up for five years to a strange financier was sheer lunacy. Worse than lunacy, it was craven cowardice, a mean clutching at expedience, an abysmal ad-mission of defeat! Faced with this unexpected vehemence I was forced to take stock of the situation all over again from a different angle. The contract between Jimmy Dunn and me was to be drawn up on his return to London on the following lines: that he guaran-teed to pay me twelve hundred pounds a year for five years, on the understanding that he was to take twenty per cent of anything I happened to earn during that period. This arrangement had seemed fair enough to me in Deauville, but in the cold light of Gladys's reasoning the glow of philanthropy faded from it. It seemed less munificent and more like a business deal than I had hitherto imagined it, and after further discussion I decided with a deep secret sense of relief that she was unquestionably right.

Having made this decision I nourished for quite a while a re-sentful anger against Jimmy Dunn. I can only suppose that my conscience was uneasy. I was ashamed somewhere inside because I had so nearly allowed myself to be made a fool of, not by him, but by myself through him. His charm, personality, perception and generosity changed, in my mind, into sinister sheep's clothing, and it wasn't until much later that I was able to see him as he really was; a man of blustering tempers, kind impulses and excellent business acumen.

(12)

In looking back now on those months, August, September and October 1924, I can detect a glow of nostalgia upon them. They mark in my life such a definite end to a chapter. The weather was fine and clear, and nothing seemed to be happening. Whether or not I felt frustrated I cannot remember, but for that little while I was undoubtedly suspended, irritably, I expect, in a sort of vacuum. Several plays were written and ready for production, but nobody was interested enough to wish to produce them. My position was equivocal. As far as the theatre world was concerned I was well-known and moderately popular. I was not yet 'unspoiled by my great success', but in danger of being distinctly spoiled by the lack of it. The Press regarded me as 'promising' and were waiting, without any undue signs of impatience, for the day when they could tie on me a less ambiguous label. The general public, on the whole, were ignorant of my existence. Meanwhile, the leaves fluttered down from the trees in Dockenfield, mist lay along the meadows in the evening, and London managers announced lists of interesting plays for the autumn, not one of them by me. Yes, the nostalgia is there all right, I can feel it strongly. It is like a sensation that every traveller knows when his ship steams away from a place to which he is sure he will never return. Not perhaps that he wants to. Not perhaps that he has been particularly happy there, but he feels a pang as the land slips down below the horizon. The little café where he used to have coffee. That boring walk along by the sea and back. The view from the balcony. The conversations with the barman. The hotel wallpaper. All part of living Time, never to be known again, the closing of a phase.

PART SIX

THE EVERYMAN THEATRE, Hampstead, was, in its infancy, a drill hall, but by the time I knew it all military flavour had departed, and it was firmly and almost defiantly a theatre. Under the management of Norman Macdermott it had achieved an excellent reputation, and several plays had been successfully launched there, later to slide down the hill into the West End.

The theatre itself was small, intimate, and draughty. Its auditorium, foyer and corridors were carpeted austerely with coconut matting, and there was a subtle but determined aroma of artistic endeavour pervading the whole place.

Norman Macdermott was a short, affable man with nice eyes and a faintly unreliable expression. He invited me to go to see him after he had read *Hay Fever* and *The Vortex,* and announced, to my joy, that he would produce one of them, but that he had not quite decided which would stand the greater chance of success. He had a slight bias towards *Hay Fever,* but as there was no good part for me in that I managed to sheer him over to *The Vortex.*

Casting was even more difficult than usual owing to the rule of the Everyman Theatre that all actors appearing there must agree to do so, regardless of their position, at a fixed salary of five pounds a week. Naturally if the play was successful enough to be transferred to a West End theatre, they reverted to their normal London salaries. This was actually an admirable arrangement but it limited our choice to actors who were sporting enough to take a chance. We finally collected a cast headed by Kate Cutler and myself, which included Helen Spencer, Mary Robson, Millie Sim, Bromley Davenport, Kinsey Peile, George Merrit and Alan Hollis.

Macdermott, after a little argument, agreed that Gladys Cal-throp should design the scenery and dresses, and it wasn't until all the contracts were signed and we were about to start rehearsals that he called me to his office and told me that he was sorry to say that he couldn't do the play at all as he hadn't enough money, and that unless two hundred pounds were procured immediately the whole thing would have to be abandoned.

This was the first of the many horrible setbacks attending that production. I was in despair, and spent a black twenty-four hours racking my brains to think of someone whom I could ask for the money. Ned Lathom was out of the question as I felt that I had already sponged on him enough. I scurried miserably through my address-book marking with crosses the names of my richer acquaintances and later discarding them all on the fairly accurate assumption that, being rich, they wouldn't be good for more than a fiver, if that. Suddenly, on turning back to the beginning of the book again, I lighted on the name Michael Arlen. I had not seen him for a year or so, and during that time *The Green Hat* had been published and was a triumphant Best Seller. I remembered our casual meetings during the last few years. I remembered our occasional heart-to-heart talks sometimes in corners at parties, sometimes in his little flat in Shepherd Market. He knew all about being poor. He knew all the makeshifts of a struggling author. He also must have known, many times, the predicament I was in at the moment, that dismal resentment at being forced by circumstances into the position of being under obligation to people. He was the one to approach all right. Success was still new to him, and the odour of recent shabbiness must still be lingering in his nostrils. I telephoned to him straight away and he asked me to dine with him that night at the Embassy.

It was a smart evening at the beginning of the winter season. We had cocktails in the newly decorated bar and smiled with affable contempt upon the newly decorated clientele. Half-way through dinner I blurted out my troubles, and without even ques-tioning me about the play or making any cautious stipulations about repayment, he called for a cheque form and wrote out a cheque for two hundred pounds immediately. After that the evening seemed even more charming than it had been in the beginning.

Rehearsals started and all went well for a few days. Then Helen Spencer developed diphtheria, and despair set in again. This was a bitter disappointment. However, Mollie Kerr was engaged to take over the part and played it excellently.

Our next obstacle appeared to be insurmountable and reared itself up in the most unexpected quarter. Kate Cutler, for whom I had written the part of Florence, suddenly refused flatly to go on rehearsing. I have never quite known to this day what strange devil got into her. We were close friends and she had been my strongest and wisest ally through all the vicissitudes of *I'll Leave It to You* and *The Young Idea*. At all events, she became surprisingly angry because upon realising that the last act was too short, I had re-written it, enlarging my own part considerably in the process. It was a painful and, I still think, unreasonable quarrel. Norman Macdermott was away for the week-end, and there was no one to whom we could appeal for arbitration. After a violent scene in which Kate and I both held our ground sturdily and refused to give way an inch, Kate left the theatre, and there I was, a week away from production, faced with two alternatives. I could either stick to my guns, in which case I should have to find a new leading lady immediately and rehearse her from the beginning, even supposing that I could persuade any first-rate actress to undertake such a task at such short notice. Or I could surrender to Kate by reverting to the original last act which I knew to be too short and lacking the correct emotional balance in the conflict between the mother and son. The fact that Kate seemed to imagine that I had re-written it only in order to give myself better material as an actor made me extremely angry. I remember roaring out several grandiloquent phrases about my 'literary integrity', etc., which, although pompous, were certainly justifiable in the circumstances.

Gladys and I drove back to Ebury Street in my red car, much too fast and sizzling with indignation. When all rage was spent and blood had resumed its normal circulation, I decided, quite firmly and without passion, that neither then, nor at any time in my life, would I allow myself to be dictated to in the age-old battle between actor and author; a resolution, I am proud to say, that I have kept more or less shining and unsullied to this day.

In the meantime, a new mother had to be found, and all through that night a grotesque ballet of middle-aged actresses whirled through my dreams. The next morning, having been forced to discard for various reasons all those who were even remotely suitable to the part, I decided to work from another angle and make a list of actresses as far removed from the type of Florence as possible. This list was headed by Lilian Braithwaite. She was tall and dark. Florence should be small and fair. She was well-bred and serene. Florence should be flamboyant and neurotic. Lilian Braithwaite had been associated in the public mind for some years with silver teapots in Haymarket comedies. She was almost inextricably wedged in a groove of gentle, understanding motherhood. Her moral position was clearly defined, and her virtue unassailable. Even in *Mr. Wu* a few years back, when by a hair's breadth she had, nightly for over a year, escaped dishonour at the hands of a Chinaman, she had still managed to maintain an air of well-bred integrity. All of which went to prove the foolish incongruity of casting her for Florence. On the other hand, there was the finally important fact that she happened to be a first-rate actress. And so, waving aside all obvious objections, I telephoned to her and about twenty minutes later was sitting in her drawing-room in Pelham Crescent reading the play to her.

Before starting, I had explained the Kate Cutler situation and told her that before anything definite could be decided, Kate must be given one more chance to say either yes or no. Lilian also told me that she was about to start rehearsals for a new play, *Orange Blossoms,* in which her part was bad but her salary extremely good. She added, however, with a slight glint of her eye, that she had not yet signed the contract.

That being such a portentous interview, I am sorry that I cannot remember more details of it. I recall that the room was dimly green, and that there were well-arranged flowers and several silver photograph frames; I remember Gladys's hat which was brown and perky; also her rather screwed-up position in an armchair. Lilian wore a far-away expression during the reading, she was looking out of the window beyond the trees of the Crescent, at herself in a blonde wig, rather *outré* clothes, with perhaps a long cigarette holder. I knew by the occasional nods she gave that she was liking the play and recognising the value of the part. At the end, without any quibbling, she said that if Kate refused finally, she would play it. I explained about the regulation salary being only five pounds a week at the Everyman, and that unless the play were successful enough to be transferred to the West End the engagement would only be for a fortnight; to which she replied that she was willing to take the chance providing that we let her know definitely within a few hours. It was a nice clean morning's work. There were no blandishments and no superlatives, no time wasted on inessentials. Gladys and I gulped down some sherry, dashed out of the house, and drove straight off to see Kate. It was only a short way but to our strung-up minds it seemed miles. By that time we had bolstered ourselves into the belief that Lilian was absolutely ideal casting for the part and must play it at all costs. This was actually unfair to Kate, but it provided us with a certain necessary impetus. We burst in on Kate and found her still angry and still adamant. This was, of course, a relief superficially, but I felt horrid and sad inside as though I were playing her a dirty trick by allowing her, and at this moment definitely encouraging her, to throw away one of the best opportunities of her life. But there it was. It had to be done. I told her that, after careful reflection, I had decided to keep the play exactly as I had re-written it, and that I wished her to say finally whether or not she would play it. She said 'No, no, no,' with rising inflections, and that was that. Gladys and I left the house, thankful that the scene was over, and went back to Lilian for another glass of sherry.

Before the Monday morning rehearsal I had a stormy interview with Norman Macdermott, who, furious that an important decision had been made while his back was turned, struck the desk firmly with his clenched fist and said that Lilian Braithwaite was utterly wrong for the part, and would ruin the play, and that if she played it he would wash his hands of the entire production.

I tried to reason with him and was at length forced to remind him that as I had scraped up a good deal of the backing, the production was no longer his anyway, and, leaving him to his hand-washing, I went down on to the stage to rehearse Lilian.

That week was almost entirely beastly, and I should hate to live through it again. The weather was icy, damp and foggy. The roads were so slippery that driving to and from Hampstead was a nightmare. Gladys worked like a slave over the scenery and dresses, assisted by Mrs. Doddington, 'Doddie', the housekeeper at the Everyman. Doddie was a darling; fat and warm and dressed in untidy black. It was she who kept the fire going downstairs in the subterranean cavern where we all dressed. The dressing-rooms were little more than cubicles with a passage running between them which opened out into a small draughty space in front of the fireplace on either side of which were two frowsy, comfortable settees. Here, at any time of the day or night, Doddie brought us cups of strong tea.

Lilian learned her part in two days and devoted the rest of the time to developing and polishing her performance, with a dry, down-to-earth efficiency which was fascinating to watch. It was the only brightness in those cold, hurrying days. I knew, after her second rehearsal, that she was going to be superb, but in addition to all the extraneous details I had to attend to I was dreadfully worried about my own performance. The play as a whole I had, of course, never seen, as I was on the stage myself most of the time. I had no way of telling whether I was over-playing or under-playing, or whether my emotion was real or forced. Gladys emerged seldom from the basement, and as Macdermott remained up in his office, there was nobody out front to give me the faintest indication as to whether I was going to be good, bad or indifferent. Lilian remained a rock and allowed me to dash my miseries and hopes and fears and exaltations against her. Over and over that last act we went when everyone else had gone and the lights were reduced to one working lamp on the stage. That memory is vivid enough, anyway. Those blank rows of empty seats in the foggy auditorium; Lilian and I wrapped up in coats and tearing ourselves to pieces. 'That speech was bad —let's go back'—'I must start crying later, if I start too soon the scene's gone'—back again—then suddenly an uninterrupted flow for a little—'it's coming this time'—triumph!—then back again just once more, to set it—no life—no flow—despair! So on and so forth until gradually there began to grow into the scene the shape and reality we had been working for. Gladys came up one night towards the end of the week and saw it through. She was clearly excited by it, and we all went downstairs exhausted and drank tea by the fire.

The dress rehearsal staunchly upheld theatrical tradition by being gloomy and depressing to the point of suicide. The acting was nervous and unbalanced. The dresses looked awful, and the lighting was sharply unbecoming. The theatre cat made a mess in the middle of the stage, which everybody said was lucky but which, to me, seemed to be nothing so much as a sound criticism of the entire performance.

An incident occurred which was remarkable only because it marked the first and last time that I have ever seen Gladys shed a tear over a production. At the end of the second act she appeared suddenly in my dressing-room trembling with rage and clutching a proof of the programme. The cause of her rage was a little paragraph which announced that the scenery of act one and act three had been designated by G. E. Calthrop, and that of act two by Norman Macdermott. Considering that the whole essence of Gladys's scheme of décor lay in the contrast she had made between the highly-coloured modernism of the first and last acts and the oak and plaster simplicity of the country house in act two, her anger was understandable. True, Macdermott had contributed an idea for the construction of the fireplace, but apart from this the whole structure, colour, and conception of the set had been Gladys's. We immediately went up into the stalls and tackled him about it, whereupon he said blandly that the complete set had been designed by him and that the programme must remain as it was. We then left him and went straight upstairs to his office, where we ransacked his desk and finally unearthed Gladys's original sketch with Macdermott's O.K. scribbled across it in his own handwriting. We took it down to him triumphantly and he was very cross, and became crosser still when I said that I would not rehearse any further until the programme was changed. He ultimately gave in, however, and ordered his personal fireplace to be hacked out of the scene. This was done, and we were left with no fireplace at all for the opening night.

The next day Gladys was at the theatre early in the morning with the carpenter and George Carr, our stage manager, and by about seven in the evening, an hour before the play was due to begin, the set was fixed satisfactorily.

Meanwhile, I was having a spirited duel with the Lord Chamberlain (Lord Cromer) in his office in St. James's. He had at first refused point-blank to grant a licence for the play because of the unpleasantness of its theme, and it was only after a long-drawn-out argument, during which, I must say, he was charming and sympathetic, that I persuaded him that the play was little more than a moral tract. With a whimsical and rather weary smile he finally granted the licence, and with this last and most agitating of all obstacles safely surmounted, I jumped into my car and drove up to Hampstead to help Gladys with the set.

We spent a couple of hours with hammer and nails, hanging pictures and tacking bits of material on to the last-act furniture, and at seven o'clock allowed ourselves a quarter of an hour to rush over the road and have some tomato soup which, for the first time in the history of that particular café, happened to be so scorching hot that we were almost unable to drink it. Then back to the theatre again. Gladys changed into evening dress in my dressing-room while I made up. The call boy called Half an Hour, then Quarter of an Hour, then Beginners.

The stage was reached by a spiral iron staircase; I can feel the ring of it now under my feet as I went up, my heart pounding, to see that everything was in order and to listen, with a sort of dead resignation, to the scufflings and murmurings of the audience at the other side of the curtain. Gladys, with a tightened expression about her mouth, moved about the set arranging flower vases and cigarette boxes on small tables. George Carr made a few little jokes and animal noises in order to make us giggle and forget for a moment the lifts going up and down in our insides. Lilian appeared resplendent in pillar-box red and a blonde wig, wearing her 'emu' face, a particular and individual expression of outward calm masking inward turmoil. She was apparently placid; as cool as a cucumber. First nights were nothing to her, she had known too many of them! But yet there was a little twitch that occurred every so often at the side of her jaw, as though she were biting very hard on something to prevent herself from screaming. Presently Kinsey Peile, Mary Robson, Millie Sim and Alan Hollis came on to the stage in various stages of alert misery. George Carr glanced at his watch and said 'Clear, please' very softly, as if he were scared that we might all rush madly out into the street. Gladys gave one last hopeless look at the set. We all cleared to the side of the stage and, amid a sickening silence, the curtain rose on the first act.

That evening was altogether an extraordinary experience. There was a certain feeling of expectancy in the air, an acceptance almost that the play would be a success. The audience looked distressingly near, owing to there being no orchestra pit and no footlights. Familiar faces suddenly jumped out of the darkness and accosted us in the middle of a scene. Lilian was cool and steady and played beautifully. I was all over the place but gave, on the whole, one of those effective, nerve-strung, *tour-de-force* performances, technically unstable, but vital enough to sweep people into enthusiasm.

At the end of the play the applause was terrific. I happened to cut a vein in my wrist when, towards the end of the last act, I had to sweep all the cosmetics and bottles off the dressing-table. I bound it up with my handkerchief during the curtain calls, but it bled effectively through my author's speech.

The first person to clutch my hand afterwards was Michael

Arlen. His face was white with excitement and he said: 'I'd be so proud, so *very* proud, if I had written it.'

After him came the deluge. And a very gratifying deluge it was, too. There was little or no empty politeness about it. People had obviously been genuinely moved and Lilian and I held court for a long time until finally the last visitor went away and we could relax.

There it was real and complete, my first big moment. I don't remember exactly how I felt. I do know that I was tired. We were all tired. I know also that I recognised a solidity underlying all the excitement; this time I really had done it. The cheering and applause had been no louder than it had been for *I'll Leave It to You* and *The Young Idea*. If anything it had been a trifle less, owing to the smallness of the Everyman Theatre. The backstage enthusiasts had used the same phrases; their superlatives were still in my ears; the same superlatives as before; the same 'divines', 'darlings', 'brilliants', and 'marvellouses'. The same fervent embraces and handshakes; the same glistening eyes. But this time there was a subtle difference. Lilian said wearily: 'Do you think we are all right?' And I knew, and she knew that I knew, that that question was merely rhetorical, a routine gesture of diffidence. We were all right, more than all right. We were a smash hit.

(2)

The Press notices the next day were, on the whole, enthusiastic, although most of the critics deplored the fact that the characters of the play were 'unwholesome' which, of course, was perfectly true. Their insistence, however, on the cocktail drinking, decadence and general smart-settishness of the play was good for the box office, and we played to packed houses.

Those two weeks at the Everyman were exciting. Bit by bit I improved my performance technically; controlling my emotion, holding tears in reserve until the right moment. Different scenes took shape and became more complete. Never in my life had I looked forward so much to getting down to the theatre at night. Lilian and I discussed, sharpened and polished our last act until it became almost as good as people said it was.

Meanwhile, there was the anxiety of wondering which management would take us over in the West End. Finally Alban Limpus and Charles Kenyon offered us the best terms and the Royalty Theatre was decided upon.

Our last night at the Everyman was almost as exciting as our first. There was more cheering and speech-making and we felt sentimental and sad to be leaving that draughty, uncomfortable and loving little theatre. Doddie cried copiously and deluged us with tea and Gladys and I drove away down the hill for the last time, waving valedictions to our various landmarks. The pillar-box that we had run into after the dress rehearsal. The private gateway where we had had to leave the car all night in a pea-soup fog. The corner just by Lords cricket ground where we had once missed a lorry by inches. Those drives from Ebury Street to Hampstead and from Hampstead to Ebury Street, so fraught with agitations and emotions, were now just part of the past, along with all the early rehearsals, the snatched meals at the café opposite the stage door, the arguments, the agonies, the crises. It was again the nostalgia of leaving a familiar shore. Several weeks of fever pitch, strung-up heavens and hells, hours of desperate concentration, slipping away behind us as the road was slipping away behind us into the mist. I remember saying dolefully to Gladys: 'And now what?' But, oddly enough, I cannot recall her reply.

(3)

Success altered the face of London for me. Just for a little the atmosphere felt lighter. I'm not sure whether or not the people who passed me in the street appeared to be more smiling and gay than they had been hitherto, but I expect they did. I do know that very soon life began to feel over-crowded. Every minute of the day was occupied and I relaxed, rather indiscriminately, into a welter of publicity. No Press interviewer, photographer or gossip writer had to fight in order to see me, I was wide open to them all; smiling and burbling bright witticisms, giving my views on this and that, discussing such problems as whether or not the modern girl would make a good mother, or what would be my ideal in a wife, etc. My opinion was asked for, and given, on current books and plays. I made a few adequately witty jokes which were immediately misquoted or twisted round the wrong way, thereby denuding them of any humour they might originally have had. I was photographed in every conceivable position. Not only was *I* photographed, but my dressing-room was photographed, my car was photographed, my rooms in Ebury Street were photographed. It was only by an over-sight, I am sure, that our lodgers escaped the camera.

I took to wearing coloured turtle-necked jerseys, actually more for comfort than for effect, and soon I was informed by my evening paper that I had started a fashion. I believe that to a certain extent this was really true; at any rate, during the ensuing months I noticed more and more of our seedier West End chorus boys parading about London in them.

I found people difficult to cope with in my new circumstances. Their attitude to me altered so swiftly and so completely. Naturally my intimates and the few friends I happened to know well remained the same, but ordinary acquaintances to whom I had nodded and spoken casually for years, gummed strong affection to me like fly-paper and assumed tacit proprietary rights. Apparently they had always known that I was clever, talented, brilliant and destined for great things. 'How does it feel,' they cried, 'to be a genius?' To reply to this sort of remark without either complacency or offensive modesty was impossible, and so I chose the latter as being the less troublesome course and wore a permanent blush of self-deprecation for quite a long while. I can indeed still call it into use if necessary. Sometimes I became so carried away by my performance that I alluded to my success as luck! This monumental insincerity was received with acclaim. People were actually willing and eager to believe that I could throw out of my

mind all memories of heartbreaks, struggles, disillusionments, bitter disappointments, and work, and dismiss my hard-earned victory as luck. Just glorious chance. An encouraging pat on the back
from kindly Fate. I can only imagine that this easy belief in a
fundamental schism in my scale of values must have been a comfort to them, an implication that such a thing might happen to
anybody.

The legend of my modesty grew and grew. I became extraordinarily unspoiled by my great success. As a matter of fact, I still
am. I have frequently been known to help old friends in distress
and, odd as it may seem, I have actually so far forgotten my glory
as to give occasional jobs to first-rate actors whom I knew in my
poorer days. Gestures such as these cause wide-spread astonishment. The general illusion that success automatically transforms
ordinary human beings into monsters of egotism has, in my case,
been shattered. I am neither conceited, overbearing, rude, nor insulting to waiters. People often refer to me as being 'simple' and
'surprisingly human.' All of which is superficially gratifying but,
on closer analysis, quite idiotic. Conceit is more often than not
an outward manifestation of an inward sense of inferiority. Stupid
people are frequently conceited because they are subconsciously
frightened of being found out; scared that some perceptive eye
will pierce through their façade and discover the timid confusion
behind it. As a general rule, the most uppish people I have met
have been those who have never achieved anything whatsoever.

I am neither stupid nor scared, and my sense of my own importance to the world is relatively small. On the other hand, my
sense of my own importance to myself is tremendous. I am all
I have, to work with, to play with, to suffer and to enjoy. It is
not the eyes of others that I am wary of, but my own. I do not
intend to let myself down more than I can possibly help, and I
find that the fewer illusions that I have about me or the world
around me, the better company I am for myself.

Naturally in 1925 my reasoning on myself was not as clear as
it is now, but the nucleus was fortunately there. I opened my arms
a little too wide to everything that came, and enjoyed it. Later on,

just a little while later, three years to be exact, circumstances showed me that my acceptance has been a thought too credulous. The 'darling' of the London Theatre received what can only be described as a sharp kick in the pants. And while my over-trusting behind was still smarting, I took the opportunity to do a little hard thinking.

Perhaps, after all, in the above paragraphs I have been a little stingy with my gratitude. I hereby render deep thanks to those booing hysterical galleryites and those exultant, unkind critics and journalists for doing me more constructive good than any of their cheers or their praises have ever done.

As all this, however, belongs to a later part of the book, I will stop digressing and return to the Royalty Theatre in December 1924.

(4)

The Vortex opened at the Royalty Theatre on December 16, 1924. The first performance felt to all of us a little dull after the intimate excitement of the Everyman. The audience, although much larger, was further away, separated from us by an orchestra pit and footlights; also the nervous strain was lacking. We knew from our Press notices and from the advance sale that we were already an established success. The audience seemed to be conscious of this, too, and so we just played the play as well as we could, and they appreciated it as well as they could, and despite the fact that many of them were obviously suffering from bronchial catarrh during the first two acts, they overcame their wheezings and coughings and cheered quite lustily at the end.

My dressing-room was large and comfortable, and there I sat nightly at the end of the play receiving people and giving them drinks and cigarettes and listening to praise. So much praise. So many various ways of expressing it. It was fascinating. Some would come in sodden with emotion and break down and have to be soothed. Others would appear to be rendered speechless for a few minutes and just sit nodding at me. The majority were

With LILIAN BRAITHWAITE
in The Vortex

With Lilian Braithwaite, Mary Robson, Mollie Kerr, Millie Sim, Bromley Davenport, Alan Hollis, Kinsey Peile and Ivor Barnard in THE VORTEX
Everyman Theatre, 1924

voluble. There had apparently never been such acting or such a play in the history of the theatre. Many of them had friends who were the exact prototypes of Florence and Nicky. It was extraordinary, they said, how I had managed to hit off so-and-so with such cruel accuracy. No amount of protesting on my part that my characters were imaginary and that I barely knew the person in question convinced them in the least.

I arranged a series of code signals with Waugh, my dresser, by which means we contrived to get rid of visitors when the delight of their presence was wearing thin. He would vanish and re-appear again with urgent telephone messages, and on one occasion became so carried away by his own virtuosity that he announced in ringing tones that Lady Biddle's car was waiting for me. I must have appeared rather over-excited at this news because in order to control my laughter I was forced to embark upon a sea of explanations relating to my lifelong connection with the Biddle family. However, it all passed off quite successfully, and from then onwards Lady Biddle and her car were used *ad nauseum*.

It must not be imagined that I was blasé and lacking in proper gratitude towards all those kind people who said so many charming things to me. I loved it all, but I had learned from experience that dressing-room opinions, unless based on sound theatrical knowledge, are actually worth little beyond the amiable impulse that prompts them. When fellow actors or authors came back-stage to see me it was quite different. It is deeply gratifying to be praised by one's peers, to know that that little bit of business by the window in act one and that crushing out of the cigarette in act two was not only noticed, but appreciated and remembered. Laymen cannot be expected to note these small subtleties; indeed, it would be disconcerting if they did, but never let it be said that their appreciation, however untechnical, is unwelcome; far from it. It is warming and delightful and most comforting. It is only occasionally, after the performance of a strenuous part, that an actor may feel a little tired, a little hungry and a little anxious to get his make-up off and get out of the theatre to have supper.

The supper routine during the run of *The Vortex* is one of my pleasantest memories. There were two clubs flourishing at that time, clubs where it was not necessary to dress and where one could eat the kind of food one wanted to eat in comparative peace and quiet. The Gargoyle was practically next door to the Royalty Theatre and specialised in sausages and bacon and a small dance band consisting of a pianist and a trap-drummer who caressed, tenderly, the latest tunes, without imposing the slightest strain either upon the ears or the digestive tract.

The Fifty-Fifty was rather more flamboyant but equally theatrical in atmosphere. It was run by Constance Collier and Ivor Novello and catered exclusively to 'Us.' I put 'Us' in inverted commas advisedly, for although 'Us' were happy and contented with it at the beginning because we really could come in after the show in sweaters and old clothes without being stared at, this congenial state of affairs lasted only a little while. All too soon the news got around and various social liaison officers began to appear with representative groups, and the small-part actors, who were the basic reason for the club's existence, were seen to be shrinking away into the shadowy corners of the room until finally they no longer came at all. Personally I mourn to this day the loss of the Fifty-Fifty Club. I spent so many happy hours there. Constance, of course, was the spirit of it. Her table was enchantingly insular; an island of theatre, washed only occasionally by wavelets from the outer sea. Conversation was amusing and gay and bound together by old understanding. Memories of early days suddenly took life again for a little. No one can talk theatre like Constance. There is a percentage of her tinsel quality in her book of memoirs, but inevitably only a small percentage. Anecdotes, particularly theatrical anecdotes, lose charm in print. Stage reminiscence needs a close intimate audience of stage people; people for whom it is not necessary to translate jargon; people from whom the mention of Crewe Station or Ackers Street, Manchester, will bring forth appropriate chuckles of recognition. Constance's principal asset as a raconteuse was self-laughter. Her humour rippled as lightly over tragic years as over gay ones. She was, I often suspected, an outrageous liar, and yet I found more truth in her than in many people. She has always epitomised for me the theatre world that I love and honour, and she will always have for me, like the glow of footlights on a red plush curtain, a deep and lasting glamour.

(5)

The house in Ebury Street blossomed perceptibly with the success of *The Vortex*. The feet of the lodgers on the high steep stairs trod more lightly. The water became more swiftly hot in the taps, and even the depressing little lobby separating the bungalow from the hall acquired a sheen of complacency.

I ordered new chintz covers for my sitting-room and had my bedroom done over in pillar-box scarlet, a decision which I afterwards regretted. Gladys set her seal on this by painting, out of the goodness of her heart and the deeps of her erotic imagination, a few murals to brighten up the room in case the scarlet paint became too monotonous. There were two pink nudes over the fireplace, and a third doing its languid best to disguise what was quite obviously a po cupboard. It was in the midst of this misguided splendour that I was unwise enough to be photographed in bed wearing a Chinese dressing-gown and an expression of advanced degeneracy. This last was accidental and was caused by blinking at the flashlight, but it emblazoned my unquestionable decadence firmly on to the minds of all who saw it. It even brought forth a letter of indignant protest from a retired brigadier-general in Gloucestershire.

Lorn, who had been my secretary intermittently for two years since the death of our much-loved Meggie Albanesi, for whom she had officiated before, was now established permanently. Every morning she arrived with my breakfast tray and sat on the side of the bed while we smoked, drank coffee and transacted what we were pleased to call the business of the day.

Later on, another room in the house was taken over and transformed into an office. We had two letter files, known as 'Poppy' and 'Queen Anne' respectively, and a sinister cardboard-box labelled 'Shortly' into which we put all the letters we felt incapable of answering at the moment. About once in every month or so it overflowed and we had to concentrate, finding, to our delight, that at least three-quarters of its contents lapse of time had made unnecessary to answer at all. This admirable system founded far back in 1924 we still employ with success. Of course, there is occasionally a slip-up, and I am attacked by some irate acquaintance whose urgent invitation to do something or other has been completely ignored, but, on the whole, our percentage of failure is small.

I indulged immediately a long-suppressed desire for silk shirts, pyjamas and underclothes. I opened up accounts at various shops, happy to be able to charge things without that inward fear that I might never be able to pay for them. I wasted a lot of money this way, but it was worth it. My clothes certainly began to improve, but I was still inclined to ruin a correct ensemble by some flashy error of taste.

I went to a lot of lunch parties in the most charming houses which, in retrospect, appear all to be exactly the same. This may be a trick that Time has played upon me, but I have a uniform memory of pickled oak, modern paintings, green walls, a strong aroma of recently burned 'Tantivy' from 'Floris', and eggs, mushrooms, cutlets, sausages, and bacon sizzling in casserole dishes. The conversation, I am sure, was distinguished, but that, too, has become lost in transit. I only remember that I felt happy and confident and very pleased to be eating such nice food with such nice people. I loved answering the questions put to me by eminent politicians. I loved noting that fleeting look of pleased surprise in people's eyes when it was suddenly brought to their attention that, in spite of theatrical success and excessive publicity, I was really quite pleasant and unaffected. This, of course, was all nonsense, but I was at least no more affected than anyone else. A social intermingling of comparative strangers automatically imposes a certain strain, an extra politeness which is not entirely real. This, I think, may be described simply as good manners. I had been brought up by Mother in the tradition of good manners, and so had they, therefore everybody was extremely agreeable to everybody else. I think possibly what surprised them was that I could play the game as well as they could, but then, after all, I had learned many different parts by heart long before I had ever met them.

(6)

Soon after the opening of *The Vortex* I started work on a revue for Cochran. This had been tentatively discussed before. There had been an interview with C. B. in his office in Old Bond Street in course of which we bickered for about two hours because he wanted me only to write the book of the revue, and I wished to compose the entire score as well. Finally his armour of evasive politeness cracked, and he was forced to say that he was very sorry but he frankly did not consider my music good enough to carry a whole show, and that he intended to engage Philip Braham as composer. That settled it for the time being, and I retired, vanquished, to concentrate on ideas for sketches and burlesques.

The ideas came swiftly and, oddly enough, nearly every idea carried with it its accompanying song. In my planning of the show almost every scene led up to a number, and so when the revue was complete it was discovered, to the embarrassment of everyone but me, that with the exception of three numbers by Philip Braham for which I had written the lyrics, a few odd pieces of classical music for use in ballets, etc., and one interpolated song for Delysia, the whole score, book and lyrics were mine. A few days before we were due to open in Manchester I tackled Cochran and asked him to raise my percentage, which was for the book and lyrics alone. He explained painstakingly, with great charm but implacable obstinacy, that he could not in any circumstances ask his backers for any more money, but that I was to leave it to his discretion to decide upon some additional reward for me if the show happened to be a success.

In the face of his confidential gentleness and impressed by his
financial dilemma which he outlined so clearly to me, I felt that
there was nothing for it but to give in. It was altogether an exas-
perating interview and took place in a rehearsal room in the
Helvetia Club. For the benefit of the untheatrical public I would
like to describe here, briefly, the general horror of rehearsal rooms.
There are several crops of them all over London, and they are a
necessary evil, particularly in big musical productions. Stages are
not always available, and even when they are it is usually only
during the last week of rehearsals that they are occupied by the
entire company. Until then a show is rehearsed in bits, dialogue
scenes in one place, dance numbers in another, and vocal numbers
in another. This frequently necessitates members of a company
scudding miserably from one side of the West End to the other.
Touring companies are rehearsed almost exclusively in rehearsal
rooms, seldom achieving the dignity of a stage at all until a hurried run through on the day of the opening night.

Cochran productions alternate monotonously between the Poland Rooms and the Helvetia Club. There is little to distinguish
between the two except that the Poland Rooms are slightly larger.
Both places are equally dusty and dreary. Each room in each
place contains a tinny piano, too many chairs, a few mottled
looking-glasses, sometimes a practice bar, and always a pervasive
smell of last week's cooking. Here rows of chorus girls in practice
dress beat out laboriously the rhythms dictated by the dance producer. The chairs all round the room are festooned with hand-
bags, hats, coats, sandwiches, apples, oranges, shoes, stockings
and bits of fur. It is all very depressing, especially at night in the
harsh glare of unshaded electric bulbs.

My interview with Cochran occurred during a morning rehearsal
to the accompaniment of 'Cosmopolitan Lady', which Delysia was
rather irritably running through with the chorus. The general
din was no aid to coherent thought, and I remember my attention
being constantly distracted by wrong notes and sharp cries from
the dance producer. I tried hard to remain adamant and business-

like, but Cochran and the atmosphere and a certain bored weariness got the better of me, and the whole question was shelved.

We all travelled to Manchester on the following Sunday for the orchestra rehearsal, dress rehearsal and opening night. I had arranged to stay off for the Monday and Tuesday performances of *The Vortex* and allow my understudy to play for me. I would never behave so casually to the public nowadays, but then I was new to stardom and unencumbered by any particular sense of responsibility. Incidentally, my understudy happened to be a keen young actor named John Gielgud, so in the light of later events the public were not really being cheated at all.

On with the Dance, which was the title finally selected for the revue, was lavish to a degree and very good in spots. There were two ballets created and danced by Leonide Massine and an excellent cast including Douglas Byng, Nigel Bruce, Hermione Baddeley, Ernest Thesiger and several others. The star, of course, was Delysia. Everything she did she did well, with a satisfying authority and assurance. She was occasionally temperamental and flew into a few Continental rages, but to me she was always easy to work with and extremely agreeable.

Those three days in Manchester were on the whole unpleasant, although fraught with incident. In the first place, I discovered soon after my arrival that my name was not on the bills at all. The show was labelled 'Charles B. Cochran's Revue', which, considering that I had done three-quarters of the score, all of the lyrics, all of the book, and directed all the dialogue, scenes, and several of the numbers, seemed to be a slight over-statement. I went roaring back from the theatre to the Midland Hotel and attacked Cockie in his bathroom. I'm not at all sure that I didn't deprive him of his towel while I shrieked at him over the noise of the water gurgling down the plug-hole. I will say, however, that he retained his dignity magnificently, far more so than I, and in due course calmed me down and gave me some sherry. It is odd that in all the years I have since worked with Cockie, that show was the only one over which we have ever quarrelled. I think the psychological explanation must be that then, in those early days of our association, we had neither of us estimated accurately enough our respective egos. And a couple of tougher ones it would be difficult to find.

The dress rehearsal started at ten o'clock on Monday morning and continued without a break until lunch-time on Tuesday. I can never quite put out of my mind the picture of that large auditorium in the early hours of the morning. The limp, exhausted bodies of chorus girls and boys strewn all over the stalls, some lying in the aisles, small miserable groups of people huddled in corners drinking coffee out of thick cups and trying to digest even thicker sandwiches. Meanwhile, Frank Collins, Cochran's most admirable of Admirable Crichtons, dealt calmly with lighting men, property men, carpenters and stagehands, never raising his voice and preserving to the end an expression of unrelieved gloom and an unquenchable sense of humour. Cockie himself sat in the front row of the dress-circle supervising operations, with a grey felt hat at a rakish angle on the back of his head and a large cigar jutting truculently out of his mouth.

Cockie and I had still one more battle, this time over 'Poor Little Rich Girl', which he considered too dreary and wished to take out of the show. I fought like a steer, backed up by Delysia, and fortunately for all concerned we won, as it turned out to be the big song hit of the revue.

Sibyl Cholmondeley travelled from London for the first night, and she and Mother and Gladys and I sat tremulously in a stage box. The dress rehearsal had ended only a few hours before, and we were taut with nerves and weariness. Cockie in his box was suave and calm. I know his first-night face now so well, but then it was new to me, and I must say that all my small angers and resentments were immediately swamped by admiration of his courage. There he sat with a beaming smile, occasionally waving a welcome to some acquaintance in the stalls, as though everything were smooth and in the best of order. Nobody could possibly have guessed from his bland expression that hardly one scene had gone through without a hitch at the dress rehearsal, that it was probable that every quick change in the show would last twenty minutes instead of thirty seconds, that the lighting men knew little or nothing about the running order of the scenes, that the stage hands and the company were dropping from exhaustion, and that Delysia was liable to lose her voice completely on the least provocation. Cockie continued to smile as he always does in a crisis, and also, as usually happens with a Cochran production, his smile was justified. The show went through without any noticeable accidents. There were spontaneous bursts of applause and cheering at frequent intervals during the evening, and a great deal of enthusiastic hullabaloo at the end. Cockie made a speech and led Delysia forward and me forward, and we all bowed and grinned over baskets of flowers. There was a festive party at the Midland afterwards, where all rancours and harsh thoughts were submerged in champagne, and a great many photographs were taken of everybody for the *Daily Mail*. Not only was all anger forgotten, but, I may add, the possibility of my getting a larger percentage of the gross was also completely forgotten.

(7)

Almost simultaneously with the production of *On with the Dance* in Manchester came the rehearsals of *Fallen Angels* in London. This play had at last been bought by Anthony Prinsep as a vehicle for Margaret Bannerman. Edna Best was engaged to play opposite her, and the producer was my old friend Stanley Bell. Bunny Bannerman, one of the kindest-hearted and least troublesome leading ladies I know, was dead tired and heading for a nervous breakdown, having played a series of long parts at the Globe, none of which, with the exception of *Our Betters,* had been successful enough to enable her to relax. She tried bravely to remember her words, but every day they receded further and further away from her. This, not unnaturally, made her more and more hysterical and nervous until finally, four days before production, she had a brain storm and said that she couldn't play it at all. We had advanced too far to be able to call the whole thing off which might have happened if her breakdown had occurred earlier. Edna, as usual, was word perfect and calm, and we were faced with the necessity of finding someone at once with a name of more or less equal drawing power. Once more that endless weighing of names in the balance. So-and-so was too old, So-and-so too young, So-and-so far too common, and So-and-so just about to have a baby. Finally, after a brief telephone conversation with Tony Prinsep and a slightly longer one with me, Tallulah Bankhead came flying into the theatre. Her vitality has always been remarkable, but on that occasion it was little short of fantastic. She took that exceedingly long part at a run. She tore off her hat, flipped her furs into a corner, kissed Edna, Stanley, me and anyone else who happened to be within reach and, talking incessantly about *Rain,* which Maugham had just refused to allow her to play, she embarked on the first act. In two days she knew the whole part perfectly, and on the first night gave a brilliant and completely assured performance. It was a *tour de force* of vitality, magnetism and spontaneous combustion.

Edna pursued an orderly course of accurate timing and almost contemptuous restraint and skated knowledgeably over the holes in the script.

There was no sense of struggle between the two leading ladies. Their teamwork was excellent. They also remained entirely friendly towards each other all through the run which, considering that their parts were about equal and that they had to play the whole second act alone together, was definitely a strategic triumph.

The Press notices for *Fallen Angels* were vituperative to the point of incoherence. No epithet was spared. It was described as vulgar, disgusting, shocking, nauseating, vile, obscene, degenerate, etc., etc. The idea of two gently nurtured young women playing a drinking scene together was apparently too degrading a spectacle for even the most hardened and worldly critics. The *Daily Express* even went so far as to allude to these two wayward creatures as 'suburban sluts.'

All this was capital for the box office and the play ran for several months. It had one disagreeable effect, however, which was to unleash upon me a mass of insulting letters from all parts of the country. This was the first time I had ever experienced such a strange pathological avalanche, and I was quite startled. In the years that followed, of course, I became completely accustomed to anonymous letters dropping into the letter-box. They have come in their hundreds, crammed with abuse and frequently embellished with pornographic drawings. Then I was still ingenuous enough to be amazed to think that there were so many people in the world with so much time to waste.

With *Fallen Angels, On with the Dance,* and *The Vortex* all running at once, I was in an enviable position. Everyone but Somerset Maugham said that I was a second Somerset Maugham with the exception of a few who preferred to describe me as a second Sacha Guitry.

On with the Dance had opened at the London Pavilion and was a big success. 'Poor Little Rich Girl' was being played in all the restaurants and night clubs. I went to too many parties and met too many people. I made a great many new and intimate friends, several of whom have actually lasted. My old ones were still nearly all with me with the exception of Stoj whom I saw only every now and then. She had married, had a baby, published two or three novels and embraced Christian Science with tremendous ardour. This depressed me but apparently gave her a great deal of pleasure, a pleasure, I may add, that was not entirely free from superciliousness. To this day we still meet occasionally and have a good time, but the paths back into the past are long and tortuous, and new faiths like new policemen are over-zealous in obstructing traffic.

The Vortex, having moved from the Royalty to the Comedy, was transferred once more, this time to the Little Theatre, where I had made my first appearance in *The Goldfish* in 1910. This was the fourth theatre in which we had played it; a quiet intimate house peopled for me with ghostly hordes of small children dressed as fish. It was a far cry from Prince Mussel in *The Goldfish* to Nicky Lancaster in *The Vortex*. I sometimes imagined how the fond matrons of 1910, blissfully regarding the antics of their progeny, would have shuddered could they have visualised the podgy little boy with the throbbing treble voice posturing on that same stage fifteen years later as a twisted, neurotic drug addict.

The theatre was so small that we were able to jog along for ages to adequate business. Our routine was set and, although the last act was a slight strain when we were tired after a matinée, we managed to uphold a pretty good standard of performance. On one occasion Seymour Hicks, that most generous of actors, came to a matinée, and stood up on his seat at the end, cheering wildly. This was thrilling to us because we had been long resigned to rather dim audiences and no 'bravos' had rung in our ears for many months. On another occasion Madge Titheradge came and fainted afterwards in Lilian's dressing-room, which was equally gratifying.

One night in May a young man in the front row of the stalls caught our attention early in the first act. His rapt absorption in the play inspired Lilian and me to renewed efforts, and at the final curtain we both conceded him a gracious bow all for himself. This situation frequently occurs when actors have been playing a play for a long run. The routine has become dull, the repetition of the same words night after night has become so monotonous as to be almost automatic, when suddenly, out of the gloom of the auditorium, a single face emerges. Just for a fleeting second you note the attitude of intense interest, the gleam of enthusiasm in the eye, and if you are a conscientious actor, you refrain from looking again except only very occasionally, and even then obliquely as though you are not looking at all. But the difference it can make to your performance is extraordinary. You play exclusively in your mind to that one stranger, and by the end you find that your most boring scenes have passed in a flash, and that you have probably played better than you have played for weeks. There are many unknown people in the world to whom I shall always be grateful because on some night in some play in some theatre somewhere or other their little extra interest caught my eye and set a spur to my imagination, causing me to give a fresh and vital performance of a part which I had played and played until my nerves were sick and tired of it.

On that particular night in the Little Theatre the young man responded nobly to our bow by applauding even more loudly, I remember remarking to Lilian that he must be an American because he was wearing a turn-down collar with his dinner jacket. A few days later a mutual friend told me that he knew a young American who was very anxious to meet me, and could he bring him round to my dressing-room one night, and the next evening Jack Wilson walked nervously, and with slightly over-done truculence, into my life.

Gladys was in my dressing-room and we both considered him amiable enough but rather uppish. He left after a drink and a little commonplace conversation, having asked me to lunch with him in New York when I came over with the play. We promptly forgot all about him, no clairvoyant being present to tell us that my trio of closest, most intimate friends, Gladys, Jeffrey, and Lorn, was fated, in those few minutes, to become a quartette. We should, I think, have laughed at the idea that that almost defiantly American stockbroker would become so much part of our lives that scarcely any decision could be made without him. That, however, is what ultimately happened.

(8)

My final efforts of that full season were concentrated upon *Hay Fever*, which, having mouldered sadly in a drawer for months, was suddenly taken out, dusted off and put into rehearsal at the Ambassadors' Theatre.

This all came about because Alban Limpus and Charles Kenyon wanted a play for Marie Tempest, who was no longer under her own management, but under theirs. I told them that I didn't think she would do it as she had already turned it down once. They insisted, however, that it would be a good idea for her to read it again. This she did, and, much to my surprise, said that she was delighted with it and that I must produce it. This scared me somewhat because, although my opinion of my own talents was reasonably high, I hardly, even in my most bumptious moments, visualised myself showing Marie Tempest how to act. Nevertheless, I agreed and arrived at the first rehearsal probably more nervous than I have ever been in my life.

Actually, I needn't have worried; moreover, I should have known that an artist as fine and experienced as Marie Tempest automatically takes direction with more graciousness and docility than a dozen small-part actresses rolled into one. She stamped her foot at me early in rehearsals and said sharply with the utmost decision: 'Come up here, Noel, and play this scene for me. You wrote it and you know it, I didn't write it and don't!' I clambered obediently on to the stage and played the scene as well as I could, whereupon she kissed me and said: 'Excellent, my dear, you've shown me exactly where I was wrong. Let's go back.'

She touched me, thrilled me, and enchanted me all through those rehearsals, and she has touched, thrilled and enchanted me ever since. I have seen her on occasion snappy and bad-tempered, particularly with actors whose lack of talent or casualness in the theatre exasperated her. She has a personal imperiousness that demands good behaviour in others, but if you give in to her too much she'll bully the life out of you. She is lovable as a person and unique as an artist, and her charm is ageless. And if it were not that my intention in this book is to write about me, I should probably continue indefinitely to write about her. In any event, she is bound to appear again, for even the most impersonal book dealing with the theatre could not avoid frequent reference to the first lady of it.

We gave an invitation dress rehearsal of *Hay Fever* to which all the actors in London came. They greeted it with hilarious enthusiasm although the general consensus of opinion was that the play was fundamentally too theatrical in flavour and too thin in plot ever to be a success with the public. On the first night I remember dear Eddie Marsh, that dean of first-nighters, wobbling his head sorrowfully at me and saying: 'Not this time, Noel. Not this time.' He was fortunately wrong. And I went on at the end in response to the calls for 'Author' with a slightly less modest demeanour than usual. I was still smarting from the insults I had received over *Fallen Angels,* and I announced, with some tartness, after I had correctly thanked Marie Tempest and the company, that although the audience and the critics may have found the play a trifle dull, they would at least have to admit that it was as clean as a whistle. This called forth delighted laughter and was later alluded to in the Press as being amusing and witty, thereby proving that my stock that winter was still obstinately high.

The bulk of the notices referred to the play variously as being dull, amusing, thin, slight, tedious, witty and brittle. It ran to excellent business for over a year.

Since *The Vortex* had opened in November I had received several offers from different American managements who wished to present it in New York. For a long while I was undecided which to accept and, also, which way to do the play. Either with an all-American cast and an American star to play Florence, or else with Lilian and the principals from the English cast. I had a shrewd suspicion that, all personal feelings aside, it would have to be a very fine actress indeed, star or no star, to give a better, or even as good a performance as Lilian. Also, the thought of re-rehearsing from the beginning and playing that heavy last act with somebody else depressed me, and so finally I arranged with Basil Dean that he should take over the play and produce it in New York under the auspices of Charles B. Dillingham and Erlanger. This seemed really to be the most satisfactory arrangement. I knew Basil well and admired his work, and I didn't want to carry the burden of producing the play myself as well as acting in it.

It was ultimately agreed between Basil and me, after a lot of dogged haggling over percentages in course of which Basil became more and more business-like, and I became more and more vaguely artistic, until I finally won from sheer dreamy stubbornness, that we would take with us, in addition to *The Vortex, Easy*

Virtue, and *Nadya.* (This was later re-titled *The Queen Was in the Parlour.*) *The Vortex* was to open first with Lilian, Mollie Kerr, Alan Hollis, and me, and new people for the other parts, and the other two plays were to come later. September the 7th was set for our try-out week in Washington, and as it was now only June I set about making plans for a holiday. I was certainly in need of one, and I persuaded Alban Limpus to let me leave the cast of *The Vortex* and go away. John Gielgud took over my part and played it beautifully, and the play continued for a considerable while after I left. Lilian, I need hardly add, stood staunchly to her post and never missed one performance.

(9)

I sailed for New York on the Majestic in the middle of August. It was a gay, nervous voyage and far from peaceful. In addition to Lilian, Alan Hollis, Basil Dean, Mercy (his wife), Mother, Gladys and me, there were on board, Leslie Howard, Ruth Chatterton, Laura Hope Crews, Mercedes de Acosta and Eva Le Gallienne. Laura was delightful, and we seemed to know each other well at once. Ruth Chatterton was still and reticent, and it wasn't until long afterwards that I grew to know her as a devoted friend. Eva I had known before. She and Mercedes had been in Paris presenting, rather disastrously, Mercedes' play on Joan of Arc. I think they were sad about it; at any rate they alternated between intellectual gloom and feverish gaiety and wore black, indiscriminately, for both moods. Leslie was vague and amiable and spread his own particular brand of elusive charm over every gathering. The whole trip consisted of gatherings. We had bathing parties, cocktail parties, dinner parties and poker parties. We discussed the theatre exhaustively and from every angle. We were all anxiously looking forward to the autumn season. Leslie was going to play *The Green Hat* with Katharine Cornell. Laura was to do *Hay Fever,* Eva had plans for a few Ibsen revivals. Ruth was going to do *The Man with a Load of Mischief,* Basil and Gladys and I were twit-

With MOLLIE KERR in The Vortex
Everyman Theatre, 1924

NEW YORK
1925

tering with our own projects. The sea was calm and the weather fine, but the air on that ship felt definitely electric.

New York looked more beautiful than ever in the early hours of the morning, but by the time we docked most of the colour had been drained away by the full glare of noon. We went to the Plaza for the first few days, and then moved to a singularly inappropriate apartment in East 54th Street, which seemed to have been designed exclusively for the blonde plaything of a tired businessman. It was dainty to the point of nausea; however, we saw very little of it, as rehearsals started almost immediately, and there were lots of things to be done. Gladys and I left Mother to deal with the intricacies of American housekeeping, and she shopped, mastered the frigidaire, and engaged coloured maids without turning a hair.

Those first few days were over-crowded and breathlessly hot. I was received with genial kindliness by Charlie Dillingham who lent me his car and sent us masses of flowers. Everyone we met welcomed us with the utmost enthusiasm and seemed cheerfully convinced that *The Vortex,* although most of them had never seen it, could be nothing but a tumultuous success. Nevertheless, in spite of all this encouragement, an unpleasantness happened very soon. Charles Dillingham and Abe Erlanger were to present the play in conjunction with Basil Dean, and, in due course, a conference was called in the Erlanger offices. This was my first meeting with Mr. Erlanger, and I had not been in the room five minutes before he informed me that the play could not open in New York until I had re-written the last act. Although he never removed his feet from his desk throughout the entire interview, he was patient and fatherly with me, explaining that mother-love in America was a real and universally recognised ideal, and that the public would assuredly rise as one man and leave the theatre at the spectacle of a son so vilely abusing the woman who gave him birth. He added, gently, that the little question of reconstruction would not be difficult as he could come to rehearsals and tell me what to do.

He talked for a considerable time. I regarded the over-furnished office; his perspiring form leaning back in shirt-sleeves with a cigar stub in one hand and lily cup of ice water in the other; the dusty beams of sunlight slanting through the open windows catching refractory gleams from a gargantuan spittoon in the middle of the floor; the 'We must be tactful at all costs' expression on the faces of Basil Dean and Charlie Dillingham; and my spirit revolted.

I remembered that *The Vortex* had been turned down cold by many managers in London and New York, and that I had had finally to borrow money from Michael Arlen to get it produced at all. I remembered the obstacles we had had to overcome during rehearsals. The difficulties, the disappointments, the battles and the despairs. I remembered also the impact of that last act upon the first-night audience. And here was this theatrical magnate, soggy with commercial enterprise, prattling smugly to me about the ideal of mother-love, and imagining that I would agree to re-write my play at his dictation. I knew, in that moment, that I would far rather go back to England the next day and not do the play in America at all than submit to such insolence.

I must say, to my credit, that I controlled any outward display of temper and waited, politely, until he had finished. Then, ignoring Dillingham's frantic grimaces, I said quite calmly that I intended to play the play exactly as it was, and that far from listening to any of his suggestions for the altering of the script, I would not even allow him inside the theatre while I was rehearsing. With which I made a swift exit. Not too swift, however, to miss a gratifying roseate suffusion of Mr. Erlanger's face and neck. I was overtaken by Basil and Charlie Dillingham in the passage, where they assured me that I had been over-hasty, and that they would guarantee that Erlanger wouldn't worry me at all during rehearsals, and that, with a little tact, he was perfectly easy to manage.

I replied that I had not travelled three thousand miles to manage Mr. Erlanger, but for him to manage me, and left them to go back to the office and be as tactful as they liked. The upshot of the whole thing was that Sam Harris and Irving Berlin took over the play, and Erlanger and Dillingham absolved themselves, misguidedly, from any connection with it.

The important additions to our New York cast were Leo Carroll as Pawnie and Auriol Lee as Helen. Auriol was an old friend. She had a witty mind and gave a fine performance.

We had been fortunate in getting the Henry Miller Theatre. It was one of the nicest theatres in New York and perfect, both in size and atmosphere, for the play.

Henry Miller himself was extremely hospitable, and on the first day turned over his private office to me. It was well furnished and comfortable, and had its own shower bath and dressing-room, and I looked forward to cooling myself luxuriously in it after tiring rehearsals. A few days later, however, Henry Miller went away, and from then onwards the office was inexorably locked, and all my protestations to the house manager were unavailing. He said that there was only one key, and *that* Mr. Miller had taken away with him. This seemed to be rather eccentric of Mr. Miller, but I remained deeply appreciative of his initial gesture.

Gladys had only two weeks in which to collect all the furniture and get the scenery built, and so we seldom met until evening. She disappeared early each morning into the maw of New York in search of scene-painters and standard lamps and sofas and chairs. It will always be a mystery to me how she managed to get everything done in time, but she did, and with apparent ease.

During the first week of rehearsals I had a letter from Jack Wilson asking me to lunch. Flushed with pride at having even remembered his name, I dictated a letter of acceptance and waited, in a mounting rage, for three quarters of an hour on the day specified, and finally was forced to lunch alone in a cafeteria. It later transpired that my secretary had never posted the letter.

(10)

In later years I have travelled extensively. I have sweated through the Red Sea with a following wind and a sky like burnished steel. I have sweated through steamy tropical forests and across arid burning deserts, but never yet, in any equatorial hell, have I sweated as I sweated in Washington in September 1925. The city felt as though it were dying. There was no breeze, no air, not even much sun. Just a dull haze of breathless discomfort through which the noble buildings could be discerned, gasping, like nude old gentlemen in a steam room. The pavements felt like grey nougat and the least exertion soaked one to the skin.

We floundered through a dress rehearsal on the Sunday night with the make-up streaking down our faces, every extra dab of powder creating gloomy little rice puddings round the corners of our nostrils, and every word we uttered crackling in our throats like brown paper. We prayed ardently for a thunderstorm. Prayers to which the Almighty responded with unparalleled thoroughness, granting us not just one thunderstorm during the day to cool the air, but one every night of the week without cooling the air. The first one was timed, with perfect accuracy, to burst in the middle of the second act on the opening night, and from then onwards, in spite of our frantic shrieks, not one word of the play was heard. On the second night the storm broke at the beginning of the last act, and so on throughout the week with monotonous regularity, until we were forced to conclude that God shared Mr. Erlanger's views on the sanctity of mother-love and that by offending one I had obviously offended the other.

The only coolness in that unpleasant week was supplied by the Press. The notices referred to the play as unwholesome, dull and mediocre. One critic even went so far as to say that if, as he had heard on good authority, I was considered to be the white hope of the English theatre, God help the English theatre.

We played on the week to a little over six thousand dollars and returned to New York on the Sunday miserably prepared for certain failure. Lilian, I believe, actually had the forethought to make tentative steamship reservations.

We were due to open on the Wednesday night, and Mother and Gladys and I occupied those agonising days by going to plays and moving into a new apartment.

The apartment we had taken was in the Hotel des Artistes on West 67th Street, and belonged to Miss Mae Murray. Its assets were that it was spacious and high up, and commanded a grand view over Central Park. Its defects were that it was exceedingly expensive and rather trying to the eye. The main studio was Italian Gothic in intent, but papier-mâché in reality. There were two elaborately wrought-iron gates which flew away lightly at a touch, and a set of really wrought-iron chairs which were quite immovable. There was a stained-glass window depicting a ship at sea, which lit up at night unless we were careful. There was also a tall Renaissance chair with a red velvet cushion under which lived an electric victrola.

There was a wooden trellis in the dining-room over which clambered festoons of tin ivy. I remember looking at it abstractedly as I tried to eat a light meal at six o'clock on the evening of September the sixteenth, 1925.

(ii)

I remember driving from West 67th Street through Central Park and down Sixth Avenue trying, with all the will-power I could exert, to coax myself into a more detached frame of mind. The play was going to be a failure, of that I was convinced. It would be a horrible evening, tense and depressing; certain people I knew would come back-stage afterwards and be as sympathetic and comforting as they could, saying, with almost defiant enthusiasm, that I had given a wonderful performance and that they had liked the play anyhow. I knew that behind their kindness I should be able to detect the truth, and have to steel myself to the additional strain of putting up a good show for them; not letting them know that I knew; accepting their politeness with as good a grace as possible; betraying, neither by bitterness nor over-jocularity, that my heart was sick inside me.

I strove vainly to project my mind a few weeks ahead when I should be able to view this dreadful night in perspective, set in its right proportions. After all, it didn't matter as much as all that. My whole career was not going to be blasted by one failure in New York. I had written other plays and intended to write still more. The fact of failure would not, in this instance, necessarily mean that the play was bad; it had been a proven success in London and, dealing as it did, with an extremely small and typically English social group, there was no earthly reason why a New York audience should recognise its values at all; the dialogue, to them, would be nothing but an alien jargon; Washington, by all accounts the most cosmopolitan of cities, had regarded it with blank distaste; the New York reaction would be just so much blanker and, after some bad notices and a week or two of bad business, the show would close, and that would be that.

In this mood of dreary resignation I arrived at the theatre and went in to talk to Lilian for a little while. She was making up lethargically with a white cloth tied round her head, looking remarkably like an early photograph I had seen of her as the Madonna in *The Miracle,* but wearing an expression that was less tranquil and a good deal more pessimistic. 'We can only do our best,' she said, slapping her face viciously with a powder puff, 'and if they don't like it they can do the other thing!'

Both our dressing-rooms were crowded with boxes of flowers and there was a pile of about a hundred and fifty telegrams on my table; many of them from total strangers. All the managers, all the stars, everyone, it seemed, connected with the American Theatre, wanted me and the play to be a success. It was my first professional experience of the tremendous warmth and kindness that New York theatre people extend to strangers, and I was touched by it almost beyond endurance. There was a lot of time, far too much time, and I made up slowly and methodically, opening fresh batches of telegrams as they came, and occasionally wandering round the room looking gloomily at the cards on the flowers. Mother and Gladys arrived in due course, dressed up and scented and looking as though they might break if anyone touched them. Basil appeared, too, in an opera hat that was a little too small for him. His manner was pathetically breezy, and he slapped me on the back rather harder than he meant to and made me choke. Eventually the 'Five Minutes' was called, and they all went round to the front of the house.

My dressing-room was on the stage level, and I heard the curtain rise. A few minutes later I heard, to my astonishment, a laugh from the audience; then, almost immediately, a bigger one. I could only conclude that either Leo Carroll or Auriol Lee had fallen flat on their faces. A little while later there was a prolonged round of applause. That was Lilian's entrance. I got up then and after a final dab at my face and the usual nervous gesture to discover if my fly buttons were properly done up, I went on to the stage. Lilian was playing her scene at the telephone; I noted a certain strain in her voice, but she was timing beautifully and getting laugh after laugh. Remembering the damp unresponsiveness of Washington, I could hardly believe it. I paced up and down gingerly on the strip of coconut matting at the side of the stage and was told by the theatre fireman to put out my cigarette. At last it was near my time to go on, and I stood holding the door knob with a clammy hand, frowning in an effort to keep my face from twitching. My cue came and I made my entrance. There was a second's silence, and then a terrific burst of applause which seemed to me to last for ever. Fortunately the first thing I had to do was to embrace Lilian, which I did with such fervour that her bones cracked. The applause continued, and there we stood locked in each other's arms until I felt her give me a little reassuring pat on the back, and I broke out of the clinch and managed, in a strangulated voice, to speak my first line.

Never before or since in all my experience have I received such a direct personal stimulus from an audience. First nights are always over-strung and nerve-racking. There is always a certain tension and, for leading actors, always a reception on their first entrance. This comes to be regarded less as a tribute than as an inevitable part of a first performance. Some actors like it and say so, some like it and pretend they don't, some really hate it. I belong to the first contingent. To me a round of applause, even though it may interfere for a moment with the action of the play, even though it be conventional rather than spontaneous, almost always sets my performance off on the right foot. On that particular night, however, it did more than that, it saved me. I had expected a little clapping—after all even Washington had accorded me that—but this sound was of such a different quality, and the genuine ring of it uprooted my deep-set conviction of failure and substituted for it a much stronger conviction of success.

There was no false modesty in my astonishment at such an ovation. I had never appeared in New York before. They had no reason to make the smallest demonstration until the end of the evening when they could decide whether or not I merited it. As it was, they made me feel as though I were one of their most beloved and established stars, and I tried with everything I had in me to deserve it. I do know, to my lasting satisfaction, that I gave the best performance that night that I have ever given in my life.

In *The Vortex* we had made it a rule not to take any curtain calls until the end of the play. This was not a new idea in America, although in London, where the public were inured to watching a row of actors bowing and smiling after every act, it was considered to be quite an innovation. It is now, I am thankful to say, usual in both countries. On that first night in New York the play ran more smoothly than it had ever run. Everyone in the cast seemed to be inspired, and when the curtain fell after the piano-playing scene at the end of the second act, there was prolonged cheering, so prolonged, indeed, that we could still hear it while we were changing in our dressing-rooms.

We had now only the last act to be got through, but it was technically the most difficult of all, and we enjoined each other urgently to keep clear and cool, and to hold everything in reserve until the last few minutes.

We played it with the utmost wariness, feeling the audience completely with us. There wasn't a fidget or a sneeze or a nose blow, or even a cough. The whole act was received in absorbed silence. The curtain fell and rose again on the final picture of me kneeling with my head buried in Lilian's lap while she mechanically stroked my hair, still in dead silence, until, just as it fell for the second time, the cheering broke over us, and we struggled trembling to our feet.

I had rehearsed a polite little speech in my mind in case it should be called for, but when the time came for me to say it, my throat was so constricted that I was able only to mumble a few incoherent words of thanks and clench my hands tightly to prevent myself from breaking down.

We stood in our dressing-rooms afterwards for over an hour receiving. A few faces in that procession stand out in my mind; Mother's, very pink and powdered over tear-stains; Gladys's, aloof and almost expressionless except for a triumphant glint in the eye; Jeanne Eagels's, with little rivulets of mascara trickling down her cheeks. I was hugged and kissed and crowned with glory, and that night is set apart in my memory, supreme and unspoilt, gratefully and for ever.

(12)

The Press notices the next day were enthusiastic and the advance sale tremendous. Ticket speculators bought up seats and sold them, sometimes on the sidewalk outside the theatre, for as much as twenty and twenty-five dollars a pair. It was obviously a violent and glittering success, and I became, extremely happily, the talk of the town. I was photographed and caricatured and interviewed and publicised with even more thoroughness than in London. I was the guest of honour in all directions and made brief speeches at immense ladies' luncheons. I was invited to restful week-ends in large houses on Long Island, but these I had to give up very soon, as they were far too strenuous, and I was too tired after such clamorous relaxation to be able to give a good performance on Monday evenings.

Jack Wilson appeared at the stage door of the Henry Miller after the first matinée. He had been to a cocktail party where he had drunk enough to give him enough courage to come and attack me for not having answered his invitation to lunch. Fortunately I remembered his face and, after a moment's scurried thinking, his name, which mollified him somewhat and after a few high words in the alley, I took him back to dine at the studio where Gladys, with royal thoroughness, also remembered him at once, so that his outraged feelings were soon smoothed out.

From then onwards we became close friends, and a few months later he gave up being a stockbroker in order to be my personal manager, in which capacity he has bullied me firmly ever since.

The Vortex being safely launched, I had to start work immediately on *Hay Fever*. There had been a considerable muddle over the casting owing to the eccentric behaviour of the Shuberts who were given to engaging people recklessly without even a cursory knowledge of the types required by the script.

On the morning of the first rehearsal I walked on to the stage of the Broadhurst Theatre and was startled to find a company of over thirty which, for a comedy of nine characters, seemed excessive. I weeded them out gradually, but one lady gave me a great deal of trouble. She was a brassy blonde in a décolleté afternoon dress of black lace, and was lying on her back on a wooden bench chewing gum with an expression of studied languor. At first she replied to my questioning laconically, but even in her monosyllables it was not difficult to detect a strong Brooklyn accent. I asked her what part Mr. Shubert had promised her and, shifting the gum from one side of her mouth to the other, she replied 'Myra', and turned her head away wearily as though the whole interview were distasteful to her. Out of the corner of my eye I observed Laura Hope Crews at the prompt table convulsed with laughter. I persevered, with as much tact as I could manage, and said that I was extremely sorry, but that as Myra was such a typically English character she could obviously not be played with such a thorough-going American accent; whereupon the blonde rose in a sudden fury, spat her gum neatly into a chiffon handkerchief, said: 'Accent hell! I've got a contract,' and flounced off the stage.

The fact that she had indeed got a contract cost me many wasteful hours in the Shubert office later.

Eventually after days of argument the cast was set, never, I must say, to my satisfaction, but I was at a loss in New York, and had, more or less, to accept actors on other people's recommendation.

Hay Fever played a trial week in Brooklyn, and opened in New York at the Maxine Elliott Theatre to a specially invited audience on a Sunday night.

I had decided, with careless optimism, to give a large party at my studio after the show, to celebrate its success, and I sat, during the performance, wishing with all my heart that I hadn't. It was, without exception, one of the most acutely uncomfortable evenings I have ever spent in the theatre. Everyone of artistic importance in New York was there. All the stars, all the writers, and all the critics. Not only were they there in the theatre, but most of them were coming to the party afterwards, and I, being in a box with Mother and Gladys and Jack, had an uninterrupted view of their faces as the play proceeded majestically, and with measured tread, towards complete failure. The cast, never inspired at best, seemed utterly crushed by the splendour of the audience, all of them, that is, expecting Laura, who, in a praiseworthy but misguided effort to lift the play and her fellow actors out of the lethargy in which they were rapidly congealing, gave a performance of such unparalleled vivacity that it completely over-balanced everything.

The critics tore her to pieces the next day for over-acting, which indeed she did, but what they didn't realise, and what I realised fully was, that in the circumstances it was certainly excusable. She lost her head a bit and hit too hard, but she was surrounded by a cast who were lying down and not hitting at all.

The applause at the end was polite and the atmosphere in Laura's dressing-room strained. She knew and I knew, and everybody knew, that the play was a flop; however, there was the party to be got through, and Laura gallantly agreed to come to it in spite of everything.

Many of the guests had already arrived by the time I got back to the studio, having left the theatre as quickly as they could in order to evade back-stage condolences. Apprehensive social smiles seemed to be glued on to the face of everyone, and the preliminary gaiety was forced, to say the least of it. Looking back at it, that party was hilarious; at the time, however, it was pretty dreadful, especially for the first hour or so before the dampness of the play had been dispelled by liquor. Laura's social performance was superb; this time she didn't overact a fraction; she was gay and gracious and accepted guarded compliments with the most genuine of smiles.

The Press notices the next day were extremely depressing and the advance sale non-existent, and the play, having played to rapidly diminishing business for about six weeks, gently expired.

(13)

Christmas came and went with its attendant festivities, and, owing to a throat infection, my voice went with it, and I was forced to stay out of the cast for a whole week. My understudy was a boy called Allen Vincent, who played the piano excellently.

Basil Dean was busy producing John van Druten's first play, *Young Woodley,* and when that had been successfully launched we devoted ourselves to Jane Cowl and *Easy Virtue.*

Although Jane Cowl has been described with amusing malice by Mr. Joseph Reed in his book *The Curtain Falls,* I should like to have a slap at her, too; my slap, however, will be more in the nature of a loving pat, as I found her, both in spite of and because of her temperament and capriciousness, a most enchanting personality. To begin with, she is everything a famous theatrical star is expected to be: beautiful, effective, gracious, large-hearted, shrewd in everything but business, foolishly generous, infinitely kind to lesser people of the theatre, extremely annoying on many small points, and, over and above everything else, a fine actress. She and Basil inaccurately measured each other's quality early on, and proceeded firmly to misunderstand each other on every possible occasion.

The production of *Easy Virtue* was tricky, especially the dance scene in the last act which Basil, with his usual passion for detail, polished within an inch of its life. The cast, on the whole, was excellent, and the play opened, after a trial week in Newark, at the Empire Theatre where it was received with only moderate acclaim. Jane's performance was smooth and touching, but she always played the big scene at the end of the second act too dramatically, thereby jerking the play too far back into the Pineroism from which it had originally sprung. My object in writing it had been primarily to adapt a story, intrinsically Pinero in theme and structure, to present-day behaviour; to compare the déclassée woman of to-day with the more flamboyant demi-mondaine of the nineties. The line that was intended to establish the play on a basis of comedy rather than tragedy comes at the end of the second act when Larita, the heroine, irritated beyond endurance by the smug attitude of her 'in-laws', argues them out of the room and collapses on to the sofa where, suddenly catching sight of a statuette of the Venus de Milo on a pedestal, she shies a book at it and says: 'I always hated that damned thing!'

Jane invariably delivered this line in a voice strangled with sobs and brought the curtain down to tremendous applause. If, however, she had said it and played the scene leading up to it with less emotion and more exasperation, I don't think that the play would have received quite so much criticism on the score of being old-fashioned. On the other hand, there would probably not have been so much applause, and so I expect that Jane, from her point of view, if not from the play's, was quite right.

At all events, she made an enormous personal success, and if I had to bear the gleeful laughter of Alexander Woollcott and a few stinging comments from the other critics, I had, at least, the satisfaction of knowing that Jane was filling the theatre to virtual capacity, and that the play would certainly run for months.

(14)

I remember drinking-in the year 1926 alone with Mother. We had a bottle of champagne all to ourselves, and stood at the window looking out over Central Park. There had been a heavy fall of snow, but the night was clear and starry; the traffic far below us looked like a procession of toys illuminated for some gigantic children's party, and when we opened the window the noise of it sounded muffled and unreal.

All along upper Fifth Avenue and West 59th Street the buildings glittered with lights; it was a beautiful sight, but so alien to us that it made us homesick. We both sighed for the gentle familiarity of London. Mother kept on saying: 'I wonder what Eric and Arthur and Vida are doing,' and, refraining from the obvious surmise that they were probably bickering like mad, I allowed the sentimentality of the moment to have its fling, and pictured the Ebury Street house *en fête,* left-over Christmas decorations looped from the ceiling of the bungalow and festooned over Grandfather's sword, Father sipping inferior port and cracking nuts, and Eric and Auntie Vida wearing firemen's hats and laughing immoderately.

We stood with our glasses correctly poised while the ice-cold air blew over us through the open window; sirens were blowing and bells were ringing, and a wave of depression engulfed us. I knew, from the trembling of Mother's lip, that she was remembering too much, but my own thoughts were occupied more with the future than with the past. I think I realised in that moment how warily I should have to go; how infinitely more dangerous the achievement of ambition was than the struggle to achieve it. Here we were, Mother and I, having survived many despairs, at last safe, financially safe at any rate, for quite a while, providing we weren't too foolishly extravagant and providing that my grip on my talents didn't become loosened with too much success. How dreadful it would be, having got so far, to sink slowly back;

not perhaps this year, nor even the next year, but later, when praise and publicity and 'stage centre' had insidiously become necessary to me, too necessary to be discarded without heartbreak. The picture of a one-time white-headed boy advancing bitterly into middle-age with yesterday's Press headlines yellowing in a scrapbook, and only an occasional Sunday-night performance by the Stage Society to remind him of past glories, seemed far from improbable and almost too depressing to be borne. Perhaps I was over-tired. Perhaps I was wiser than I knew, but instead of welcoming that new year with a grin of triumph, which in the circumstances I had every right to do, I greeted it suspiciously, with guarded politeness, like a newly crowned king receiving the leader of the Socialist party at his first levée.

However, natural resilience and another glass of champagne dissipated the mood, and we both began to giggle at the spectacle of ourselves, hovering on the verge of sentimental tears in a Metro-Goldwyn-Mayer mausoleum. We retired to bed early in a gale of hiccups, and the next morning 1926 seemed happily indistinguishable from 1925.

(15)

By this time I had whittled down my large circle of New York acquaintances to the small group of people I really liked. I had for some weeks been gradually eliminating big parties, finding them tiring and almost always disappointing. Before, I had accepted every invitation with a little thrill of anticipation; So-and-So was going to be there, and also Such-and-Such, and it would be sure to be gay, and I should probably meet someone new and exciting. It didn't take me long to realise that there was little or no novelty in any large party; people looked the same and talked the same and sang the same songs and made the same jokes. Only very occasionally, for a brief hour or two, generally round about three in the morning when most of the guests had gone, a certain magic occurred, and the few who were left really relaxed and enjoyed themselves; but these moments were rare, and you could never be sure that the various elements were really going to fuse success-fully. Even if they did, awareness that there was a rehearsal the next morning, or a matinée to be played the next afternoon, made the dreary hours of waiting hardly worth while.

Frances Wellman, whom I had known since my first visit to New York, administered, like Elsa Maxwell in Paris and Sibyl Colefax in London, the best social mixtures. At the crack of her whip Park Avenue clapped Broadway on the back, and Broadway generously went through its hoops for Park Avenue. I soon dis-covered, however, that Park Avenue, like Mayfair, had not yet acquired the estimable habit of keeping quiet when someone was entertaining them. It appeared that life was too swift for them, too crowded with excitement and endeavour, to permit them to sit still and listen to some fine musician such as George Gershwin or Vincent Youmans or Richard Rodgers, without breaking the spell by whispering shrilly, or demanding, over-loudly, the few songs they happened to know. It was on account of this odd restlessness that one had to wait so long for most parties to become good. However, Frances organised well as a rule, and professionals were allowed to show off to their heart's content, without too much competition from amateurs.

My own entertaining was usually confined to small suppers after the show, when nobody was expected to dress, and music and conversation were possible without strain.

(16)

After a run of just over five months *The Vortex* closed in New York, and we went off on a short road tour. Mollie Kerr returned home to England and an excellent actress, Rose Hobart, took over the part of Bunty. With this exception, the cast remained the same.

I cannot say that I look back on that tour with any pleasure. The business was good for the first few weeks, but I was too tired of playing that heavy part night after night to care much. It was

[232]

then that I made a vow that never again, in any circumstances, would I play a play for longer than six months, preferably three months in London, and three months in New York. For an actor alone, this decision would seem to be rather high-handed, but I was a writer, too, and the routine of eight performances a week, with all the attendant obligations, precluded any chance of concentration on new ideas. Nobody but an actor knows the vitality that has to be expended during a single performance; even after months of playing, when you move through the play automatically and without nerves, you still have to be strung up to a certain extent in order to get yourself on to the stage at all. In *The Vortex* there was always the last act hanging over me; the interminable physical strain of lashing myself, on cue, into the requisite frenzy. There were bad nights when the tears wouldn't come at the right moment, or when they came too soon and dried up completely just before they were really wanted. There were scarifying moments when suddenly my mind went blank, and I had no idea what came next or what had gone before. This happens to many actors when they play long runs. The displacement of a chair; the ticking of a clock; a sudden unexpected sound, either backstage or in the front of the house; or a new intonation on one of the other actor's lines, is quite enough to dry them up dead. It is a horrible sickening sensation and leaves you shaken and insecure, not only for the rest of the evening, but for several performances afterwards.

Audiences, too, after the first month or so, begin to deteriorate in quality, and whereas during the first part of a run you can count on at least five good audiences a week, later the percentage gets lower and lower until every performance seems drearier than the last, and it is only very rarely that you feel, on your first entrance, that blessed electric tension in the front of the house which means that for once you won't have to pump the words over the footlights, and nurse and coddle every line until your nerves ache with boredom.

The Mecca of our tour was Chicago. The company reminded each other at frequent intervals of the delights of that city. 'Wait,' they said, ignoring the kindly enthusiasm of Newark, Brooklyn, and Cincinnati, 'wait until we get to Chicago. There they'll really appreciate the play. There they'll eat it up!'

We arrived in Chicago having been advertised to play a six-weeks' season, but reserving smugly to ourselves the right to prolong this indefinitely. Mother was with me and Jack; Gladys wasn't, as she was on tour with Eva Le Gallienne, working with her on plans for the formation of the famous Civic Repertory Company for which she, Gladys, was to be art director. On the advice of Mary Garden we had reserved an expensive suite at the Lake Shore Drive Hotel, in addition to which I had ordered my car to come from New York and be there to greet us when we arrived. The car had been, at the outset, a wild extravagance. It was a vintage Rolls-Royce with a shining new Brewster body which successfully concealed from the casual eye the aged dilapidation of its engine. Ravished by its appearance, I had bought it against all unprejudiced advice. After all, it was a Rolls-Royce, and Rolls-Royces were well-known to last for ever, also the drive was on the right-hand side which would be very useful in England. The fact that I had often stepped into it outside the stage door and been forced to step out on the other side into a taxi, I merely ascribed to the inadequacy of the chauffeur. At all events, it looked marvellous, and although in the long run it cost me as much as three new Bentleys, I am still grateful to it for the many plutocratic thrills it gave me.

It managed to reach Chicago all right, and met us at the station, and we drove out to the Lake Shore Drive, none too impressed with the atmosphere of the town, but determined to enjoy our long stay there as much as we could.

Mary Garden had lovingly and generously written a squib for the papers, 'My divine breezy city, you have with you four words that spell 'Genius,' 'Noel Coward *The Vortex!'* and we opened to a packed house at the Selwyn Theatre on the night of George Washington's birthday.

They seemed unappreciative of the comedy in the first act but we struggled manfully across the damp patches where the laughs should have been, deciding in our minds that they were a dramatic audience rather than a comedy one. In this we were wrong. They were essentially out for comedy, and they got their first big belly laugh at the curtain of the second act. This struck me like a blow on the head. With every audience I had ever played it to, I had always been able to rely on complete absorption at the particular moment; it was really the most tragic scene of the play, when the son plays jazz more and more feverishly in order to drown the sound and sight of his mother abasing herself before her young lover. Chicago, however, saw it only as supremely comic, and Lilian and I retired to our dressing-rooms with prolonged laughter instead of prolonged cheers ringing in our ears. I was trembling with rage; I wanted to go out before the curtain and inform that gay holiday-spirited audience that this was the first and last time that I would ever appear in their divine, breezy city, and that to save themselves and me further trouble they could go back to their dance-halls and speak-easies immediately as there was not going to be any last act at all. Lilian restrained me by gripping me by the shoulders and hissing in my face: 'Remember you are English! Remember you are English!'

The last act was worse than I could ever have imagined it to be. The sight of me in pyjamas and dressing-gown started them off happily, and from then onwards they laughed without ceasing. Never, since *Charley's Aunt* on a Saturday night in Blackpool, have I heard such uproarious mirth in a theatre. The curtain fell to considerable applause, and I even had to make a speech, which, remembering that I was English, was a model of grateful restraint.

I have regretted ever since that I didn't tell them what I thought of them; it wouldn't have made any difference as the play was a dead failure, and it would, at least, have given me a little satisfaction.

The two principal critics of the town wrote two such diverse notices that they nullified each other. Ashton Stevens said that the play was great and fine and subtle and tragic, while his confrère, whose name I forget, said it was cheap and comic and stupid and dull. Unfortunately we couldn't close at once because there was no other attraction ready to come into the theatre. Pauline Lord was playing next door in *They Knew What They Wanted,* and came popping in as often as she could to cheer us up, but apart from her my theatrical career in Chicago was miserable.

Socially, however, everyone was extremely kind. I was made a member of the Riding Club, and rode every morning with Diana Cooper and Iris Tree, who were playing *The Miracle* at the Auditorium. There were gay supper parties given almost every night, and when they weren't, we gave impromptu ones in our hotel and ran upstairs and downstairs between each other's kitchenettes bearing bacon and cheese and ginger-ale.

Diana and Iris and Rudolph Kommer were at the Lake Shore Drive; Pauline Lord, Helen Hayes and Judith Anderson were not far away, and apart from the horrible hours I had to spend in the theatre, I had quite a good time.

Before leaving the Selwyn Theatre, Chicago, I wrote on the wall of my dressing-room in indelible pencil 'Noel Coward died here', and when I visited Clifton Webb in the same room years later, I was delighted to see that the inscription was still there.

Cleveland received us kindly, and we finished our tour to good business. I don't ever remember feeling so relieved and happy as I did on that last night. I had played the part over four hundred and fifty times, and although during the tour I had forced myself to write a play, it had been a tremendous strain, and I felt that many months of creative impulse had been frustrated. The play I wrote was called *Semi-Monde,* and the whole action of it took place in the public rooms of the Ritz Hotel in Paris over a period of three years. It was well constructed and, on the whole, well written; its production in London or New York seemed unlikely as some of the characters, owing to lightly suggested abnormalities, would certainly be deleted by the censor; Max Reinhardt, however, was enthusiastic about it, and it was translated into German by Rudolph Kommer and taken in due course to Berlin, where for years it escaped production by a hair's breadth until eventually Vicky Baum wrote *Grand Hotel,* and *Semi-Monde,* being too closely similar in theme, faded gently into oblivion.

[236]

With EDNA BEST in THE CONSTANT NYMPH
New Theatre, 1926

With EDNA BEST
in THE CONSTANT NYMPH
New Theatre, 1926

Mother and I had reservations on the Olympic which didn't sail for two weeks, and so I left her in New York and went to Palm Beach to stay with my old friends, Florence and John Magee. It was an uneventful but lovely holiday. The air was soft and the sea blue, and I bathed and lay in the sun. There were dinner parties, lunch parties and picnic parties. Perhaps they were dull, perhaps they weren't; I only know that I enjoyed every minute of them. I was out of prison; free! Not for as long as I liked would I again have to be in any theatre every night at a certain time. I could have a nice strong cocktail before dinner with a clear conscience, and no fears that it might spoil my performance. Of course it was conceivable that too strong a cocktail might spoil my performance at dinner, but I don't think it ever did, and I returned to New York decently tanned and feeling a great deal better.

(17)

Jack, having already wisely invested a lot of my money in American securities, and having convinced his family that a career as my business manager would ultimately prove more lucrative than that of a stockbroker, was sailing to England with Mother and me. We had drawn up an elaborate contract in a lawyer's office, bristling with legal technicalities, options and percentages, so that in the event of sudden unforeseen mutual hatred, we could still continue to work together, however dourly, on a business basis.

Happily that situation has not, to date, occurred and as during the last ten years we have weathered more storm and stress than the average business association has to combat in a lifetime, I think it can safely be said that our original summing up of each other's characters was fairly shrewd. During that voyage home I remember feeling a little apprehensive over Lorn. I wondered how she would welcome the introduction into our slap-dash business lives of a hard-headed and extremely uncompromising American. Fortunately, however, my fears were groundless as they took to each other on sight; in fact the only scenes that have ever taken place since have been the result of both of them, for some reason or other, basely combining against me.

(18)

The Rolls-Royce was brought over to London at great expense, and on the rare occasions when it was not being over-hauled at Derby, I drove about in it with considerable satisfaction and found that the streets of London, although retaining their well-worn familiarity, took on a new sheen viewed through Rolls-Royce windows. Bouncing along on gracious, buff-coloured upholstery, I noted with a thrill of conscious pleasure various landmarks of my still very recent past. Garrick Street, Bedford Street, Leicester Square, Shaftesbury Avenue, St. Martin's Lane, looking, in the warm May sunlight so exactly the same, still, in the mornings, thronged with actors hurrying in and out of agents' offices, stage doors, and rehearsal rooms. Even the chocolates and cakes in the windows of the Corner House seemed unchanged except for the difference that now I no longer yearned for them. It felt strange after months in America to be back again as an established star. True, I had been that when I left, but now Time had allowed the sediment of novelty to settle a bit, and I could accept the situation more tranquilly. The success in New York seemed to have added assurance to my position. This was all right, concrete. The sense of unreality had faded, and I no longer felt as though I were flying faster and faster through a nervous dream.

Easy Virtue was playing its last weeks in New York, and Basil had arranged to present it in London with Jane and practically the same cast in June. Meanwhile, there was nothing much to do, and so I went off for a trip to the South of France, Sicily and Tunis. While in Palermo I wrote a new comedy called *This Was a Man*. It was primarily satirical and on the whole rather dull; the bulk of its dullness lay in the second act which was an attenuated duologue between two excessively irritating characters. The fact that the characters were intended to be irritating in no way mitigated the general boredom, and this vital error in construction ultimately cost the play its life.

On my return to London I showed it to Basil who thought it excellent, and so we sent it to Lord Cromer for a licence with the intention of producing it immediately after *Easy Virtue*. The licence, however, was refused, principally I think because of a scene in the last act when the husband, on being told that his annoying wife had committed adultery with his still more annoying best friend, bursts out laughing. The fact that the circumstances of the story made this behaviour more than permissible weighed not a jot with the board of censors who like their commandments broken solemnly or not at all; and so, after a little gleeful publicity in the Press, the play was shelved for later production in America.

Jane arrived three days before we were due to open *Easy Virtue,* and we travelled up to Manchester. The Manchester Watch Committee, for some strange reason known only to itself, refused to allow us to use the title *Easy Virtue,* and so it was announced merely as *A New Play in Three Acts.* At the cinema next door to the theatre a film entitled *Flames of Passion* was complacently advertised for the whole week: perhaps, however, the vigilance of the Watch Committee did not extend to mere celluloid. *A New Play in Three Acts* was a big success, and Jane made a gracious first-night speech, explaining that she was a stranger and rather scared, but that she already felt absolutely at home in dear Manchester. She was appropriately mobbed by the gallery girls at the stage door and conveyed in triumph to the Midland.

London fell into Jane's lap like a ripe plum. She made a tumultuous success and was immediately adored. She still played the end of the second act too emotionally, and the dramatic impact she gave to it still brought forth terrific cheering. The bulk of the critics sniffed superciliously at the play, but I was prepared for this and didn't mind much. The business was excellent, and everybody rightly felt that the London Theatre was the richer by the presence of a new and glamorous star.

(19)

Almost immediately after the production of *Easy Virtue, The Queen Was in the Parlour* went into rehearsal at the St. Martin's Theatre. The cast, headed by Madge Titheradge, included Herbert Marshall, Francis Lister, C. M. Hallard, Ada King and Lady Tree. The rehearsals were remarkable for the fact that Madge and Basil worked together in complete peace and harmony. By this time, having worked with Basil a good deal, I had grown to know him very well, not only as a producer but as a person. The two were in no way synonymous. As a man he was pleasant, occasionally gay with an almost childish abandon, and in his more relaxed moments exceedingly good company. As a producer he could be and frequently was a fiend. It was not that he meant to be in the least, but his genuine passion for perfection of detail, his technical thoroughness, and his tireless energy as a rule completely shut him off from any personal contact with his companies. He often blinked at me in amazement when I told him how bitterly he had offended So-and-So, or how unnecessarily cruel he had been when poor Miss Such-and-Such had been unable to get the right intonation. I don't think it ever occurred to him that actors' feelings are notoriously nearer to the surface than average people's; if they weren't they wouldn't be good actors. Every good surgeon knows that no operation, however swift and brilliant, can ultimately be considered a complete success if sensitive membranes and organs and viscera have been handled carelessly in the process. A first-rate theatrical producer should learn early on in his career that most actors wear their intestines on their sleeves. Basil's only real failing in the theatre was lack of psychological perceptiveness. His actors, on the whole, were terrified of him, frequently even stars of big reputation quailed before him. True, their fear took various forms, but it was there all right, under their blusterings and ragings and tearful refusals to do this or that. His knowledge and efficiency were undeniable and his personality was strong, but, generally, rehearsals under Basil were nerve-racking. Jane, who had fought him stubbornly step by step, finally won hands down, slightly at the expense of the play. Madge never fought him at all. She took his direction with enthusiasm, automatically changing anything she didn't approve of, but with such expert technique that I don't believe he ever noticed. She agreed with everything he said and emerged triumphantly at the end of it unruffled by anything but her own temperament. Her performance of *The Queen Was in the Parlour* was flawless both in its comedy values and its moments of tragedy. She gave to the play more reality and pathos than it actually deserved, and although as an experiment in Ruritanian romanticism it wasn't so bad, it was Madge, I am sure, aided by a brilliant cast and production, who made it the success it was.

(20)

We gave up the little house in Dockenfield and set to work to find somewhere less cramped and villa-ish and in deeper country than Surrey. There were many kindly memories attached to it. The first day when it had risen out of a thick fog to welcome us; long spring evenings when we had made toffee on its inadequate stove and listened to the rain dripping through the bathroom ceiling into a tin basin; lovely summer nights when we had driven down late from London, tearing much too fast over the long straight stretch of the Hog's Back, whirling through Farnham with only a few lights winking at us from the sleeping houses, finally arriving at that kind, silly little villa squatting on its haunches in a field.

I wanted, if possible, to be near the sea, and I naturally turned towards Kent where we had been so happy before. We stared at advertisements of houses to let in the *Kentish Times* until our eyes ached. None of them were any good. They were either too old and falling to pieces, or so new that they were horrible. Finally we were on the verge of fixing upon a more or less passable-looking red-brick house at Stone near Rye, when we had a letter from Mr. Body, our one-time neighbour at St. Mary's. He wanted to let his farm-house at Aldington and move into one that he had just built on the Marsh. Mother went down and saw it first and said it was all right, but rather poky; I went down a little later on and agreed with her, but as the rent was only fifty pounds a year and it had six acres of ground, electric light, and a garage, it seemed a good idea to take it for a year or so, still keeping a look-out for something better. It was called, floridly enough, 'Golden-hurst Farm.' There was the house proper which was lop-sided and had a Victorian air; jammed up against this was the 'new wing', a square edifice wearing perkily a pink corrugated tin roof and looking as though it had just dropped in on the way to the races. There was a muddy yard enclosed by thatched barns which were falling to pieces, there were two small ponds, five poplars, a ramshackle garden consisting almost entirely of hedges, and an ancient, deeply green orchard with thick grass and low-growing apple trees. At the end of the garden the land sloped away to the Military Canal and you could see across miles of marshes to Dymchurch and the sea wall. Beyond this the sea looked high as though it were painted on the sky; on clear nights the lights on the French coast glimmered along the horizon.

The house itself was indeed poky and quite hideous, made up into dark little rooms and passages, but there was a certain atmosphere about the place that felt soothing and somehow right, and so we decided to move in the moment the Bodys moved out in October.

(21)

Easy Virtue and *The Queen Was in the Parlour* ran along together for a little, and when *Easy Virtue* closed because Jane had to go back to America, *The Queen Was in the Parlour* was transferred from the St. Martin's to the Duke of York's. In the meantime, Basil was planning *The Constant Nymph* and suggested that I should play Lewis Dodd for the first month of the run. I wasn't at all keen as it was a heavy part and I was feeling exceedingly tired, also it meant postponing until November our production of *This Was a Man* in New York. However, Edna Best was to play Tessa, and after a good deal of argument both she and Basil prevailed upon me and we started rehearsals.

It was a crowded play and Basil tore himself and us to shreds over the production of it. As an actor it was excellent experience for me, being utterly unlike anything I had ever played before. Basil adamantly refused to allow me to use any of myself in it at all. I wasn't even permitted to smoke cigarettes, but had, with bitter distaste, to manœuvre a pipe. I had grown my hair long and put no grease on it for a month, consequently it was dry and fluffy and sparks from the pipe frequently blew up and set fire to it. In addition to the pipe, I wore purposely ill-fitting suits, and spectacles through which I peered short-sightedly; altogether I don't remember ever having been so thoroughly uncomfortable on the stage in my life. I hated Lewis Dodd whole-heartedly from the first rehearsal onwards. In the book his character was clearly defined and understandable; in the play he seemed to me to be a clumsy insensitive oaf with little to recommend him over and above the fact that he was supposed to be a musical genius. I say 'supposed to be' because, beyond a few modern piano chords and a burlesque opera in the first act and a little Scarlatti and a doggerel rhyme in the second, he betrayed no marked talent whatsoever. I was told, even by my most uncompromising critics, that I gave a fine and convincing performance, which still comforts me as I was under the impression then, and am still, that I was awful.

Edna gave a tender, exquisite portrayal of Tessa and was so gallant and moving in the death scene at the end that she almost made me forget my own dreariness.

The whole production with its multitude of small parts, ensemble scenes and minute details was magnificently done; the doing of it, however, was gruelling work. The party scene was Basil's pet, and we went over and over it endlessly until whatever spontaneity there might have been at the beginning set like cement in our joints, and we were unable even to remember our words. There was also a supper scene in the first act to which he was extremely attached. It had more props in it then *Ben Hur*. Plates, mugs, knives, forks, spoons, bread, jam, cheese, biscuits, ham, all of which had to be manipulated on cue. Wooden benches and tables and chairs had to be moved on to their correct marks for the opera scene immediately following it. Owing to there being so many of us there were no consecutive sentences lasting for more than a few lines, and so we had to listen like hawks and spear our cues out of the general chaos like fish from a boiling cauldron. The effect from the front was of course masterly, but the strain on the stage was unbelievable.

In the second act alone I had three two-minute changes; lounge suit to tails, back to lounge suit, and back to tails again; these changes were achieved frenziedly at the side of the stage usually in the pitch dark. Before the death scene I had only one minute in a black-out in which to change completely from evening clothes to flannel trousers, shirt, tie, thick socks, shoes, hat and coat, with the result that I generally shot on to the stage like a rabbit with no breath at all. It was worse than revue because once on, the scenes were long and difficult, whereas in revue nothing lasts longer than a few minutes.

That rehearsal period was a bad time for my unfortunate intimates. Lorn and Jack bore most of the brunt of it. I gave up the part publicly on Mondays, Wednesdays and Saturdays, and privately every night of the week. Basil, impervious to my wailings, kept my nose firmly to the grindstone, and I know whatever good there was in my performance was entirely due to him. Margaret Kennedy, the authoress, twittered in and out, endeavouring, with sudden bursts of the most obvious tact, to persuade me how good I was going to be, although I am certain that she had an unshakable conviction that I was as much like her beloved Lewis Dodd as the Queen of Sheba.

Mrs. Patrick Campbell rang me up on the day of the last dress rehearsal and implored me to allow her to come, explaining at

JACK

length that she was a poor unwanted old woman and couldn't afford seats for the first night. She arrived rather late, bearing in her arms a Pekinese which yapped insistently through the quieter scenes. The next morning, the actual day of production, she rang me up again. Her voice sounded sympathetic over the telephone, she said that she had enjoyed the play very much and that the little fair girl (Edna) was quite good, but that why, oh, why had I ever consented to play the part. 'You're the wrong *type!*' she moaned. 'You have no glamour and you should wear a beard!'

The play opened and was an immediate smashing success. I moved through the opening performance in a dull coma of depression. Jack appeared in my dressing-room after the second act and told me that everyone was saying how marvellous I was; this I took to be a well-intentioned but transparent lie, and asked him gloomily to go away and leave me alone, which, to my considerable irritation, he did. I played Lewis Dodd for just over three weeks, and then my nerves, resenting at last the strain that had been imposed upon them for the past two years, finally snapped and I went through one whole performance weeping for no reason whatever, to the bewilderment, not only of the audience, but of the cast as well. Edna guided and upheld me as well as she could, and at the end I subsided on to the floor of my dressing-room where I remained until my doctor arrived and gave me a strychnine injection and put me to bed.

I stayed in bed for a week without seeing anybody, and then, feeling slightly rested, insisted against the doctor's advice on sailing for New York.

I was certainly in no condition to enjoy the rehearsals of *This Was a Man;* indeed, even if I had been as radiant with health as a Phospherine advertisement, I doubt if I could have derived much pleasure from that dreariest of dreary productions.

My withdrawal from the cast of *The Constant Nymph* made no more difference to the business than if an aunt of Margaret Kennedy's had died in Scotland. John Gielgud took over Lewis Dodd and played it successfully for a year, pipe and all.

My first serious play, *The Rat Trap,* was produced at the Everyman Theatre while I was on the Olympic bound for New York, and so I never saw it; however, from what I gathered later from eyewitnesses, I didn't miss much.

The leading parts were played by Robert Harris, Joyce Kennedy and Mary Robson, and the smaller ones by Adrianne Allen, Elizabeth Pollock and Raymond Massey. But in spite of the effulgence of the cast, the play fizzled out at the end of its regulation two weeks. I was not particularly depressed about this; *The Rat Trap* was a dead love. Seven years had passed since I wrote it with so much ardour, and during those years its glory had been eclipsed by more balanced and mature work. It had achieved publication at least, and I could read it in my first volume of *Three Plays* with indulgent cluckings of the tongue at its youthful gaucheries. The two big scenes were still good, but the first act with its strained epigrams and laboured exposition of character, and the last act in which the heroine bravely admits that she is going to have a baby, thereby tying up the plot with a bow on the top, made me shudder, nostalgically, but with definite embarrassment. It was neither good enough nor bad enough to merit a West End run, and it was perhaps a mistake to have allowed it to be produced at all; however, no harm was done, and I am sure that it was admirable exercise for the actors.

On arrival in New York we set to work to find an attractive star to play the extremely unattractive part of Carol in *This Was a Man.* This was difficult, and it was only after considerable blandishments that we persuaded Francine Larrimore to do it. As a type she was miscast, but her name was a draw and she was a first-rate actress. The other principals were Auriol Lee, Nigel Bruce and A. E. Matthews.

The rehearsals were slow and uncomfortable and the tension increased by the fact that Basil's effect on Nigel Bruce was much the same as that of a python on a rabbit. Like so many large, bluff and hearty actors, Nigel was acutely sensitive and tremulous with nerves. He knew his lines perfectly until he stepped on to the stage, when, confronted by the menacing figure of Basil in the stalls, his moral legs became like spaghetti, his tongue clove to the roof of his mouth, and all coherence was lost in a flurry of agonised stammering. Francine was calm and doggedly efficient, although occasionally tearful; A. E. Matthews ambled through the play like a charming retriever who has buried a bone somewhere and can't remember where, and Auriol Lee snapped in and out like a jack-knife.

The first night was fashionable to a degree. Everybody who was anybody was there; that is, they were there up until the end of the second act, after which they weren't there any more. Jack and Gladys and I sat with neatly arranged first-night faces in a box and watched the theatre slowly emptying until the stall floor was almost deserted except for a few huddled groups of the faithful. We had the feeling that even they were only staying because the theatre was warm.

I must say that Basil had not done his best with the play; if the writing of it was slow, the production was practically stationary. The second-act dinner scene between Francine Larrimore and Nigel Bruce made *Parsifal* in its entirety seem like a quick-fire vaudeville sketch. The scene between Nigel Bruce and A. E. Matthews in the last act might have livened things up a little if A. E. Matthews had not elected to say the majority of his lines backwards; however, it didn't really matter for by then the play was down the drain anyhow. Gladys and Jack and I, after a few jocular condolences with the company, went back to the Ritz where we lapped up neat brandy in order to prepare ourselves for the inevitable party which was being given by Schuyler Parsons ostensibly in my honour.

It turned out to be a highly successful party where fortunately the glaring failure of the play was quickly dimmed by the arrival of the Queen of Roumania.

We all had some more brandy, and recent agonies receded

farther and farther away until suddenly George Jean Nathan appeared from behind somebody, shook me warmly by the hand, and said that he thought the play was excellent and had enjoyed it thoroughly. This was so unmistakably the crack of doom that I gave up even pretending to be cheerful and went disconsolately home to bed.

That two months' sojourn in America was altogether unsatisfactory. I felt far from well and lacking in energy when I arrived, and soon my nerves began to get really bad again. For so many hours of each day I felt all right and then, suddenly without warning, melancholia enveloped me like a thick cloud, blotting out the pleasure and colour from everything. It was a difficult malady to explain; a bursting head that didn't exactly ache but felt as though it were packed tightly with hot cotton wool; a vague, indefinable pain in my limbs when I lay down to rest, a metallic discomfort as though liquid tin had somehow got mixed up with my blood-stream, making sleep impossible and setting my teeth on edge.

I went off for two weeks to White Sulphur Springs with Jack in order to get fresh air and rest. I was unused to being in anything but the best of health, and was irritable and unhappy. We got up early every morning and rode peaceful horses up and down the mountain trails until lunch. There was nothing to do in the afternoons but lie about and read or write, and so I, of course, wrote.

I really should have rested completely, but I had promised Marie Tempest that I would write a comedy for her, and as an idea had been kicking about inside me for some time, I huffed and puffed and poured out nervous energy which I should have been conserving, and finally completed a pleasant little eighteenth-century joke called *The Marquise*. The last act was a bit weak, but I thought on the whole it would make a good evening's entertainment.

When it was finished I sent it to England and came back to New York in time to attend, with resigned lassitude, the last performance of *This Was a Man*.

There was no reason for me to stay any longer in America, and I didn't feel equal to going back to the cold and damp of London and facing the casting and rehearsing of *The Marquise*. I felt suddenly sick of the theatre and everything to do with it, sick of cities and high buildings and people and screeching traffic. I decided that the time had come for me to go away, right away from everyone I knew and everything that was familiar, so I procured hurriedly, before my determination cooled, passport visas, typhoid inoculations, some new suitcases, and a ticket for Hong Kong.

This sudden drastic decision jumped me for a little out of my nervous depression, and I set off across the continent with Jack, who, disapproving of the whole idea, insisted at least upon coming as far as San Francisco with me. He was right to disapprove because I was actually too tired and out of condition to make such a long trip all by myself, but I argued and insisted and finally convinced him that it was a case of kill or cure. If I didn't make a clean break and let a little new air into myself, I should probably, within a few months, subside into some gloomy mental nursing home in a state of complete nervous collapse. By going boldly out into the blue the very adventure of the thing would uphold me for a little while, and although I was fully prepared for days, perhaps weeks, of acute loneliness, Time in the long run, together with new sights and sounds and climates, would be sure to cobble up the rapidly widening holes in my nervous fabric.

Finally, on Christmas Day in the evening, I sailed for Hong Kong on the President Pierce. It was foggy and cold and, up to date, the wretchedest, most forlorn moment of my life. Sirens were blowing and a brassy band was playing. The air was filled with loud, sharp noises, and coloured paper streamers fluttered and stretched between the ship and the dock.

I watched Jack, my last link with familiar life, disappearing down the gangway wearing my fur coat which he was taking back to New York. He turned and waved once, with a very forced, gay smile, then as I couldn't see any more I went below to my cabin.

PART SEVEN

THE RECONSTRUCTION of despair is difficult. I find that now it is only with the utmost concentration that I can catch for a moment or two a clear memory of the profound unhappiness I suffered during those seven days on the President Pierce between San Francisco and Honolulu. It is grey and nebulous in my mind like the cloudiness on an X-ray photograph that marks a diseased area.

I can remember a few hours when I emerged from my cabin and, with almost hysterical vehemence, endeavoured to fling my miseries over the rail and into the past. But I was too tired and weak to sustain the gesture and back came the hosts of darkness, crowding me down into my cabin again, twitching my nerves with sharp fears for my sanity, and clouding the future with the most dismal forebodings.

Too much had happened to me in too short a time. I had written too much, acted too much, and lived far too strenuously. This was the pay-off; possibly, I thought, the full stop to my creative ability which I had strained and over-worked beyond its strength. My talent or flair for formulating ideas and dressing them up with words was squeezed dry and I felt convinced that I should never be able to write again. To add to my troubles, sleep evaded me and I spent many hours of every night trudging round the deserted decks until finally I persuaded the ship's doctor to give me some sort of sedative.

He was an amiable man but obtuse and offered me, in addition to the sedative, some kindly meant but irrelevant words of comfort. He seemed to be obsessed with the idea that lack of money was the only vital ill that the flesh was heir to, and regaled me with sad little stories about the engineer who only got so much a month and had three children, and the stoker who got even less and had five children and a wife with diabetes.

If my illness had been of the variety that profits from a counter-irritant, that foolish man would undoubtedly have effected a complete cure. As it was, his dullness and lack of understanding only served to emphasise my loneliness. I do not know if there were any amusing people on board, because I rarely came on deck except at night when everyone was asleep. I had a couple of radios from Gladys and Jack, whose intent to cheer made me almost suicidal, and I landed in Honolulu on a pearly blue-and-grey morning, with a temperature of a hundred and three, and a black loathing for the President Pierce, the ship's doctor, my Chinese room steward, the entire Dollar Line and everything connected with it.

Florence Magee had telegraphed to her friends the Walter Dillinghams, who lived in Honolulu, asking them to entertain me, and I was met on the dock by a smart Japanese chauffeur, who placed a *lei* of sweet-smelling flowers round my neck and informed me that Mrs. Dillingham was expecting me at the Peninsular. I, of course, had no idea where the Peninsular was, and he omitted to tell me that it was twenty miles away. We drove out through the town and into the country. I noted feverishly and without particular enthusiasm the luxuriant foliage and bright new colours. Bananas, palms, sugar canes, flame-in-the-forest, poinsettias and hibiscus flashed by, and the air was soft and cool for it was still early. I wondered what Mrs. Dillingham would be like and whether she would think I was drunk when I fell flat on my face at her feet. I had definitely decided not to continue my journey in the President Pierce, but I doubted whether I could hold out long enough to explain coherently that I was ill and wanted to go to bed.

We arrived at a Japanese house in a Japanese garden and Louise Dillingham came flying out, surrounded by dogs and children. She was a woman of abundant vitality, charming looking and smartly dressed, and almost before I had finished my halting explanations she had bundled me back into the car together with herself, the dogs and the children, and back we went at a great rate to the town I had just left. She expressed a hope en route that I was not too ill to come to the lunch party she had arranged for me; she said that the people she had invited were all absolutely delightful, and that I couldn't possibly fail to adore every one of them. After lunch, she added, we would see about getting me a comfortable room in the hotel, unless of course I preferred to come and stay with her. I gave a hurried glance at the dogs and the children and said in a weak voice but with a firm intonation that I would rather go to the hotel.

We whirled through the town and along a coast road fringed with gigantic palms until we reached La Pietra, the Dillingham home on Diamond Head. Even ill as I was I couldn't fail to notice the loveliness of that cool, pink house with its terraces and patios and tinkling fountains. The children and dogs disappeared miraculously the moment we arrived and I was left alone on the terrace with a strong whisky and soda, while Louise Dillingham changed her dress to receive the lunch guests. I lay in a swing chair under a 'Hau' tree looking out over a green valley to the deep-blue sea; the town was in the middle distance and purple mountains lay along the horizon. The whisky went to my head at once, and I could hardly stand up to receive the first guest, who happened to be a doctor. His name was Withington and, sensing sympathy in his manner, I explained quickly how dreadful I felt, and he promised to keep his eye on me. Then other people arrived and I have only a vague recollection of summer dresses, small talk, and hot little sausages on sticks.

We went into lunch and sat down at a shiny table. I concentrated on my plate because, whenever I looked up, people's faces seemed to rush close to me and then recede again like a badly cut film. About half-way through the meal I happened to see through the window the car turn into the drive and, suddenly realising that I could bear it all no longer, I got up from the table with a mumbled apology to Louise Dillingham, rushed downstairs and, jumping into the car, directed the chauffeur to drive to the boat. There I dismissed him and staggered on board and down to my cabin. The boat was deserted, and there was nobody to help me, but I managed by degrees to pack everything, collect a couple of deck hands, and get my luggage off and into the Customs House. I had to wait for about half an hour because another ship had just arrived, so I sat down on the ground with my back against a trunk until the officials were ready to deal with my bags. When they had passed them I had them piled on to a taxi and drove off to the Moana Hotel. By then I think my fever must have mounted still higher, because there were strange noises inside my head and I could hardly see. However, I contrived by a great effort of will to register my name at the desk and send a cable to Jack explaining my change of plans; after that I don't remember any more until I woke up in bed. Paul Withington, the doctor I had met at lunch, was in the room. He was calm, reasonable and wonderfully quiet; everything about him was quiet—face, movements and voice. He explained to me gently that I had a slight fever that was nothing to worry about and which would go down soon, and that he had given me a strong sleeping draught and something to make me sweat.

Of the two concoctions, the 'something to make me sweat' won easily. I woke up soaked every hour or so during the night and had to rub myself down and change beds.

The din outside on the beach and in the streets was terrific owing to it being New Year's Eve; it seemed as though the entire Chinese population of Honolulu had chosen the immediate vicinity of the Moana Hotel to blow their squeakers and let off their fire crackers.

The next morning, and several times a day for a week, Paul Withington appeared bringing me books and more sedatives and bunches of vivid tropical flowers from the Dillingham's garden. My fever gradually subsided and towards the end of the week I was able to sit up for a few hours a day and watch from the window the beach boys riding the surf. They came flying in over the rollers like animated bronze statuettes; and marvelling at their grace and agility, I wondered miserably whether I should ever be able to lift a hand or a foot again without gasping with exhaustion.

Paul Withington gave me a meticulously thorough examination when I was strong enough to get to his office. Everything about me was tested in order to discover the cause of my fever for which there seemed to be no apparent reason whatever. Finally, in the X-ray photographs, he pounced on the long-since healed tubercular scar on my lung and announced with clinical triumph, but strange lack of psychological consideration, that I had T.B.

This I didn't really believe for a moment, but it was an unpleasant possibility to go to bed with. Fortunately my earlier T.B. experiences at Dr. Etlinger's sanatorium and with Ned Lathom at Davos reassured me a good deal. As far as I could see, I had none of the symptoms. I had lost only a little weight from the fever and now that it had gone I didn't sweat at night at all; my breathing was sound and I had no cough. All the same, my imagination worked over-time for a few days, visualising the future years as an attenuated procession from sanatorium to sanatorium surrounded by the well-known T.B. paraphernalia; doctors, nurses, lung inflations, sputum cups, and chill beds on snow-covered verandas. It was not a cheerful vision, but it gave me something definite to fight and, oddly enough, stimulated my nerves. I decided that however long it took I would lie in the sun and fresh air until all possibility of such horror should be completely eliminated.

The Dillinghams, with infinite kindness, told me that their ranch at Mokuleia on the other side of the island was at my disposal for as long as I liked. A French caretaker and his wife lived near by and would cook meals for me; apart from them nobody would speak to me or worry me and I had nothing to do but sleep and relax and get well.

I accepted gratefully and a day or two later Paul Withington drove me there, with a suitcase and a few books packed into the back of his car.

There are some places in the world that charm the spirit on sight; Mokuleia was one of them. A soothing graciousness seemed to emanate from it.

The ranch itself lay at the foot of a high mountain and was built on three sides of a square. The middle part was one big room opening on to a veranda; the bedrooms were on either side. At the back an avenue of enormous royal palms led to the foot of the mountain. In the front was a sweep of grass, a tall eucalyptus tree, and then a banana and sugar plantation, through which a little road led to a small copse of pines and then to the sea. Although it was over a mile away, you could hear from the veranda the noise of the surf pounding ceaselessly on the reef like muffled thunder. The beach itself was a semi-circle of gleaming white sand that shelved steeply into deep water and in which it was perfectly safe to bathe because the reef was a protection against barracudas and sharks.

We arrived in the evening, just after sundown. Mme. Thevenin, the caretaker's wife, greeted us with an omelette and coffee and freshly baked bread. She was a round little woman with a kind, comfortable face.

The twilight changed swiftly to darkness and then the moon came up as suddenly as though someone were jerking it through the sky on a string. After supper we drove down to the sea; the pinewood was ghostly with shadows but the beach was almost as light as day and we took off our clothes and swam out through the warm surf into deep water.

Presently it was time for Paul Withington to go back to Honolulu, so he dropped me at the ranch and drove off. I watched the taillights of his car disappearing down the road and when the noise of it had died away I stayed for a little, sitting on the veranda rail and listening to all the various unfamiliar sounds of the night. There were tree fogs and cicadas and lizards and some strange hooting little bird in a tree not far off. The air was heavy with the sweet scent of night-blooming cereus, and presently, fearing that the spell might be broken by a sudden attack of scare or loneliness, I went to bed and slept deeply and dreamlessly for the first time for weeks.

(2)

I stayed at Mokuleia for several weeks. Occasionally Paul Withington and Constance, his wife, drove out to visit me, and we had picnics on the veranda or on the beach; apart from them I saw no one but the Thevenins. Their house was at the end of the garden, and I had all my meals with them; breakfast at six-thirty, lunch at one, and dinner at seven. Although their English was reasonably good, we spoke mostly in French. M. Thevenin had a fine face, white hair, and piercing blue eyes which flashed cold fire whenever he was propounding his extremely violent political opinions; and as this was practically all the time, they flashed a good deal. My French was not fluent enough for me to be able to argue really satisfactorily, and so I filled in agreeably with enough *'ouis'* and *'c'est vrais'* to make him feel that his eloquence was not being entirely wasted.

There was a ferocious bull-terrier chained up in the yard who bared his teeth and snarled whenever anyone went near him. The Thevenins assured me that he was dangerous, but I had a feeling that he was bluffing and so one day I boldly offered him my hand to bite. This embarrassed him horribly, and he seemed at a loss to know what to do with it. Finally, he licked it apologetically and from then onwards he spent most of his time with me, accompanying me down to the beach every morning, sleeping on my chest during my afternoon siesta on the veranda, and walking with me through the plantations in the cool of the evening.

The big moment of every morning was eleven o'clock, when one train a day rattled across the little wooden bridge just behind the beach, and disappeared into the hills. Owgooste always heard it before I did and started barking, whereupon I sprang up from the sand and raced to the top of a dune in time to wave my towel, forgetting in the excitement of the moment that I was stark naked. This, the Dillinghams told me later, shocked immeasurably many of the native passengers and also the engine driver.

Frequently, during the early part of my time there, I had bad hours when the peaceful charm of the place turned suddenly sour and I felt neglected and far away. These black patches were usually caused by the arrival of a cable from Mother or Gladys or Jack asking how I was and when I planned to return. In the instant of reading them peace slipped away from me and a troubled restlessness took its place. My mind's eye blinked resentfully at the vivid colours all round me and ached for the gentle greens and greys of Kentish marshes, the familiar procession of red buses trundling down Piccadilly, or the garish lights of Broadway at night. A longing to be within reach of the things and people I knew tugged at my heart-strings, robbing me of my appetite and making me irritable and snappy with the Thevenins.

I could, of course, go back quite easily. There was nothing to hold me there except my own private vow not to budge until I felt, beyond doubt, that I was completely cured.

There were many things to be adjusted before I could consider myself really fit to plunge once more into the strenuous life that had so nearly wrecked me. Not only my physical health; that was coming along beautifully; I was already burnt black by the sun and sleeping and eating well, but my mind needed a great deal more solitude and a great deal more time before it could safely be guaranteed to function as I intended it to function. I meant to take no more chances. Never again would I allow myself to sink into that pit of unreasoning dreads and despairs. I had scrambled out by the skin of my teeth and intended to stay out for the rest of my life. In those long hours alone, lying on the hot sand with the noise of the sea in my ears, or on the veranda, rocking gently in the swing chair, or wandering along the dark roads in the evening, I had had time to round up an imposing array of past mistakes. It seemed that I had not only burnt the candle at both ends, but in the middle as well, and with too strong a flame. From now onwards there was going to be very little energy wasted, and very little vitality spilled unnecessarily.

People, I decided, were the danger. People were greedy and predatory, and if you gave them the chance, they would steal unscrupulously the heart and soul out of you without really wanting to or even meaning to. A little extra personality; a publicised name; a little entertainment value above the average; and there they were, snatching and grabbing, clamorous in their demands, draining your strength to add a little fuel to their social bonfires. Then when the time came when you were tired, no longer quite so resilient, you were pushed back into the shadows, consigned to the dust and left to moulder in the box-room like a once smart hat that is no longer fashionable.

I remembered the chic, crowded first night of *This Was a Man* in New York. Three-quarters of the people present I knew personally. They had swamped me, in the past, with their superlatives and facile appreciations. I had played and sung to them at their parties, allowing them to use me with pride as a new lion who roared amenably. I remembered how hurriedly they left the theatre the moment they realised that the play wasn't quite coming up to their expectations; unable, even in the cause of good manners, to face only for an hour or so the possibility of being bored. True, there was no reason why they should stay. They had paid for their seats, most of them, and they were under no obligation to me or the management. I felt no bitterness towards them, no bitterness, that is, beyond a realisation of their quality, a forewarning of what to expect if I continued to fail.

I sorted them out, those names and chinchilla wraps and piqué evening shirts, and stacked them neatly along the rail at the end of the veranda. On the other side, a few more dimensional individuals sat at ease. These were a little cleverer, more reliable, and could be counted on for certain hours of pleasant companionship providing one didn't ask too much or allow the burden of acquaintanceship to weigh too heavily on their shoulders. In the centre of the lawn, against the shadow of the eucalyptus tree, half-a-dozen figures moved into the light moonshine. These were my friends and I was glad that there were so many.

(3)

I firmly resisted the temptation to work during those weeks. This was difficult, as I had soon got through most of the books in the ranch that were readable, and there was nothing whatever to do in the evenings.

A tune certainly did slip through the barricade one day while

I was on the beach and, between waking and dozing in the sun, I lazily fitted words to it. It lay forgotten at the back of my mind for many months until it emerged, nearly a year later, as 'A Room with a View.'

Apart from this, my vegetation was complete, until one day the urge to return home became too insistent to disregard any longer, and I went back to Honolulu to make plans for sailing.

At last, on a still, crystal-clear evening, I sailed on a stumpy little ship called The Wilhelmina. Few passengers were on board, but those were nice, particularly the Paepckes, a young American couple whom I had already met with the Dillinghams. Lots of people came down to see us off and we were loaded with leis of every flower imaginable.

The Wilhelmina sailed out of the harbour to the strains of 'Aloha', played and sung by a band of Hawaiians on the dock; the coloured streamers snapped and broke, and the plaintive music followed us out over a sea that looked like grey oiled silk. There was so little breeze that the tall palms on Waikiki could only wave languidly as we passed.

I stayed on deck looking out through the gathering dusk until Diamond Head loomed over the port bow. I could see lights in the Dillingham house and others springing up along the coast.

There is a superstition in Hawaii that travellers who are sailing away, and wish to return to the islands, must drop the flower leis that have been given them into the wake of the ship.

I remembered Mokuleia, the little road winding down through the plantations, Owgooste, the light shining from the cosy sitting-room of the Thevenins' house and making shadows across the lawn, the pinewood, and the thunder of the surf on the reef, and with a nostalgia that a few weeks ago I could not have believed possible, I dropped my leis one by one into the sea.

PART EIGHT

DURING THE ENSUING YEAR the realisation that my nervous disorders, fevers and despairs, culminating in those rejuvenating weeks in Honolulu, had come at a very opportune moment, was brought forcibly home to me. I discovered that I had need of every ounce of the moral and nervous stamina that the rest had stored up in me.

My various reunions went off satisfactorily. Jack and Gladys met me in New York, both looking much younger and nicer than when I had left them. The Olympic, in which Jack and I sailed to England, had been repainted. Lorn was gay and in the best of spirits, Mother was well and delighted with Goldenhurst, and *The Marquise* had opened at the Criterion Theatre and was a big success. I went to it on the night of my arrival. It was beautifully played by Marie Tempest, W. Graham Browne and Frank Cellier, and William Nicholson had designed an accurate and charming setting.

The spring and summer passed agreeably and without agitation. To begin with, Jack and I discovered during the first weekend we spent at Goldenhurst that, beneath its tiled fire-places and hideous wallpapers, it was really a fine old seventeenth-century farm-house groaning with oak beams which a surveyor from Folkestone told us were free from dry rot and in perfect condition. We immediately bought the house and grounds freehold at a ridiculously small price and set to work to make improvements.

We knocked walls down right and left and banished all family horrors of sentimental value into Mother's and Auntie Vida's bedrooms, substituting for them solid oak furniture from every antique shop within a radius of fifty miles.

Mother and Auntie Vida wailed a good deal at first, but we over-rode their protests; later on they admitted that they were very proud and pleased that we had.

In the late spring Jack and I went to Vienna to see the first performance of *The Marquise* at the Volkstheater. It was played by a celebrated German actor named Albert Basserman, who, I believe, only consented to play it because the Marie Tempest part provided a fine opportunity for Frau Basserman, his wife. She, I gathered from current gossip, was not quite such a public idol as he was.

The whole thing was rather bewildering. We arrived only an hour before curtain time, dressed hurriedly at the Bristol Hotel, and were escorted to a stage box by several directors and the translator, who, in the scramble, had omitted to explain to me that he had taken the liberty of transposing the period of the play from the eighteenth century to the present day.

My lack of knowledge of German prevented me from discovering this until about ten minutes after the beginning of the first act; up to then I had been under the impression that we were watching a curtain raiser. When finally I caught the word 'Eloise', which was the heroine's name, and observed Frau Basserman enter in a red leather motor coat, the truth dawned upon me and I laughed so much that I nearly fell out of the box.

I gathered from Albert Basserman's performance that he was primarily a tragedian, as his idea of comedy consisted of little beyond sudden bull-like roarings and noisy slappings of his own face. Frau Basserman, on the other hand, was going to be a comedienne or die. This, apparently, was her big opportunity to establish herself once and for all as a light soubrette, and it was clear that she intended to leave not a stone unturned. Unfortunately her stage experience, like her husband's, had obviously been hitherto confined to heavier rôles and her comic resources were limited to a repeated wrinkling of the nose, as though she were going to sneeze, and an incessant giggle.

There was, however, an utterly delightful performance of the ingénue part by a comparatively unknown young actress named

Paula Wessely, who, I am gratified to know, is now one of the greatest stars in her own country.

At the end of the play I was called on to the stage and, hand-in-hand with the Bassermans, took endless curtain calls. Finally a group of students clambered over the footlights with a zeal that I could not but feel was out of proportion to the merits of either the play or the performance, and we all signed autographs, thereby setting the seal of success upon what had been, for me at any rate, a thoroughly hilarious evening.

(2)

During the summer I wrote a comedy called *Home Chat*. It had some excellent lines and a reasonably funny situation, but I was not entirely pleased with it. However, I read it to Madge Titheradge, for whom I had visualised the leading part, and she liked it, and as Basil, also, thought it good, we settled to do it in the early autumn.

Gladys came back from America with a hard black hat and mumps, having severed finally her connection with the Civic Repertory Company.

Lynn and Alfred appeared, too, later on in the summer and came down to Goldenhurst. They had just finished playing S. N. Behrman's comedy *The Second Man* for the Guild, and were extremely enthusiastic about it as a play for me. A cast of only four characters made it comparatively simple for them to play the whole thing through for me in the drawing-room, which they did immediately. A certain amount of argument sprang up between them, and Alfred forgot one of the most important scenes and burst into tears, but I gathered enough inspiration from their performance to set about getting hold of the rights of the play at once.

I discovered that Macleod and Mayer held the English rights and were planning to do it in the late autumn, but I managed to persuade them to wait for me and do it in January instead.

Basil had for a long while been anxious to produce *Sirocco*, the play I had written in New York in 1921, and after we had had a series of discussions about it, I re-wrote a great deal of it and we decided to put it into rehearsal directly after we had launched *Home Chat*.

Having thus light-heartedly sealed my doom, I spent a charming holiday with the Cole Porters in Venice and returned home fairly crackling with health and optimism to start work. The cast of *Home Chat* was good and rehearsals proceeded with sinister smoothness.

On the first night I suspected, early, with growing certainty, that we were in for a bad failure. The audience was restless, particularly in the cheaper parts, and I recognised danger in their whisperings and scufflings. Basil had not been insistent enough on tempo during rehearsals, with the result that the play moved with admirable realism, but too slowly. Poor Nina Boucicault, who was playing Madge's mother, and had not acted for some time, was horribly nervous and dried up on several of her lines, thereby creating long pauses which, in addition to those that Basil had put in purposely, brought the action frequently to a standstill. I writhed about on my chair in the box, sniffing disaster and seeing no way of averting it. Madge, with her unfailing ear, did her best to quicken things up, but it was of no avail, and at the final curtain there was booing from the gallery and the pit.

I dashed through the pass door and on to the stage as quickly as I could, feeling that it was unfair for the company to bear the brunt all by themselves. Basil was nowhere to be seen and the stage manager was in a panic.

The moment I appeared the booing became a good deal louder and then subsided as I advanced to the footlights. My intention was to ignore all hostility, thank the audience briefly but insincerely for their kind reception, and get the curtain down as quickly as possible, but just as I was about to speak, a voice yelled 'Rotten' from the pit and another one shouted from the gallery: 'We expected a better play!' whereupon I snapped back that I expected better manners, and the curtain fell amid considerable tumult.

The notices the next day were all bad. Some contented themselves with supercilious patronage while the rest were frankly abusive and the business, needless to say, did not profit by them.

(3)

The two principal parts in *Sirocco* were played by Ivor Novello and Frances Doble, and the only theatre available was Daly's which had housed nothing but musical comedies for many years.

Basil took infinite pains over the production, and although the *festa* scene in the second act was considered by some to be over-elaborate, I personally thought it a superb piece of ensemble work.

Ivor was a difficult proposition. Although his looks were marvellous for the part, and his name, owing to film successes, was a big draw, his acting experience in those days was negligible. I must say, however, that he worked like a slave and endeavoured, to the best of his ability, to do everything that Basil told him. Unlike Nigel Bruce, he was not in the least fussed or nervestricken and, although Basil at various times brought up all his artillery, gentle sarcasm, withering contempt, sharp irascibility, and occasionally full-throated roaring, Ivor remained unimpressed, behaving on the whole gaily, as though he were at a party.

Frances Doble was frankly terrified from beginning to end. She looked lovely, but, like Ivor, lacked technique. On the whole, she gave a good performance, although it ultimately transpired neither she nor Ivor had at that time strength or knowledge enough to carry those two very difficult parts. The play, I think, was fairly good. The characterisation was clear, and although the story was a trifle thin in texture, it seemed to me that it should be strong enough to hold.

On the evening of the first performance Mother, Gladys, Jack and I, elaborately dressed and twittering with nerves, dined at the Ivy. Abel, the proprietor, stood us champagne cocktails, and we drove to the theatre in good time to go back-stage and wish everybody success.

When we went into the box, I noticed, over the squeaking and scraping of the refined quintet in the orchestra pit, the familiar sound of restlessness in the upper parts of the house. The gallery was jammed—mostly, I suspected, with Ivor's film fans. The atmosphere in the theatre was certainly uneasy, and when the house lights went down, my heart went down with them.

(4)

Probably nobody not connected with the theatre could appreciate fully the tension and strain of that dreadful evening. The first night of any play is uncomfortable enough for those who are intimately concerned with it.

And in the case of *Sirocco* it was a losing battle from the word 'go.'

The first act was received dully. Ivor got a big reception from the gallery when he came on; apart from that there was nothing but oppressive stillness, broken, only very occasionally, by two or three half-hearted titters on certain comedy lines.

The curtain fell to scattered applause, and in the orchestra pit a quintet, with almost shocking vivacity, struck up the Henry the VIII dances. G. B. Stern came to my box and said that she was sitting at the back of the stalls close to the pit, and that there was going to be trouble.

Jack's face assumed a slightly greenish tinge, Gladys's chin shot up so high that I was afraid she would rick her neck. Mother, unaware of impending disaster, waved to Mme. Novello Davies at the opposite side of the theatre, and the second act started.

The storm broke during Ivor's love scene with Bunny Doble. The gallery shrieked with mirth and made sucking sounds when he kissed her, and from then onwards proceeded to punctuate every line with catcalls and various other animal noises.

The last act was chaos from beginning to end. The gallery, upper-circle and pit hooted and yelled, while the stalls, boxes and dress-circle whispered and shushed. Most of the lines weren't heard at all. Ivor and Bunny and the rest of the cast struggled on doggedly, trying to shut their ears to the noise and get the torture done with as quickly as possible.

The curtain finally fell amid a bedlam of sound, and even Mother, who was slightly deaf, was forced to realise that all was not quite as it should be. I remember her turning to me in the darkness and saying wistfully: 'Is it a failure?'

I replied, without quibbling, that it was probably the bloodiest failure in the history of the English Theatre, and rushed through the pass door on to the stage.

During the first act I had felt utterly miserable. The sense of hostility was strong in the house and I knew it was directed against me. The second-act commotion jumped me from misery into anger, and by the last act I was in a white-hot fury. I don't ever remember being so profoundly enraged in my whole life. I could think of no way to account for this violent change of public feeling towards me. The failure of *Home Chat* had not been important enough to cause it, and *Sirocco* as a play, although far from perfect, was at least superior in quality and entertainment value to many plays running successfully in London at the moment.

Whether or not the demonstration was organised by personal enemies I neither knew nor cared, I was conscious only of an overwhelming desire to come to grips in some way or other with that vulgar, ill-mannered rabble. When I reached the side of the stage, Basil, who never attended first nights of his own productions, and had been quietly dining somewhere, was standing in the prompt corner smiling and ringing the curtain up and down. From where we stood, the tumult in the front of the house might conceivably be mistaken for cheering and he, having no idea of the horrors of the evening, was happily convinced that it was.

I quickly disillusioned him and walked on to the stage. Without once looking at the audience I went along the frightened line of the company to the centre, shook hands with Ivor, kissed Bunny Doble's hand, presenting my behind to the public as I did so, and walked off again.

This, as I expected, increased the booing ten thousandfold. I whispered hurriedly to Basil that I was going on again and that he was to take the curtain up and keep it up until I gave him the signal. If we were to have a failure I was determined that it should be a full-blooded one.

I went on again and stood in the centre, a little in front of Bunny and Ivor, bowing and smiling my grateful thanks to the angriest uproar I have ever heard in a theatre. They yelled abuse at me, booed, made what is known in theatrical terms as 'raspberries', hissed and shrieked. People stood up in the stalls and shouted protests, and altogether the din was indescribable.

It was definitely one of the most interesting experiences of my life and, my anger and contempt having reduced me to a cold numbness, I was able almost to enjoy it.

I stood there actually for about seven minutes until their larynxes became raw and their breath failed and the row abated a little. Then someone started yelling 'Frances Doble'; it was taken up, and she stepped forward, the tears from her recent emotional scene still drying on her face, and, in the sudden silence following what had been the first friendly applause throughout the whole evening, said in a voice tremulous with nerves: 'Ladies and gentlemen, this is the happiest moment of my life.'

I heard Ivor give a gurgle behind me and I broke into laughter, which started a fresh outburst of booing and catcalls. Bunny stepped back, scarlet in the face, and I signalled to Basil to bring the curtain down.

Ivor's behaviour all through was remarkable. He had played a long and strenuous part in the face of dreadful odds without betraying for an instant that he was even conscious of them, and at the end, with full realisation that all his trouble and hard work had gone for less than nothing, his sense of humour was still clear and strong enough to enable him to make a joke of the whole thing. Nor was he apparently in the least ruffled by the inevitable Press blast the next day. He made no complaints, attached no blame or responsibilities to anyone, and accepted failure with the same grace with which he has always accepted success.

The evening for me, however, was not quite over. The fireman sent a message to me in Ivor's dressing-room, where we were all drinking champagne in a state of dazed hysteria, to say that there was a hostile crowd outside the stage door and that it would be wiser for me to leave by the front of the house. This information refuelled my rage and I went immediately up to the stage door. The alley was thronged with people who yelled when I appeared. I surveyed them for a moment from the steps, wearing what I hoped was an expression of utter contempt, and then pushed my way through to the car. Several of them spat at me as I passed, and the next day I had to send my evening coat to the cleaners.

(5)

The next morning Lorn appeared early in my bedroom and peered at me sympathetically over an armful of newspapers. 'This time, my darling,' she said, 'we have undoubtedly bought it!'

I read carefully through every notice and was interested to discover that in not one of them was there so much as a kindly word. I noted also, however, that the notices themselves were much longer than those usually accorded to failures.

There was an unmistakable note of glee discernible in most of them. It seemed that all along, for the past three years, since *The Vortex,* the bulk of the critics had known that my success was ephemeral, merely a foolish whim of the public's, and based upon a little merit beyond a superficial facility for writing amusing lines. There was little or no surprise that a play of mine should be so appallingly bad, for, in their minds at least, I had never been anything but a flash in the pan, a playboy whose meteoric rise could only result in an equally meteoric fall into swift oblivion. In fact, so general was the conviction that I was done for, that several journalists announced it in so many words.

There were, however, two notable exceptions. One was St. John Ervine, who wrote an impartial, careful criticism of the play with no malice, and even a certain amount of praise, and the other was Edgar Wallace who, although we had never met, took the trouble to write a long article in my defence, warning the gentlemen of the Press that their announcements, in his opinion at any rate, were not only unsporting but distinctly premature; this heartened me a great deal.

We certainly passed a gloomy enough morning; Lorn, Jack, Gladys and I, sitting round in my bedroom, drinking coffee, and deciding what was best to be done. Even the comfort of knowing that the house was sold out for three days was denied us, for when we rang up the box office we were told that more than half the seats already booked had been returned.

My first instinct was to leave England immediately, but this seemed too craven a move and also too gratifying to my enemies, whose numbers by then had swollen in our minds to practically the entire population of the British Isles.

We finally came to the conclusion that the best plan was for me to brazen things out for a week, to be seen everywhere, and to try, as convincingly as possible, to make light of the whole fiasco. After that it seemed best to go away, preferably to America, writing first, of course, to Macleod and Mayer asking them to release me from my *Second Man* contract, and also to Cochran, for whom I had agreed to write a new revue.

It seemed absurd to embark on further theatrical enterprise in London with the Press and the public so obviously against me. An absence of a year or so would give them time to forget and enable me to make a come-back with a more reasonable chance of success.

Having decided upon this, we strapped on our armour, let down our visors, and went to the Ivy for lunch.

The Ivy looked much the same as usual. Perhaps it was our over-wrought nerves that sensed a sinister quality in the atmosphere. So often, after success, we had filed in triumphantly to our usual table in the corner, just to the right of the door, receiving congratulations modestly, and trying not to allow too much cocksureness to colour our jokes. This time our task was more difficult. A line had to be drawn between what we felt and what we wanted people to think we felt. It wasn't unfriendliness exactly that we had to combat. Most of the Ivy's clientele were essentially well disposed towards us; indeed, on this occasion, kindly sympathy was all too apparent in every eye.

This had to be accepted with tempered gratitude. Condolences were harder to handle than congratulations, particularly as we felt them to be more whole-heartedly sincere.

Our table was in no way isolated. We were not ostracised for a moment, in fact the rush was quite flattering. Expressions of shocked horror, revilings of the shameful manners of first-nighters, scornful recriminations of the Press, rattled on to our plates and splashed into our dry Martinis. If I had expected even the most embittered character actresses to rise up and spit at me, I was doomed to disappointment. In fact, the whole thing, after the first few difficult moments, went with a swing.

Realising that the eyes of Lorn and Gladys and Jack were set upon me with an almost clinical watchfulness, I was constantly wary that no undue bitterness should sully my replies, nor, on the other hand, any over-done jocularity either. A too-casual attitude would be obviously false and recognised at once, whereas any indication of the real anger and humiliation I felt would not be in keeping with the gay, cynical, playboy-of-the-theatre tradition which had proved such a useful façade for so long. Also, I considered, without rancour, that my real feelings were nobody's business but my own.

Doubtless the reader will wonder why, in the circumstances, we went to the Ivy at all. Why, in addition to the strain and anxiety of the night before, and in the face of such thorough-going disaster, we elected to make ourselves the target for possibly still further slings and arrows. The reader will also probably say to himself or herself: 'How foolish, how unnecessary, and, above all, how conceited to imagine that the mere failure of a play was of such importance. To believe, for an instant, that the Press and the public were really interested enough in so small an event as to feel exultant.'

In this the reader would be completely justified. Even at the time we realised in our hearts that the bulk of the public knew nothing about *Sirocco* and cared less. The theatre world, however, was different, and it was with the theatre world that we had to deal. We went to the Ivy that day as a gesture. Not to our friends, nor our acquaintances, nor our enemies, but to ourselves. Nor was it entirely a gesture of defiance. To hang our heads in private and not be seen about anywhere would only make our ultimate emergence more embarrassing, and it seemed much more sensible to take the bull, however fetid its breath, by the horns at the outset.

Ivor, we were delighted to see, had decided upon the same course, and was sitting, surrounded by his coterie, at a large table just opposite to us. His gaiety seemed, even to me, to be genuine, and we all joined up for coffee and discussed the miseries of the night before with growing hilarity, and it wasn't until we had separated and gone our different ways that I realised that, on the whole, I had enjoyed myself.

(6)

After an unpleasant week in London, a week of lunches and dinners and suppers during which *Sirocco* was discussed interminably, by me with an air of semi-humorous resignation, nicely adjusted and not too semi-humorous, and by everyone else with various degrees of anger, conjecture, pleasure, wit, shocked astonishment, and sympathy, I went to Paris, where Jack and I stayed with Edward Molyneux in Neuilly for a while before going on to St. Moritz for Christmas.

Macleod and Mayer had gallantly refused to release me from my contract for *The Second Man* and Cochran had almost laughed at me for wishing to postpone doing his revue. He said, with a kindly wisdom born of many years of battling with success and failure, that in a few weeks' time any hubbub over *Sirocco* would be entirely forgotten and that he was quite sure that the revue would turn out to be a triumphant one in the eye for the lot of them.

I was grateful to him for this. His faith in me was so genuinely unimpaired, and although I wouldn't have blamed him if it hadn't been, I was extremely glad. It was altogether a sentimental interview, sentimental in the best sense of the word. He, more than most people, perceived beneath my business-like nonchalance a certain vague scurry of apprehensions. I was scared inside, scared that perhaps, after all, the Press were right, that I was really nothing better than the flash in the pan, the over-bright little star they had so caustically described. These fears were far from concrete, and received from me, even in my dimmest moments, no actual recognition. But, on looking back, I know they were there, swimming about in my subconscious, trying to clamber out and shake themselves like beetles striving to escape from a bathtub. I rescued them later, quite a while later, and, after scrutinising them thoroughly, squashed them with murderous satisfaction.

Then, however, I needed outside manifestations of confidence in my ability, and Cockie bolstered me generously. No gleam in his eye indicated that he remembered my past shrill quarrels with him; no suggestion of veiled patronage. It was, as I said before, a thoroughly sentimental interview because, above all things, Cockie's sentiment rises supreme in failure. It is, I am sure, through his failures that he has made his friends. No other theatrical manager that I have ever known can rally adherents so swiftly in catastrophe. Temperamental stars demand to be allowed to pawn their jewelry for him. Chorus girls, stage managers, members of his office staff, eagerly offer him their services indefinitely for nothing. Even hard-boiled backers rush through the flames with their cheque books over their mouths to aid him, regardless of the fact that the flames are probably consuming many of their own investments.

We discussed some of my already formulated ideas for the revue. This time there was no question raised as to the advisability of anyone else having anything to do with it. The whole show was to be mine; music, book, lyrics and supervision of production. The cast was to be headed by Maisie Gay, Jessie Matthews, Sonnie Hale and a Viennese dancer called Tilly Losch, whom Cockie had seen with Reinhardt and considered brilliant.

I remember leaving his office much cheered and with a new tune whirling round in my head, a tune to which the words 'Dance, Dance, Dance, Little Lady' had resolutely set themselves even before I got home to the piano.

I fear, however, that Jack and Edward had a bad time with me in Paris as for many hours of the day I was what is known as 'a prey to melancholy.' My moods of depression were in no way mitigated by the English papers, which can be obtained far too easily in that gayest of gay cities.

In everyone I chanced to look at, daily or weekly, I was confronted by either unpleasantly veiled or direct allusions to my recent débâcle. I should, of course, far from being upset, have congratulated myself on the stringy persistence of my news value; no other dramatist that I could remember, with the exception of Bernard Shaw, having been the object of such a sustained attack for many years. However, I was upset, exceedingly upset. It seemed strange that the various editors should permit such redundant flogging of a dead donkey, unless perhaps they had a suspicion that, after all, the donkey might not be quite dead, and wished to make sure. At all events, I formed a vicious little resolution then and there that in the future, however many triumphs I might achieve, I would never again, in any circumstances, give an interview to the London Press.

Never again should their readers be gratified by my opinion of 'The Modern Girl.' Henceforward, my views on Birth Control, Television, Long Skirts, D. H. Lawrence, Free Love and Bicycling Waitresses should be locked in my own bosom and, strange as it may seem, good resolutions as a rule being so frequently trodden into the dust by the march of Time, I have adhered to that vow ever since.

With the passing of the years, of course, even the memory of my disgust has evaporated and my feelings towards the Press are friendly in the extreme and I hope will remain so. But the resolution still holds firmly and gratefully, for the simple reason that it saves me an incalculable amount of time.

Edward's quiet, lovely little house in Neuilly presently began to soothe me down a bit. It had been at one time a royal pavilion attached to the French court, and there was enveloping it an atmosphere of departed glory. The high trees in the garden bowed sadly in the winter wind; they seemed tremendously dignified and long since resigned to the shock of a revolution which had swept away all familiar charm and elegance, a revolution, I could not help reflecting, whose impact on world history had on the whole been more serious than the screeching of a few gallery girls in a London theatre.

(7)

The Second Man was a witty comedy, with only four characters in it and my part, Clark Storey, a cynical, intelligent dilettante, was the pivot around which the play revolved. It was, in consequence, extremely long and, owing to the author's unrestrained passion for the Oxford Dictionary, very difficult to learn. There was, however, much wisdom and charm in the lines, and by devoting a few hours of every day to it in St. Moritz, I managed to learn it by the time rehearsals started.

The other three parts in the play were played by Zena Dare, Ursula Jeans and Raymond Massey. Basil Dean produced with commendable gentleness which was only occasionally ruffled into irritability by the fact that Zena Dare was constantly bathed in tears.

This happened to be one of her peculiarities and really reflected very little on his directorial manner. She was the victim of a desperate inferiority complex, which was enhanced rather than minimised by a strong sense of humour directed principally against herself, with the result that every time she cried, she laughed at herself for crying, becoming in the process more and more hysterical until eventually rehearsals were brought to a standstill. Owing to early and arduous training in musical comedy, her first ingrained instinct was to smile; this smile often persisting even while the tears were cascading down her face. I think one of the most entrancing spectacles I know was Zena's expression when something untoward occurred on the stage, or when she lost a line and knew that she hadn't the remotest idea what to say next. On would flash the smile immediately, stretching into a mirthless grimace, meanwhile her eyes, in deathly panic, searched wildly the ceiling, the floor and the furniture for inspiration. Still smiling, she would hiss out of the corner of her mouth: 'For God's sake, dear, agony dear, what do I say, dear?'

At rehearsals, of course, such contretemps were the signal for tears; in actual performance, however, the trouper spirit was too strong in her to permit collapse, and she persevered gamely until, the danger over, her smile changed from macabre ferocity to relief and wafted her off the stage. She was a darling in the theatre and we all adored her.

Raymond Massey was another slight thorn in Basil's side, owing to his eccentric habit of behaving like a windmill whenever he dried up on a speech. Horrified at the outset by the fact that I was practically word perfect, he lashed himself into a frenzy several times a day, tearing at one particular long-suffering lock of hair and rending the air with incoherent Canadian curses, not at me, which would have been understandable, but at himself. There is nothing so irritating as rehearsing scenes with someone who already knows them, and I was fully conscious that my unethical slickness was putting him off. I apologised profusely, explaining that the reason I had played such a dirty trick on him was that my part was long and I wanted to get the actual learning of it out of the way in order to give myself time to polish.

He moaned at me wretchedly, alluding to his obtuseness and slowness with a wealth of invective that was nothing less than masochistic; the fact that he was giving one of the most expert performances of his career never occurred to him, and he continued to wallow. However, long before the dress rehearsal he vanquished his troubles and became word perfect, which was, in a way, disappointing, as the picture of that tall, gyrating figure with arms and legs waving had grown dear to me.

Ursula Jeans was the fourth member of the cast. She was ebullient, quick, and only occasionally flustered. She rushed at her scenes as though she were about to vault over a high gate, but eventually, the first exuberance over, she simmered down into a charming performance.

Altogether, it was well acted. I was happy with my part and I think I was good in it, at all events when Sam Behrman, the author, arrived from America, he said that he was delighted with all of us. I trembled at his arrival even more than the others did, realising that he had known the inestimable pleasure of seeing the play acted by Alfred and Lynn. I didn't want him to say that I was better than Alfred; if he had, I should not only have disliked him for saying so, but not believed him. However, I needn't have worried; Sam Behrman was tactful and kind to a degree. He insisted that there was no comparison between the two performances, that they were completely different both in approach and technique; and if in his secret heart he considered Alfred better than I in certain scenes and me better than Alfred in certain other scenes, I am convinced that no amount of cajoling would ever have got it out of him.

He was encouraging and charming to us all and instead of hating him coming to rehearsals, which we had all been doing in anticipation, our hearts sank whenever we looked out and noticed that his shining bald head and quizzically gleaming spectacles were missing.

(8)

The first night of *The Second Man* should by rights have been particularly nerve-racking for me, but somehow or other it wasn't.

To begin with, I had so often, during the past two months, visualised the horror of it, that when it arrived I was conscious of little beyond a steely hatred of the first-night audience even before they came into the theatre. I wondered dispassionately whether they would shriek anything offensive at me on my first entrance, or just sit in sullenness, daring me to be good. As a matter of fact, they did neither. They applauded me politely when

I came on and I judged, from an early laugh or two, that they were quite willing to be amused.

By the middle of the second act I knew the play was a success. There was a pleasant tension in the house and considerable laughter and applause. No hitches occurred. The champagne bottle opened with a good resounding pop (ginger-ale professionally bottled for us by Messrs. Mumm), and Raymond's revolver in the last act went off without any of those abortive clickings which are often so mortifying to an actor. In fact, everything was smooth and satisfactory and the cheering at the end would have been undoubtedly gratifying if, through it, I had not been listening ironically to crueller noises.

The notices were good and there were many sly suggestions to the effect that there was in reality no such person as S. N. Behrman, as the play had obviously been written by me under a pseudonym, apparently in the craven hope that it would thus be received more favourably.

Several writers even went so far as to assert that they had discerned definite examples of my wit in many of the lines. They were palpably delighted to have uncovered such a juicy secret, and it seemed almost unkind to have to undermine such proud assurance, but although Sam and I both acknowledged to each other how sincerely flattered we were, truth was truth and it had to be stated that there wasn't even one phrase or word of mine in the whole play.

(9)

Rehearsals for the revue started almost immediately after the opening of *The Second Man,* beginning as usual with a week or so of auditions for the chorus and small parts.

Daily, morning and afternoon, we sat in the dust-sheet enshrouded gloom of the London Pavilion, Lorn, Jack, Gladys, Frank Collins and me, while Elsie April, perched on the stage at an upright piano, pounded out accompaniments and drank endless cups of tea. With us also in the stalls was Cissie Sewell, the ballet mistress for all Cochran productions, her job being to remember accurately all dance movements originated by me or Max Rivers, the dance producer, and rehearse the girls apart at different hours of the day. Cissie was red-haired, smart, nice-looking, and efficient. Her memory was fantastic, and enabled her to catch the most fleeting movement of the leg or shoulder or hand and reproduce it later in the rehearsal room with precision. She possessed, in addition to her other virtues, an outspoken critical faculty allied to the kindest heart imaginable. This combination frequently set up a considerable conflict within her during the audition period. She knew, from years of experience, most of the aspirants who appeared before us. She knew whether they were kept or not kept, whether they needed the job or merely looked on the stage as a side-line, whether they were good workers or bad workers.

She and Elsie, who were bosom friends, had a series of code signals which they exchanged whenever one of their particular favourites or *bêtes noires* appeared. Elsie, with one swift twiddle round of the piano stool, would shoot a knowing look at Cissie in the stalls. If genuine talent was imminent she would give a satisfied little nod; if, on the other hand, some poor inexpert creature of old repute came on, she would shrug her shoulders and fling her eyes up to heaven with an expression of such untold resignation that we knew, long before the poor thing started, what to expect.

They were usually pretty accurate in their judgments, although occasionally, owing to private knowledge of some girl's sad circumstances, they would argue tooth and nail to get her the job, even if her talents were not quite up to scratch. These kindly, sentimental efforts were generally frustrated by Frank Collins, who also knew a thing or two, but, as a rule, it worked both ways, for he, too, had his special loves and hates, and auditions were often greatly enlivened thereby.

The atmosphere of those dim auditoriums, the dust-sheets, the large brass pot for cigarette ends, the bars of chocolate contributed by Lorn, are indelibly stained on to my memory. I will always remember the weariness at the end of a long day when Elsie finally clambered down from the piano to join us in the stalls, while we added up the odd hundred people we had seen and selected dispiritedly about three possible ones. So tired were we as a rule that the effort of getting up and going home seemed too much for us, and we sat around lethargically, gossiping a little, wondering whether Phyl would be strong enough for such and such a part or whether Vera—'You remember, dear, the one that sang "Love, Here is my Heart", and did a buck and wing'— would be, although less pretty, more reliable.

Cockie himself seldom attended these general hurly-burly auditions, preferring to wait for the later ones at which, having weeded out most of the drearies, we recalled those whom we thought were really worthy of his consideration. Naturally nobody could be definitely engaged without his O.K. and we were often on tenterhooks lest our selected pets should appear less talented than we thought, and let down our faith in them.

The finding of a title for the revue caused us all many racked hours of the day and many sleepless nights. We sat round with pencils and papers, flogging our brains and shooting forth anything we thought of, however inappropriate, in the hope that the very fatuity of our suggestion might inspire somebody else with an idea. All the ideal revue titles seemed to have been done; *Vanity Fair, Bric-à-Brac, London, Paris and New York, Odds and Ends,* etc., etc. Finally Lorn said *This Year of Grace,* and we instantly knew that we were all right. *This Year of Grace* it was, and I still think it one of the best revue titles I have ever heard.

The show opened, as usual, in Manchester. This time I did not stay off and allow my understudy to play for me, but I went up all the same for the Sunday dress rehearsal, which went on, as was expected, all through the night but was not, on the whole, nearly as depressing as *On with the Dance* had been.

Arnold Bennett was with us, I cannot at the moment remember why, and appeared to be enchanted with the whole thing, enjoying keenly with detached amusement every hitch and every hold-up. It was nice having him there, because he cheered up our blacker moments with a joke or two, and generally emanated good will from every pore.

This Year of Grace opened at the London Pavilion in March, and was an immediate success. I was still playing *The Second Man,* but as this didn't begin until just before nine, and the revue, on the first night, rang up at eight, I was able to watch, from the back of the dress-circle, the first three-quarters of an hour of it.

Quite early in the first half came my series of short one-line parodies on current plays, the final one of the series being announced as 'Any Noel Coward Play', and I was particularly anxious to see the effect of this on the first-night audience. The scene consisted merely of a row of people, with an author in the centre, bowing, until at a given moment the leading lady stepped forward and, with tears in her voice, said—'Ladies and gentlemen, this is the happiest moment of my life!' whereupon she burst into sobs and the entire orchestra and any of us in the audience who happened to be in the know, booed and raspberried with the utmost fervour.

The response of the first-nighters to this was interesting. There was first of all dead silence, then a titter of shocked amazement, and then a full-bellied roar of laughter.

That night the performance of *The Second Man* must have been exceedingly bewildering to the audience. The management had kindly agreed to cut the intervals down to half, and I had primed Ray and Zena and Ursula to play as quickly as they could, in order that I might get back to the Pavilion in time for the finale.

I don't suppose that a play has ever been performed with such speed without losing coherence. We all four rattled through it like express trains and it was not until nearly the end of the last act that I was suddenly conscience-smitten by the sight of a poor old gentleman in the front row of the stalls, leaning forward with a strained expression and his ear cupped in his hand.

I slowed down for the last few minutes, but we all managed to get to the Pavilion, still in make-up, for part of the second half of the revue.

Everything in the show went well. Tilly Losch made a huge

success. Maisie Gay triumphed with 'The Bus Rush' and her channel-swimmer song 'Up Girls and At 'Em.' Sonnie Hale and Jessie Matthews were charming in 'A Room with a View', and 'Try To Learn To Love', and Sonnie brought down the house with 'Dance, Little Lady', which he did with Laurie Devine against a group of glittering, macabre figures wearing Oliver Messel masks.

A great sensation was caused by Jack Holland and Jean Barry, who danced 'The Blue Danube' in the finale of the first half, and a Spanish dance in the second half. They were certainly magnificent, swift, graceful, and handsome to look at. Everybody fared well and the notices were ecstatic. It appeared, from reading them, that I was the most brilliant man of the Theatre that England had ever known, and the delightful audacity of parodying my own recent failure shook journalistic admirers of the sporting instinct to the marrow. In fact, far from creeping back in to favour I was shot into it with the drum accompaniment and velocity of a Star Trap Act.

(10)

The idea of *Bitter Sweet* was born in the early summer of that year, 1928. It appeared quite unexpectedly and with no other motivation beyond the fact that I had vaguely discussed with Gladys the possibilities of writing a romantic operetta. She and I were staying with Ronald Peake, her family solicitor, in Surrey, and an hour or so before we were due to leave, Mrs. Peake happened to play to us on the gramophone a new German orchestral record of 'Die Fledermaus.' Immediately a confused picture of uniforms, bustles, chandeliers, and gas-lit cafés formed in my mind, and later, when we were driving over Wimbledon Common, we drew the car to a standstill by the roadside, and in the shade of a giant horse-chestnut tree mapped out roughly the story of Sari Linden.

The uniforms, bustles, chandeliers and gas-lit café all fell into place eagerly, as though they had been waiting in the limbo for just this cue to enter.

There had been little or no sentiment on the London musical

[286]

stage for a long while. The Daly's operettas, with their crashing second-act finales in which the heroines dissolved in tears, or danced with the footman, had given place to an endless succession of slick American 'vo-do-deo-do' musical farces in which the speed was fast, the action complicated, and the sentimental value negligible.

It seemed high time for a little romantic renaissance, and very soon a few of the preliminary melodies began to form in my head. However, the whole idea had to be shelved for a while owing to the urgency of other plans.

The Second Man had finished its run, and Cockie and Archie Selwyn were trying to persuade me to play in *This Year of Grace* in New York in the autumn. The idea was for me to re-write certain of Sonnie Hale's material to suit my own talents and to co-star with Beatrice Lillie, who was to use the bulk of Maisie's numbers and sketches. There would, of course, have to be an entirely new cast as Cockie wisely and resolutely refused to break up the London company, which was playing to capacity.

I was not particularly keen on the project at first, but presently the idea of dancing, singing again, and playing a series of different rôles during an evening instead of only one began to seem more attractive, and finally I decided to do it, and signed my contract.

In July Cockie and I travelled over to New York for a couple of weeks, a little outing that we both agreed should come under the heading of 'Managerial Expenses', considering that the object of our visit was to discover fresh talent and discuss with Archie various arrangements for theatres and try-outs, etc.

As a matter of fact, we didn't find much talent beyond George Fontana and Marjorie Moss, whom we had both known for years, and one girl who could do side splits and walk on her hands with an air of social nonchalance that was exceedingly fetching. But we had a pleasant time.

We stayed at the Ritz and went out constantly to theatres and parties. Constance Collier was in New York, staying at the Algonquin in her usual slightly rusty splendour, surrounded by cats, dogs, monkeys, parrots and coffee percolators. She had become close friends with the new phenomenon of Broadway, Jed Harris, who had produced already, in rapid succession, several sure-fire successes.

He was an extraordinary creature, with an authentic flair for the theatre. He talked brilliantly, and turned on, whenever he considered it worth while, a personal charm that was impossible to resist. He had made a large fortune, but, beyond a shining Packard car, the evidences of it lay only in his conversation, and then only occasionally. His was one of the most interesting self-devouring egos I had ever met, and I found him enchanting company. Now and then he suggested to my mind that strangely ruthless insect, the Praying Mantis. I couldn't help wondering how long it would be before Jed's ego, prompted by sheer passion, ate up every scrap of him. We went to his production of *Coquette* in which Helen Hayes gave an agonisingly perfect performance and tore our emotions to shreds. We saw *Funnyface* in which Fred and Adele Astaire were more electric than ever, and also the Guild production of the Negro play *Porgy,* which Cockie immediately bought for London.

In fact, theatrically speaking, that was one of the richest two weeks I have ever spent.

As all the ships were crowded, on the voyage home Cockie and I were forced to share a cabin on the Berengaria. Although we had both viewed this prospect with slight apprehension, it turned out to be extremely cosy. Neither of us snored, apparently, and conversation after lights out was stimulating.

During that voyage I wrote, roughly, the first act of *Bitter Sweet,* and when I read it to Cockie and explained to him the story of the rest of it, he became at once enthusiastic. One of his greatest qualities is his amazing flair for visualising a play completely from the barest outline, and he decided then and there that he would do it, providing that I could finish it in the time, in the spring of the following year, 1929.

(11)

Meanwhile, at home the family fortunes continued to pursue an upward course. We had sold the lease of the Ebury Street house, although as I had recently had my rooms done up at great expense I decided to keep them on.

Father, at last free from the burden of lodgers, tax-collectors, window cleaners, etc., was installed at Goldenhurst, where he gardened to his heart's content, dealing with the wider landscape problems, while Auntie Vida had charge of the bulbs, potting, and flower beds. With this arrangement, of course, a certain amount of friction was inevitable, and high words frequently winged their way across the velvet lawns.

Mother drove recklessly about the countryside in a new car. She drove well, but with an unchristian spirit of truculence towards any other vehicles that happened to be on the road. Her mishaps, on the whole, were few. She once upset the vicar of St. Mary's and his wife into a ditch in a fog, and on another occasion, owing to mistimed acceleration, she advanced triumphantly through the plate-glass window of Pearks' grocers' shop in Ashford, remaining at the wheel in a state of splendid calm, while pots of black-currant jam, light plum, dark plum, strawberry, and Golden Shred marmalade ricochetted gaily off the wind-screen on to the radiator. Her rage over this incident simmered for days and was not soothed by the fact that the local Ashford paper grudgingly awarded her only a paragraph or two instead of the full column she had expected.

My brother Eric, then aged twenty-three, was rather at a loose end. He had had two or three jobs, in none of which he had been particularly happy. I felt, and I know that he felt, too, that to be the brother of anyone as spectacular as myself was far from comfortable. True, there were certain perquisites accruing from it, but, on the whole, I fear that my shadow lay heavily upon him.

If he had possessed any outstanding marketable talent it would, of course, have been different, but, alas, apart from a genuine passion for music and sufficient ability to play it quite well on the piano, his assets were little above the average.

We discussed his prospects at length, and eventually, as he had a keen desire to see something of the world, we arranged for him to go out to Ceylon in the autumn as a tea planter.

It was about this time that the great Barn Battle took place. This campaign, started quite unintentionally by Jack and me, flared up violently and showed every indication of continuing with all the futile persistence of the Hundred Years' War.

The beginning of it was simple. There was an old barn near to the house which we had left intact, feeling that later on it might be useful to us.

In the early spring of 1928, realising that for all of us, Mother, Father, Eric, Auntie Vida and me, supplemented frequently by Lorn, Gladys, Jack or Jeffrey, to live together in one small house was really asking too much of human forbearance, Jack had evolved a plan for re-building the interior of the barn and transforming the whole into a home for the family, while I took over the house. The view from the barn was much lovelier than from the house and, with bathroom, dining-room, bedrooms and living-room, etc., we considered that it ought to be the acme of comfort.

At this suggestion the family rose to a man, alternatively furious, outraged, martyred, hurt and bitterly resigned. The basis of the trouble was apparently a deeply embedded conviction that I had grown to be ashamed of my loved ones and wished to banish them beyond sight and sound of my new-found 'grand' friends, for whom I obviously considered them not good enough.

As my new-found 'grand' friends that year had consisted solely of Bobbie Andrews, who had come down for a couple of week-ends, this argument seemed unjust. Jack and I, terrified by the storm we had created, surrendered, but as it seemed a shame that all our elaborate schemes for the expansion of Goldenhurst should be grounded on the shoals of family pride, we set to work, and, with the aid of builders and plumbers from Folkestone, made over the barn and cottage into an establishment for my exclusive use.

When ultimately finished, the family were enraptured with it, and, to this day, use it a great deal in my absence, for entertaining their new-found 'grand' friends.

(12)

My determination that in this narrative the reader shall take the rough with the smooth impels me to relate that, two days before rehearsals for the American production of *This Year of Grace* were due to begin, I was operated on for piles.

This meant postponing everything for two weeks, during which I lay, in bad pain and a worse temper, in a nursing home.

The newspapers described the affair with light-hearted reticence as 'a minor operation', and I couldn't help reflecting that if that were a minor operation, I should have been far happier with a Cæsarian.

The night before I was to go under the knife, having been respectfully shaved and offered some barley sugar, I was left dejectedly alone in a small bed in a minute white room. Realising that after the anæsthetic I should probably have all, if not more, sleep than I was usually accustomed to, I passed the long hours until dawn pleasantly enough by writing the second act of *Bitter Sweet,* and in the morning consciousness that I had accomplished a considerable job of work upheld me throughout the routine indignities that I had to endure.

The nursing home was conservative to a degree, and so nineteenth century in atmosphere that I fully expected the nurses to come in in crinolines.

There was one bathroom on the fourth floor which contained, in addition to the usual offices, a forbidding geyser. This snarled angrily at those patients who were strong enough to survive a long, frightening ascent in a lift which, I imagine, must assuredly have been the pride of the Arts and Crafts Exhibition at Earl's Court in 1842.

I had several visitors during my convalescence, all of whom were kind and sympathetic, and seldom referred, except obliquely, to the mortifying nature of my complaint.

Marie Tempest was the exception. She came a lot to see me, and we discussed every detail with enthusiasm, and I need hardly say that her visits were far and away the most welcome of all.

It was my first experience of nursing-home life, and once the acuter discomforts were over I settled down to enjoy it. There was, first and foremost, a pleasant sense of timelessness. The moment the early-morning washing and prinking were done with I could sink back in clean pyjamas on to a freshly made bed with the heavenly sensation that there was no hurry and no necessity to do anything whatever.

There came a beaten-up egg in milk at eleven, and possibly a visit from the surgeon at twelve; apart from these minor interruptions the hours stretched lazily ahead towards lunch, my afternoon snooze, one or two amiable visitors, an early supper and then the night.

The nights were the nicest of all. When the bed had been remade, the curtains drawn, the dark-green shade put over the light, and the night nurse had whisked out of the room, a different kind of peace descended. There was no obligation to sleep. I had rested a lot during the day and could rest more on the following day. A gentle dimness enveloped me, a detachment from affairs. The life outside seemed incredibly remote.

Occasionally a taxi drew up on the other side of the road. I could hear the screech of the tires, the sound of the door opening and shutting, a murmur of voices, a sharp little ting as the driver reset the fare meter, then the grinding of gears and a diminishing hum until there was silence again. I pictured, without envy, those strangers letting themselves into their houses, switching on the lights in the dining-room and finding the usual decanter, siphon, glasses, and sandwiches curling slightly at the edges in spite of having been covered with a plate.

I imagined problems for them. Jealousy perhaps, suspicions of infidelity, a business crisis to be dealt with the next day, a brief to be prepared, or a political speech. Sleep was essential to them, they must get to bed and sleep because Time was whirling them along too fast. Not for them the luxury of lying still and making faces out of the shadows on the ceiling. Not for them the delight of a sudden cup of tea at three in the morning with a couple of Marie biscuits and one chocolate one. They had to be active and energetic and get things done, as I should have to in a week or so, but in the meantime I could relax, comfortably aware that I was not imprisoned by a long illness and that I should be up and about again before this delicious enforced rest had had time to become tedious.

(13)

We rehearsed the American production of *This Year of Grace* on the Pavilion stage and in the Poland Rooms. I had, during the summer, taken the precaution of going for six weeks to a dancing school in order to get limbered up, a necessary but painful procedure, for although I was not called upon to dance much, I had to be reasonably agile.

The show was unchanged except for the interpolation of two single numbers for Beattie: 'World Weary', and 'I Can't Think' (an imitation of Gertrude Lawrence); two duets which we did together: 'Lilac Time', an *opéra boufle* burlesque, and 'Love, Life and Laughter', a sketch and song of Paris night life in the eighties, which had originally been created by Maisie Gay in one of the Charlot revues.

The cast was surprisingly good considering how difficult it always is to duplicate an entire production, and we all sailed off to America to play a try-out week in Baltimore, before coming to the Selwyn Theatre in New York.

The Lunts, who happened to be playing in the next-door theatre to us in Baltimore, came to our Sunday rehearsal and assured me that I was going to be fine, but I was depressed and perfectly certain that I was going to be nothing of the sort. In 'Lilac Time', 'Love, Life and Laughter', and 'Dance, Little Lady', which latter I did with Florence Desmond, I was all right, but in 'A Room with a View' with Madeleine Gibson, and in the ballet announcement, I wasn't half as effective as Sonnie had been, and in most of the other things I had to do in the show I felt myself to be only adequate.

Beattie was good all through, but being, like all of us, in a bad state of nerves and fright, she contrived to be completely and utterly devilish throughout the whole week. Before I continue further, I should like to say that she was then and is now a much-loved friend. The fact that she was an uppish, temperamental, tiresome, disagreeable, inconsiderate, insufferable friend during that one week of her life in no way sullies my steadfast love for her. It may have temporarily dimmed it to the extent of my wishing ardently to wring her neck, but once we had opened in New York all rancour disappeared, as the mist on a glass disappears with the application of a damp rag, the damp rag in that instance being the re-emergence of Beattie's real character. Whether it was the stimulus of the triumphant success she made, or a letter from her son at home, or the General Election, I don't know. I do know, however, that the moment the first night was over she changed miraculously back to her old self, just as though some magician had whacked her sharply over the head with a wand, and became, what I had always expected her to be, one of the most generous and delightful partners it had ever been my privilege to work with.

There was even more than the usual first-night excitement going on when we opened in New York. Everyone was running in and out of everyone else's dressing-rooms, the passages were stacked high with boxes of flowers, Frank Collins and Dan O'Neil were conducting a gloomy little conference with the heads of departments on the bare stage.

I felt as though I were in a sort of coma. The outlook was so black, the past week had been so gruelling, and although I was sure that the scenery was bound to fall down, the lights go wrong all through, and the audience walk out on us, I was really too exhausted to care.

[294]

We went through the first half in a trance, more and more astounded, as each scene concluded, that no hitches had occurred. The second half went, if possible, even more smoothly than the first. Not a light was wrong (Frank Collins had stationed himself in the limelight box in the front of the house), not a property was out of place, and the cast, stimulated by the responsiveness of the audience, played magnificently. Altogether it was a triumphant evening, and Beattie and I fell into each other's arms sobbing with relief at the end.

From then onwards Beattie and I co-starred not only theatrically, but socially in all directions. We appeared together everywhere. At large Charity Balls where we sang 'Lilac Time', at select Ladies' Clubs where we sang 'Lilac Time', at fashionable night-clubs where our entrance was the signal for an immediate flood of requests for us to sing 'Lilac Time', and at small convivial theatrical parties to which we were invited on the strict understanding that in no circumstances would we sing 'Lilac Time.'

A week or so after the opening of the revue we gave a midnight performance which theatrical New York attended en masse, and which completely unbalanced our performance for several days afterwards. However good the audience were following that midnight show, they inevitably seemed flat and uninspiring.

In order to chasten our spirits and bring us down from our high altitude with a bump, Archie Selwyn had arranged that the next night should be a 'Benefit.' This benefit business is a custom in America, and although from the point of view of the charity concerned it is unquestionably profitable, from the point of view of the actors concerned it is hell.

One of the most remunerative and popular means of raising funds for a pet cause is the buying out of the house for a performance of a successful play. Once bought and paid for, the tickets are re-sold at fabulous prices to the supporters of the charity in question. This, of course, is not effective unless the show is new and the demand for seats high.

The managements obviously have no objection to the arrangement as it ensures the house being sold out at box-office prices, which is as much as, if not more than, they can ordinarily expect. For the actors, however, it is miserable in the extreme. A 'Benefit' night means, as a rule, an audience of such soul-shattering dreariness that it is as much as one can do to give even the semblance of a good performance.

The reason of this is difficult to discover. Whether the fact that they have all paid far too much for their seats, and are consequently in a mood of sullen resentment to start with, accounts for their behaviour, I do not know. But I do know that whether I have been warned beforehand that it is a charity audience, or whether I haven't, I can tell the first moment I step on to the stage.

To begin with, the stalls are usually half empty during the first act, and one is continually distracted by the noisy arrival of late-comers, who churn down the aisles, generally in parties, and discuss loudly, with complete disregard for the performers or those already present, who is to sit next to who. Once seated, they scan the house anxiously with opera-glasses to discover whether or not their dearest enemies have better seats than they have. Their response to the play is apathetic, to say the least of it. Lines which, with an ordinary audience, always get big laughs, are unrewarded by so much as a titter, and the play proceeds with almost as little reaction as if one were playing a dress rehearsal in an empty theatre.

Generally, in one of the intervals, a lady arrives back-stage covered with pearls, sables and orchids, to make a speech before the curtain, appealing for funds, which invariably enshrouds the house in still deeper gloom, so that the effort to re-establish the mood of the play afterwards is similar in sensation to remounting a horse immediately after you have fallen off it and broken three ribs.

During the last act there is a certain awakening of activity as people rise and leave in chattering groups in order to get to their cars before the rush begins. At the final curtain there is a general exodus, and the cast is lucky if it gets one curtain call.

In This Year of Grace
Selwyn Theatre
New York, 1928

IN THIS YEAR OF GRACE
Selwyn Theatre
New York
1928

(14)

This Year of Grace continued to play to packed houses. I had originally contracted to play it only for three months, but in the face of the business and Archie Selwyn's persuasions, I agreed to carry on for longer. During that winter Alec Woollcott inaugurated his Sunday morning breakfast parties. These peculiar functions, starting at nine A.M. and continuing until three or four in the afternoon, were adorned by a varied mixture of personalities ranging from Ethel Barrymore and Harpo Marx, to lady novelists, osteopaths, *soi-disant* foreign princesses, cub-journalists, and grey university professors.

Alec, although lacking the essential grace and fragility of an eighteenth-century marquise, being as a rule unshaven and clad in insecure egg-stained pyjamas, managed in his own harum-scarum way to evoke a certain 'salon' spirit.

There was always a din of voices augmented by the crash of crockery and the rattle of dice and backgammon men, above which Alec could sometimes be heard crooning to himself in ghastly baby language—'Evwy night my pwayers I say, I learn my lessons *evwy* day'—until his opponent happened to throw double sixes, whereupon he would scream shrilly—'Bitch delivered of a Drab' in tones of such, apparently, ungovernable fury that any strangers present who were unaccustomed to his particular brand of badinage would hastily brush the breakfast crumbs from their laps and edge, nervously, towards the door.

In addition to Dorothy Parker, Ben Hecht, Charlie MacArthur, Herbert Swope, George and Beatrice Kaufman, Alice Duer Miller and Marc Connelly, you would be almost certain to find the Lunts, Margalo Gillmore, Thornton Wilder, twittering gently in a corner, Kathleen Norris, in majestic black satin and pearls with a rowdy look in her eye, and, if she and Alec happened to be on speaking terms, Edna Ferber.

It was at one of these strange galaxies that I met William Bolitho. His name I knew from his book *Murder for Profit,* and his articles in the New York *World,* and the first thing that struck me about him was his intensity. It was not an obvious intensity, in fact his manner was on the whole singularly detached. He looked, if anything, a little irritated, as if the close proximity of so many people irked him and made him uneasy. He was tall and fair with blue eyes and a biggish nose, which he had a trick of whacking with his finger when he wished to emphasise some particular point. I liked him immediately, and when he invited me to dine the following evening before the show, I accepted with pleasure.

We dined at the Plaza. He, Sybil (his wife) and me. We talked incessantly, frequently all three of us at once. It was as though we were together again after a long absence; a reunion of close friends rather than an introductory meeting.

They lived near Avignon at Montfavet. Their house, they said, was surrounded by trees and there was a swimming-pool that William was very proud of, and several fruit trees and a vegetable garden of which he was still prouder. They spent six months of every year there and were returning quite soon.

I told them to expect me some time during the summer, and left them in a rush, having allowed myself only a bare ten minutes in which to get to the theatre.

(15)

During that winter, January and February 1929, I finished *Bitter Sweet,* on which I had been working intermittently for the last few months. The book had been completed long since, but the score had been causing me trouble, until one day, when I was in a taxi on my way back to the apartment after a matinée, the 'I'll See You Again' waltz dropped into my mind, whole and complete, during a twenty minutes' traffic block. After that everything went smoothly, and I cabled to Cockie in London suggesting that he start making preliminary arrangements regarding theatre, opening date, etc.

My first choice for Sari had been Gertie Lawrence, but when the score was almost done, she and I both realised that her voice, although light and charming, was not strong enough to carry such a heavy singing rôle. She was naturally disappointed and I promised that the next play I wrote would be especially for her.

In the meantime a leading lady who could sing beautifully, look lovely, and act well had to be found. Evelyn Laye was the obvious choice in London, but she, unfortunately, owing to various previous contracts, was unobtainable.

One afternoon, in the lobby of the Algonquin Hotel, I ran into Peggy Wood. She had just come in from the country and was wearing a raincoat, an unbecoming rubbery hat on the back of her head, and horn-rimmed glasses, and she looked as far removed from my vision of Sari Linden as Mrs. Wiggs of the Cabbage Patch.

I had known her on and off for several years, in fact ever since my first visit to New York in 1921, but, oddly enough, in all that time I had never once seen her on the stage. I had, of course, heard on all sides enthusiastic accounts of her acting and her looks and the loveliness of her voice, but never having been able to judge for myself, and confronted by that rubber hat, that face devoid of make-up, and those horn-rimmed glasses, it was with some trepidation that I heard myself asking her if she would care to come over to London and do an operetta.

She replied that she'd love to, but that hadn't I better hear her sing first? And so we rushed off immediately to my studio in the Hotel des Artistes. On arrival, Peggy realised that she hadn't any music, and so she darted out and down the street where, fortunately, her music teacher happened to live, and returned in a few minutes with the score of *Manon*.

She sat down at once and started to sing, but had to stop owing to lack of breath.

After she had rested a little and had a glass of water she started again, and the first few bars she sang assured me that here was the ideal Sari.

I was impressed by her surprising lack of 'star' manner. With a long list of distinguished successes behind her she behaved as though she were being offered a good part for the first time. She was enthusiastic over the music I played to her. I knew from that moment that she would be a delight to work with, and I was right. In due course Cockie cabled a contract to Peggy, and, with that primary difficulty settled, I continued to add finishing touches to the score and lyrics, until the whole show was complete.

(16)

Bitter Sweet went into rehearsal at the Scala Theatre at the end of May. We were ultimately bound for His Majesty's, but the Guitrys were at the moment in possession of it, and as the show was booked for a three weeks' try-out in Manchester, it was more convenient to rehearse in an empty theatre, where we could set up our scenery and work at nights as well as in the mornings and afternoons.

From the beginning *Bitter Sweet* went smoothly. Cockie and I, having taken an arduous trip to Berlin and Vienna in an effort to find a foreign tenor to play Carl, had returned to London empty-handed and engaged Georges Metaxa, who had been available all the time. Ivy St. Helier, for whom I had written the rôle of Manon la Crevette was already engaged, and the rest of the cast fell into our laps with hardly any trouble on our part at all.

We had had the usual auditions, and the chorus we had engaged sang well and looked pleasant. The scenery was well under way, the first and last acts having been designed by Gladys, and the middle act by Ernst Stern. Peggy Wood arrived in good time from America and proceeded slowly but surely to build her distinguished performance. In fact, I reflected, with everything going so marvellously, the play, according to all theatrical tenets, couldn't escape being the gravest fiasco.

Cockie, who had tactfully left the production entirely to Gladys and me, came to the last rehearsal before the dress rehearsal. Before he arrived I made a little speech to the company through my microphone which I had had installed in the dress-circle, imploring them to play up for all they were worth. The scenery was up but there was no orchestra, so Elsie officiated at a piano at the side of the stage. The company wore their ordinary day clothes and the lights consisted merely of a few battens and the footlights. In fact, it was a thorough-going working rehearsal.

In due course Cockie arrived and he, Lorn, Jack, Frank, Cissie, Gladys and I took our places in the front row of the dress-circle and waited apprehensively while Elsie scampered through the overture.

Of all the performances I ever saw of *Bitter Sweet* that rehearsal was far and away the most exciting. Each and every member of that always fine company, from Peggy down to the smallest walk-on in the café scene, was perfect. There were no dry ups, no muddles in the dance routine, and no undue waits between the scenes. Dan O'Neil, even with a skeleton staff, was, like everyone else back-stage, inspired.

At the end Cockie thanked the company through the microphone in a voice husky with emotion and added that he wouldn't part with his rights in the play for a million pounds.

It was an unforgettable, glorious three hours and the dress parade the next day, according to the law of compensations, was correspondingly ghastly.

Many of the dresses had not been finished in time, and several of those that were, didn't fit. Half the shoes were missing. The stage was littered with squabbling dressmakers, shoemakers, wig-makers, fitters, and resentful chorus girls who hated their wigs and their bonnets, complained about their feet, and said they couldn't sing unless their collars were loosened. Several of them appeared with their bustles on back to front, and the smart uniforms of the Austrian officers looked as if they had only recently evacuated the front-line trenches.

Peggy sailed on and off in a series of lovely gowns, causing no trouble and minding her own business. Ivy, on the other hand, carried on like fifty prima donnas in one. She loathed her dresses, refused to wear her wigs, tried to insist on silk stockings which for the period would have been quite inappropriate, wept and wailed and entreated, until Gladys and I sprang at her like tigers and nearly murdered her.

At the dress rehearsal in Manchester she cheered up a bit, and after the opening night, when she had given a splendid performance and had made a triumphant success, she changed back, like Beattie in New York, into her old gay, humorous self.

The Manchester first night was riotous. Peggy made a gracious speech and so did Cockie, in which he touchingly and generously handed me the credit for the whole production which, I may say, without his enthusiasm, his lavishness, and his unwavering trust in me could never have been possible. The Press notices the next day were almost incoherent with praise, and the house was immediately sold out for the entire three weeks.

I think that of all the shows I have ever done *Bitter Sweet* gave me the greatest personal pleasure. My favourite moments were: the finale of the first act when Carl and Sari elope; the café scene when the curtain slowly falls on Carl's death, in a silence broken only by Manon's sobs; the entrance of Mme. Sari Linden in her exquisite white dress of the nineties; and, above all, the final moment of the play, when, to the last crashing chords of 'I'll See You Again', Sari, as an old woman, straightens herself with a gesture of indomitable pride and gallantly walks off the stage. That gesture was entirely Peggy's idea, and the inspired dramatic simplicity of it set her for ever in my memory as a superb actress.

The London first night was definitely an anti-climax after Manchester. The audience was tremendously fashionable, and, for the first part of the play, almost as responsive as so many cornflour blancmanges.

Later on they warmed up a little, and at the end the upper parts of the house cheered. I sat with Gladys at the end in the dome of the auditorium where the spotlights were housed. It was pleasant to look down upon the audience unobserved. None of them seemed anxious to leave their seats and go home, from which I gathered that they were waiting for me to appear to make a speech. But my speech-making days were over, I did not appear, and when, an hour or so later I was hailed at the stage door by a mob of vociferous gallery girls who demanded why I had not come out in response to their calls for me, I replied, with genuine irritation, that I only came on when they booed.

The Press notices the next day and on the Sunday following were remarkable for their tone of rather grudging patronage. It seemed as though the critics were ashamed of their recent outburst of enthusiasm over *This Year of Grace* and wished to retrench themselves behind a barricade of non-committal clichés. It would be too bad, after all, if I were encouraged to believe that there was anything remarkable in writing, composing and producing a complete operetta. I might become uppish again and this was an excellent opportunity of putting me gently but firmly in my place. Some praised the book, but dismissed the music as being reminiscent and of no consequence. Some liked the music, but were horrified by the commonplace sentimentality of the book. The lyrics were hardly mentioned, and although the acting and décor were favourably received, the general consensus of opinion was that the play would probably run for six weeks, or, at the most, three months.

(17)

Cockie, already occupied with plans for an American production of *Bitter Sweet* in the autumn, had persuaded Evelyn Laye to play 'Sari.' This settled, he and Gladys and I went to France to start off again on the discouraging search for a tenor to play Carl. This time, in addition to a tenor, we had to find a soubrette to play Manon.

Paris was hot and uncomfortable. We were surrounded by active theatrical agents who produced tenors and soubrettes by the score, until we were dizzy. None of them seemed anywhere near good enough.

Finally we engaged a little French comedienne called Mireille for Manon. She was actually a bit young for the part, but her English was good, and she sang well.

We were still without a Carl, and were becoming more and more disheartened, when a handsome young Roman appeared with a letter of introduction from Princess Jane San Faustino. He had a good voice, long eyelashes, short legs, no stage experience, and a violin, and although at the moment he couldn't speak a word of English, he swore with fervour that he would learn it in two months, if we would only give him the part. We all felt a little dubious, but he seemed the likeliest possibility so far and so, after a certain amount of weary discussion, we engaged him.

This achieved, Gladys went back to London to devote herself to scenic problems, and I went to Avignon to stay with the Bolithos.

There was nothing to do at Montfavet but swim in the pool, lie in the garden, and occasionally drive into Avignon. William was just completing his book *Twelve against the Gods* and was seldom visible before lunch.

The house was indeed thickly surrounded by trees, and might have been gloomy had anyone but the Bolithos been occupying it. As it was, the atmosphere was gay enough and indescribably peaceful. The food was plain and good, and we drank a sourly delicious *vin du pays* with every meal. Also, with every meal William talked, and, Time being serenely unimportant in that house, we often sat on for hours arguing and discussing and shouting at one another. He talked with fire and grace and beauty, and with apparently a profound knowledge of every subject under the sun. His vocabulary was brilliant and varied. He was often violent but never didactic, and he never appeared to monopolise the conversation or to show off or to try for too long to hold the floor.

Of all the minds I have ever encountered, his, I think, was the richest and the most loving. Those all too brief ten days I spent in his company turned me inside out, stimulated the best of my ambitions, readjusted several of my uneasy values, and banished many meretricious ones, I hope, for ever; and I went back to London strongly elated and bursting with gratitude to him for the strange new pride I found in myself.

(18)

The rehearsals for the American production of *Bitter Sweet* also took place at the Scala, and whereas with the original company everything had been easy, with this one it was exactly the opposite. The stimulus of building something new, watching the play grow, fill out, and develop day by day, was naturally lacking. Everything was set, the formula was laid down, and with no excitement and no sense of discovery, it was all dreary to a degree.

Evelyn was delightful to work with, and the one bright spot in the whole business.

Jack, Gladys, Frank, Danny, Evelyn and I travelled over on the Mauretania, while the company followed on a slower boat. Cockie, much to our dismay, was unable to come at all, which meant that I was nominally in charge, and had to deal with Selwyn and Ziegfeld. If I had realised at the time the exasperation that this entailed, I should have insisted on Cockie's coming, even if it had meant shanghaiing him. The voyage was comparatively uneventful. Ina Claire and John Gilbert, who had been staying with me at Goldenhurst in the course of a rather strained honeymoon, were on board, and enlivened the trip to a certain extent by their conjugal infelicities, quarrelling and making up and quarrelling and making up again unceasingly, all the way from Southampton to the Statue of Liberty.

Eventually we arrived in Boston for our two weeks' try-out, and embarked on a full Sunday-night rehearsal with orchestra in the Colonial Theatre.

It was at that rehearsal that we realised once and for all that our Roman tenor could never open without doing incalculable harm to the play. We had been buoying ourselves up with the hope that his English, over which he had been slaving, would improve sufficiently for him to be understood, but it was no good; up against the orchestra he was not only unintelligible but inaudible as well; also his lack of acting experience was so apparent that even if he could have been heard, his important scenes would have gone for nothing. I felt desperately sorry for him. He had worked hard and done his best, but Evelyn and the play had to be considered, and so I told him that he couldn't appear. It was a painful scene, as those scenes always are, but there was no time to waste, and I left Dan O'Neil to comfort him and devoted my attention to Gerald Nodin, whom I had decided to put in his place. Nodin had originally sung Tokay in the London production, and although quite wrong in type for Carl, he had the advantage of knowing the show thoroughly, and was ambitious enough to make the utmost of himself.

All that night and all the next day we worked. Evelyn played her scenes with him over and over again, encouraging him and helping him in every way she could think of. Watching her and knowing how tired and nervous she was, I found it easy to understand why she was so adored by every company she had ever worked with.

On the day of production Ziegfeld asked me to lunch and told me in course of it that, as I had so resolutely refused his offer of a smarter male chorus and twelve ravishing show girls (an offer, incidentally, which had been made daily since our arrival in America), he was going to refrain from any undue display over the New York first night and, contrary to his usual custom, was not even going to raise the prices. I received this dispiriting announcement apathetically, being far too exhausted to care whether he gave the seats away with a packet of chewing-gum.

The show, however, was an enormous success in Boston, and by the time the New York first night arrived, it had been so publicised that a special cordon of police had to be called out to control the traffic in Sixth Avenue. Floodlighting was used to illuminate the gratified audience as they came into the theatre. Flashlight photographs were taken of every celebrity that entered the lobby, and seats on the orchestra floor were sold by speculators for as much as two hundred and fifty dollars a pair. Ziegfeld, whom I now addressed affectionately as 'Flo', had placed his office and private box at the disposal of Gladys, Jack and me. He had generously stacked it with flowers, caviare, and champagne, and whenever, during the performance, we found a certain scene too wearisome to be borne, we retired to it and had a drink, with the result that by the end of the evening we were merrily unconcerned as to whether the show was a success or not. At a matter of fact, it was. The company, although I never felt them to be up to their London equivalents, played, on the whole, remarkably well. But it was Evelyn who turned the scale. It was Evelyn's night from first to last. She played as though she were enchanted. Never before at any of the rehearsals or at any of the performances in Boston had she given a quarter of the grace and charm and assurance that she gave that night. Early on in the ballroom scene she conquered the audience completely by singing the quick waltz song 'Tell Me What is Love?' so brilliantly, and with such a quality of excitement, that the next few minutes of the play were entirely lost on one of the most prolonged outbursts of cheering I have ever heard in a theatre.

Her performance was magnificent all through, and she fully deserved every superlative that the Press lavished upon her the next day. It would, of course, have been impossible for her to play with such inspiration at every subsequent performance, and I don't suppose for a moment that she either could or did, but it was she and she alone who put the play over that night.

PART NINE

I SAILED from San Francisco in one of the Dollar Line ships, the President Garfield, at four p.m. on the 29th of November, 1929.

The day was grey and chilly, and an angry wind swept through the Golden Gate, whipping the harbour into waves and tearing the smoke out of the ship's funnel in a straight black line.

The important fact that this holiday was an escape that I had been planning for a long while dwindled under a general sense of futility. Jeffrey, who had given up his job on the New York *World* in the spring and gone off in a freight boat to the South Seas and Australia, had arranged to meet me on the 23rd of December in the Imperial Hotel, Tokio. We had sat in the garden at Goldenhurst with a globe between us on the grass planning the places we were going to, picturing (inaccurately) the Temple of Heaven in Pekin, the Ruins of Angkor, vivid tropical jungles, and the road to Mandalay, flying-fish and all. Then, with soft Kentish greens all around us and grey Kentish sheep punctuating our imaginative flights with gentle bleats, the whole scheme seemed glamorous beyond words; now, however, in the grip of inevitable 'boat-departure' anti-climax, I was lonely and depressed, and felt that I should have been far wiser to have stayed at home and read a travel book.

I looked dismally at the packages of fruit and flowers and books which various friends had sent me, and even more dismally at a map hanging by the purser's office. Far over in the corner of it, among a welter of greens and browns, I could discern a minute reddish speck which was England and with the aid of the pin from my tie I fixed approximately the spot where, probably at this very moment, Auntie Vida was battling through the weather with a trowel to attack the weeds in the orchard.

After dinner—an interlude of polite conversation at the captain's table—I sat on deck for a little. It was getting dark, and far away astern a few lights were shimmering on the coast. The weather was clearing and the sea calm.

It was a good moment for retrospection, so I put my feet up on the rail and relaxed, aware suddenly that time was no longer exigent. I had nothing to do; hours stretched before me into the future, hundreds and thousands of hours. No more rehearsals, no more first nights, no more leading ladies to be cajoled, no more theatrical anxieties, arguments and irritations. My dramatic sense saw me picturesquely languid, wearier than I really was, and a self-conscious peace descended upon me as I lay there looking up at the stars.

I journeyed back into the past without any particular aim or direction, allowing events of the last few months to hobnob with more elderly memories. I saw myself in a sailor suit singing 'Come Along with Me to the Zoo, Dear'; in a tail suit singing, 'Dance, Little Lady'; in a sweat-stained dressing-gown in New York pounding out short stories on my typewriter; in baggy riding-breeches riding along the sands of Deauville. I heard, dimly, the cheers for *The Vortex* and, less dimly, the catcalls for *Sirocco*. I heard orchestras tuning-up and the fateful, shuffling sound of curtains rising. People, too, popped up briefly out of the limbo and then sank back again like the little white letters in vermicelli soup when you churn it with your spoon. Gwen Kelly singing 'Every Morn I Bring Thee Violets'; Mary Garden singing 'Vissi d'Arte'; Mother in grey satin and a feather boa smiling exultantly over an ice-cream soda in Selfridge's—Mother again, hot and tired, cooking in the Ebury Street kitchen; Charles Hawtrey patting me on the back; Robert Courtneidge saying: 'You're not only a very young actor, but a very bad actor!'; Stoj in a white knitted coat and skirt riding along suburban roads on a bicycle; John Ekins buying vivid artificial silk socks with me for two shillings a pair in the Berwick Market. I suddenly remembered William Bolitho

MOTHER and FATHER
At *Goldenhurst*

With JEFFREY
travelling

talking to me just before I left New York. I had told him of a novel I intended to write, rather a neurotic novel about a man who committed suicide because he was bored. William whacked his nose with his finger and said, almost sharply: 'Be careful about Death, it's a serious business, big and important. You can't go sauntering towards Death with a cigarette hanging from your mouth!'

I didn't know then that those were the last words he would ever speak to me, and he effaced himself along with the others to make room for some clamorous new friends I had found in Hollywood.

Looking back over my ten days in Hollywood made me gasp a bit and wish for a little neat brandy. I felt as though I had been whirled through all the side-shows of some gigantic Pleasure Park at breakneck speed. My spiritual legs were wobbly and my impressions confused. Blue-ridged cardboard mountains, painted skies, elaborate grottos peopled with familiar figures: animated figures that moved their arms and legs, got up and sat down, and spoke with remembered voices.

The houses I had visited became indistinguishable in my mind from the built interiors I had seen in the studios. I couldn't remember clearly whether the walls of Jack Gilbert's dining-room had actually risen to a conventional ceiling, or whether they had been sawn off half-way up to make room for scaffolding and spluttering blue arc-lamps.

I remembered an evening with Charlie Chaplin when at one point he played an accordion and at another a pipe-organ, and then suddenly became almost pathologically morose and discussed Sadism, Masochism, Shakespeare and the Infinite.

I remembered a motor drive along flat, straight boulevards with Gloria Swanson, during which we discussed, almost exclusively, dentistry.

I remembered, chaotically, a series of dinner parties, lunch parties, cocktail parties and even breakfast parties. I remembered also playing a game of tennis with Charlie MacArthur somewhere at two in the morning, with wire racquets, in a blaze of artificial moonlight, and watching him, immediately afterwards, plunge fully clothed into an illuminated swimming-pool.

I remembered Laura Hope-Crews appearing unexpectedly from behind a fountain and whispering gently: 'Don't be frightened, dear—this—*this*—is Hollywood!'

I had been received with the utmost kindness and hospitality, and I enjoyed every minute of it; it was only now, in quietness, that it seemed unreal and inconclusive, as though it hadn't happened at all.

It occurred to me that I had been living in a crowd for too long; not only a crowd of friends, enemies and acquaintances, but a crowd of events: events that had followed each other so swiftly that the value of them, their causes and effects, their significance, had escaped me. My nervous energy, always excessive, had carried me so far. My determination, ambition and almost hysterical industry had been rewarded generously, perhaps too generously. I remembered driving with Gladys down the long road from Hampstead after the first night of *The Vortex*—'And now what?'

Then there had been no time to answer; success had to be dealt with, adjustments had to be made to my new circumstances, more money, more people, more noise, more diffusion of experience, new attitudes to be acquired, a thousand new tricks to be learned. And now, after only five years, here was that offensive little query bobbing up again. The acquired attitudes were no longer new, I could slip them on and off with ease to suit every occasion. The social tricks, then so fresh and shiny, were now creaking mechanically. There were the demands I had made, miraculously granted, looking a bit smug. Most of my gift horses seemed to have bad teeth—and now what?

I comforted myself with the thought that perhaps this uneasiness, this vague sense of dissatisfaction, was a good sign. If I was as superficial as so many people apparently thought—a subtle whip this, always guaranteed to raise a weal—if my mind was so shallow, if the characters I had written were so meretricious and unreal, if my achievements fell so far short of the first-rate, surely this moment of all moments, this relaxed contemplation of recent triumphs, should fairly swaddle me in complacency. I should be able to smile, a smooth, detached smile—'People say—what do they say?—let them say!' I should be able to boast, not loudly but with a quiet satisfaction—'at least I have done this and that in a remarkably short space of time.' I should be able to defy the envious, the jealous and the unkind—'come on, if you're so critical—come on and do better!' I should be serene, content with my lightweight crown, without a headache and without doubts.

On the other hand, however, I felt no conviction that this reasoning was in the least accurate. It seemed arbitrary to assume that a superficial mind was necessarily invulnerable. Perhaps my uneasiness was the true indication of my worth, the inevitable shadow thrown by thin facility; a deeper mind might suffer more, win less spectacular laurels, and in the long run stake a richer claim.

There seemed no criterion by which I could judge my quality, or, rather, so many criteria that they nullified each other.

How, from all the written and spoken praise, blame, admiration, envy, prejudice, malice, kindness and contempt that these last few years had brought me, could I abstract a little of what was really true? Which of all those critical minds had been the most unbiased—nearest to hitting the nail on the head? How much had the precipitate flamboyance of my success prejudiced not only those who criticised my work, but the work itself? In fact, where was I and what was I? Had I done what I thought I'd done or what others thought I had done? Was my talent real, deeply flowing, capable of steady growth and ultimate maturity? Or was it the evanescent sleight of hand that many believed it to be; an amusing drawing-room flair, adroit enough to skim a certain immediate acclaim from the surface of life but with no roots in experience and no potentialities?

Among all the thousands of people I knew I searched vainly in my mind to find one who could give me an answer or, at any rate, a comment accurate and honest enough to restore my sense of direction. The simple single track of earlier years seemed far away. There had been no necessity to look either to the right or to the left then, success was the goal—'Noel Coward' in electric lights. Now I found the electric lights so dazzling that I couldn't see beyond them. It was no use asking for help, jogging policemen's elbows and enquiring the way. The lights blinding me would probably be blinding the policeman, too. Solutions and answers would fall into place in time. Nobody, however well intentioned, could find my own truths for me, and only very few could even help me to look for them. In moments of private chaos it is better to be alone, loving advice merely increases the chaos. At all events, I could congratulate myself whole-heartedly on one account. I had realised, I hoped not too late, the necessity for space, and had deliberately broken away. Perhaps the next few months would answer a few of my questions for me; perhaps new countries, sights, sounds, and smells, the complete cessation of familiar routines, this strange sense of timelessness, would release from the caverns of my mind the most gratifying profundities. It would be enjoyable to return to my startled friends with, in addition to the usual traveller's souvenirs, a Strindbergian soul. I remember leaving the sea and the sky and the stars in charge of my problems and going below to my cabin chuckling a little at my incorrigible superficiality.

(2)

We arrived at Honolulu at six a.m. on a calm opalescent sea. I looked out of my port-hole as we passed Diamond Head towering above the palm trees; perched half-way up it I could see the Dillinghams' house where I hoped, at that very moment, breakfast was being prepared for me.

It all looked so gay and different from that horrible morning three years before when I had arrived and collapsed in the Moana Hotel. Then, seen through a haze of fever and unhappiness, everything had seemed too bright and highly-coloured and somehow unfriendly. But now it was enchanting.

Walter Dillingham's secretary met me at the dock and we drove off past the outlying buildings of the town, along that lovely road with the palm-fringed surf on one side and the mountains rising, clear-cut, out of the plains on the other.

Louise was unfortunately away visiting her eldest son in the States, so Walter and I had breakfast by ourselves, sitting on the terrace and looking out over descending green lawns to the town in the distance. The wide sweep of the sea outside the reef was deep blue, but inside near the shore the water was streaked with jade green. I could hear distinctly in the stillness the cries of the beach boys riding the surf at Waikiki, although they were nearly two miles away. A freighter with a jaunty red-and-black funnel was trundling across the bay, rolling so lackadaisically in the slight swell that I almost expected it to yawn.

Walter gave a dinner party for me that night, and while we dined a small Hawaiian orchestra played and sang softly outside. After dinner we all went out on to the moon-flooded patio and lay in long chairs drinking coffee and liqueurs, listening to further music and gazing up at Diamond Head above us.

The four days in Honolulu passed swiftly. I motored over to Mokuleia and bathed from that beach where before I had spent so many homesick hours. I re-trod the road from the ranch through bananas and sugar canes where the white dust had formerly been furrowed by my tears of self-pity. I walked through the pine trees, with the roar of the surf growing louder and louder in my ears until I came out on to the sand and saw the enormous waves advancing endlessly like rolls of blue velvet, unfrilled and unruffled until they broke in thunder on the reef, sending smaller editions of themselves to splay the beach with foam. I went out at night on a fish-spearing expedition and wandered about the reef waist-deep in water, making ineffectual dabs with my spear whenever I saw anything move in the light cast by the torches until finally, in triumph, I transfixed a wriggling pink octopus and handed it graciously to the natives to kill, which they did by biting its eyes out.

I visited the Thevenins who had left Mokuleia and were living in a small house just outside the town, and learned to my sorrow that poor Owgooste had had to be destroyed owing to an outburst of indescribable savagery in which he had bitten the behind of a Filipino coolie.

Finally, a trifle exhausted, but warmed by Hawaiian sunshine and hospitality, and conscious that I had laid for ever a number of personal ghosts, I sailed on the Tenyo Maru, a distinctly passé vessel of the N. Y. K. Line, for Yokohama.

(3)

The eight days on the Tenyo were more or less uneventful, except that we completely lost a whole Saturday, which worried me rather.

I worked hard on my novel *Julian Kane,* but became increasingly discouraged by its obvious dullness, until I finally decided that if it continued as it was going the future readers of it would commit suicide from boredom long before the hero ever reached that point of defeat, and so discarding it I proceeded to concentrate on finding an idea for a play.

Gertie Lawrence, the night before I had left New York, had given a farewell party for me and, as a going-away present, gave me a little gold book from Cartier's which when opened and placed on the writing-table in my cabin disclosed a clock, calendar and thermometer on one side, and an extremely pensive photograph of Gertie herself on the other. This rich gift, although I am sure prompted by the least ulterior of motives, certainly served as a delicate reminder that I had promised to write a play for us both, and I gazed daily, often with irritation, at that anxious retroussé face while my mind voyaged barrenly through eighteenth-century salons, Second Empire drawing-rooms and modern cocktail bars in search of some inspiring echo, some slight thread of plot, that might suitably unite us in either comedy, tragedy or sentiment.

However, nothing happened. I was aware of a complete emptiness. The Pacific Ocean, bland and calm, swished by with the perpetual off-stage effect of rice in a sieve; flying-fish skittered away from the bows, skimming along the surface for a while and disappearing with little plops; my fellow-passengers paraded round and round the deck, providing me with nothing beyond a few irrelevant and purposeless conjectures, until I finally gave up. This was a holiday, after all, and I refused to allow my writer's conscience to agitate it any further. I also resolved never again to make any promises that implicated my creative ability. They were limiting and tiresome and imposed too great a strain. I would write whatever the spirit moved me to write, regardless of whether the subject matter was suitable to Gertie Lawrence, Mrs. Patrick Campbell or Grock, and in the meantime, feeling no particular urge to write anything at all, I closed Gertie's clock with a snap and read a book.

(4)

At about five o'clock on a bitter December afternoon the Tenyo Maru came to a standstill in the bay of Yokohama. There was a blizzard raging and, through it, I could see from the smoking-room window, the quarantine launch approaching like an asthmatical old lady fussing through bead curtains.

Shapes of land appeared at intervals through the driving sleet; strange nobbly mountains dotted here and there with white specks which I gathered were lighthouses.

The drive from Yokohama to Tokio takes, as a rule, about fifty minutes, but mine took longer as a wheel came off the taxi when we were half-way. I sat inside in a pool of water watching, in the downpour, several excited Japanese put it on again and feeling, on the whole, discouraged by my first view of the 'Glamorous Orient.'

The Imperial Hotel was grand and comfortable, and was renowned for having stood firm during the big earthquake. A wire was handed me from Jeffrey saying that he had missed a boat in Shanghai and wouldn't be with me for three days which, although disappointing, was a relief, as I had begun to think I was never going to hear from him at all.

[319]

The night before he arrived I went to bed early as I wanted to greet him as brightly as possible at seven in the morning, but the moment I switched out the lights, Gertie appeared in a white Molyneux dress on a terrace in the South of France and refused to go again until four a.m., by which time *Private Lives,* title and all, had constructed itself.

In 1923 the play would have been written and typed within a few days of my thinking of it, but in 1929 I had learned the wisdom of not welcoming a new idea too ardently, so I forced it into the back of my mind, trusting to its own integrity to emerge again later on, when it had become sufficiently set and matured.

We found Tokio flat and painfully ugly: a sad scrap-heap of a city, rather like Wembley in the process of demolition. The streets were all muddy and everything appeared to be in course of reconstruction owing, we supposed, to perpetual earthquakes and an excess of zeal in the way of Western improvements. Fortunately, however, Tokio is far from being representative of Japan. Nikko is only four hours away with its snow-capped mountains and gurling streams, and its temples and shrines peacefully sheltered in groves of trees.

We spent a couple of days there in a neat, shiny little hotel with paper walls, a few back numbers of *Woman and Home,* and excellent food.

After three weeks in Japan we crossed the Yellow Sea to Fusan, and travelled by train up through Korea to Mukden in Manchuria where we were met, at six in the morning, by a gentleman in furs who turned out to be not only the British consul, but the brother of Frank Tours, the musical director of *Bitter Sweet* in New York.

He gave us a delicious, thoroughly English breakfast and a hot bath, after which we went out in rickshaws to see the town; but we soon came back with tears of agony running down our faces, as the wind happened to be blowing from Siberia that morning, and the temperature was thirty below zero.

That evening we spent a pleasant hour or two in the English Club. The English and American residents, of which there were few, had organised a fancy-dress dance to celebrate the passing of 1929. It was a strange party and, beneath its gaiety, exceedingly touching. Pierrots, Columbines, Clowns, red rep Cardinals, and butter-muslin Juliets, all pulling crackers, drinking punch, and crossing hands to sing together "Should auld acquaintance be forgot', while outside the wind blew like ice over the Manchurian wastes and the snow piled high on the window-sills. If they had not all been so kind and hospitable to us we might have had time to feel a little guilty. We were only passing through. We were free to go where we pleased, whereas the bulk of the people present were condemned to stay in that grim, remote place perhaps for years.

I will spare the reader a detailed description of a twenty-four-hour journey to Pekin in an unheated train in which we sat, wrapped in fur coats, in a wooden compartment trying unsuccessfully to conquer intestinal chills by eating nothing at all and drinking a bottle of brandy each, while the frozen Chinese countryside struggled bleakly by the windows.

Lady Lampson, the wife of Sir Miles Lampson, the British minister, was particularly charming to us in Pekin. She showed us the incredible beauties of the city, organised our shopping expeditions, and took pains to prevent us from buying soapstone instead of jade, and plaster instead of Ming pottery.

We travelled as far as Shanghai with her and her little boy, who was going home to school in England. A few days later we heard that she had been taken seriously ill with spinal meningitis on her arrival in Hong Kong and, a little later still, that she was dead. This saddened us horribly. We had only known her for a few weeks, but during that time she had been so hospitable and kind that we felt we had lost a much older friend.

(5)

A bout of influenza laid me low in Shanghai, and I lay, sweating gloomily, in my bedroom in the Cathay Hotel for several days. The ensuing convalescence, however, was productive, for I utilised it by writing *Private Lives*. The idea by now seemed ripe enough to have a shot at, so I started it, propped up in bed with a writing-block and an Eversharp pencil, and completed it, roughly, in four days. It came easily, and, with the exception of a few of the usual 'blood-and-tears' moments, I enjoyed writing it. I thought it a shrewd and witty comedy, well-constructed on the whole, but psychologically unstable; however, its entertainment value seemed obvious enough, and its acting opportunities for Gertie and me admirable, so I cabled to her immediately in New York telling her to keep herself free for the autumn, and put the whole thing aside for a few weeks before typing and revising it.

With influenza and *Private Lives* both behind me I entered the social whirl of Shanghai with zest. There were lots of parties and Chinese dinners and general cosmopolitan junketings, which, while putting a slight strain on our lingual abilities, in no way dampened our spirits. We found some charming new friends, notably Mme. Birt and her twin daughters who, apart from being extremely attractive, could quarrel with each other in six different languages without even realising that they were not sticking to one; and three English naval officers, Ascherson, Bushell and Guerrier, with whom we visited many of the lower and gayer haunts of the city and sailed as their guests on our first but, as far as I was concerned, not my last voyage in one of His Majesty's ships.

Ever since then I have become increasingly indebted to the Navy. To me, the life of a guest in a warship is deeply satisfactory. I have passed some of the happiest hours of my life in various ward-rooms. The secret of naval good manners is hard to define, perhaps discipline has a lot to do with it and prolonged contact with the sea, perhaps a permanent background of such dignity makes for simplicity of mind.

Perhaps all this is an illusion, perhaps it is merely the complete change of atmosphere that so englamours me; if so, I shall certainly take good care never to outstay my welcome long enough to break it.

Ascherson, Bushell and Guerrier, having firmly inoculated me with the naval bug, obtained permission from their captain, Captain Arbuthnot, for us both to travel as far as Hong Kong with them, and we sailed down the river from Shanghai in the H.M.S. Suffolk on a cold sunny morning in February. The warships of other nations, American, French and Italian, saluted as we moved down-stream. Jeffrey and I, well placed out of everyone's way on the gun deck, stood, uncertain whether to keep our hats on or off, knowing only that we mustn't smoke and must wait there, however cold, until fetched into the ward-room for a drink. We watched the busy water-front slide away. The air was sharp and clear, and the blue of the coolies' coats on the bund took from the sun such vivid brightness that, in the distance, it looked as though the river had climbed up into the streets and was swirling among the houses.

The voyage took five days as we stopped every now and then on the way for various exercises. I think we behaved adequately well on the whole. We learnt, and remembered, various little lessons in naval etiquette and jargon as we went along. We had a comfortable cabin each, and the captain allowed us the use of his bathroom. There is a permanent humming noise in a warship which is soothing to the nerves, and a clean, efficient smell, impossible to describe, but quite unique. No one paid much attention to us and we were free to wander about and observe the life of the ship, and a very cheerful and energetic life it seemed to be. There was an incessant orgy of polishing and swabbing and scrubbing from the moment we left Shanghai to the moment we arrived in Hong Kong. There was also a great deal of bugle-blowing and fast running, crabwise, up and down narrow iron ladders. At night we dressed for dinner and sat round the shiny ward-room table while the marine band fought its way gallantly through the intricacies of *Bitter Sweet* and *This Year of Grace,* the parts of which the bandmaster had hurriedly bought in Shanghai when he heard that I was to be a passenger.

The ship changed for dinner, too. It changed its personality entirely, becoming silent, purposeful and almost sinister. There was no activity and hardly any noise except for the humming of

[323]

the engines. We usually went up on the bridge for a little while before going to bed, and put the final seal upon the drinks we had drunk in the ward-room by swallowing a mug of ship's cocoa with the officer of the watch. Then, of all moments, we were most conscious of the good old layman's romantic 'thrill of the Navy.' The ship slid quietly through the darkness and we felt the pulse of her strength beneath our feet. The water cut away from the bows and swished and gurgled alongside, occasionally streaked with phosphorus, while overhead strange and larger stars appeared. There was a slight panic one night because Guerrier, who happened to have the middle watch, sent a frantic message down to the ward-room to say that he'd mislaid an island and did anyone know where it was! A good deal of agitation ensued, and it was finally located several miles off the port bow. This joke lasted everyone for quite a while.

Finally, on the fifth evening, Hong Kong sprang abruptly at us out of a fog. The sun was just setting, and the island against a suddenly clear sky was a fantastically beautiful sight, but at that moment sad and unwelcome for us both because it meant that we had to go ashore.

We loitered on board as long as we could. Long after the captain had left in his launch, long after night had fallen, we were still standing about in the ward-room accepting with gracious melancholy 'gimlet' after 'gimlet' until finally we clattered unsteadily down the ladder behind our luggage and went bouncing off across the harbour to the Peninsula Hotel at Kowloon, where we ate some caviare and drank still more gin. Jeffrey indeed was so sunk in depression that he signed the hotel register 'Mackintosh' without my noticing, a slip of the pen which caused us considerable trouble later on.

We stayed a week in Hong Kong. I spent most of it sitting in my hotel bedroom typing and revising *Private Lives*. When it was completed I sent copies of it to Gertie and Jack in New York, and told them to cable me in Singapore what they thought about it.

The night before we left we gave a farewell dinner to all the officers of the Suffolk. They were going to sea early next morning and that evening, although tinged with regret, was, to say the least of it, a success.

We rose with cracking heads to watch from our windows the Suffolk sail away. We felt very proud to know her as she steamed with slow dignity out of the harbour, and also so low that we ordered a bottle of champagne then and there, a drink that we both detest, and drank it to the last drop sitting miserably in a hot bath.

We embarked that same afternoon on one of the filthiest little freight boats I have ever encountered. We were bound for Haiphong in Indo-China, and there were no other boats available. This one, whose name I will withhold owing to the laws of libel, was French owned, and manned by a crew of murderous-looking Annamites and three French officers with singularly untidy personalities. Our cabin contained two cast-iron bunks and a tin basin, and we shared it with hordes of cockroaches, bedbugs and fleas, and a dead mouse which we buried at sea as soon as the tragedy was discovered.

We were immured in that God-forsaken tub, with a cargo of copra and salt fish, for five days and nights.

On arrival at Haiphong we hired a car and drove to Hanoï, which is the capital of Tonkin. Here we were not allowed out of the hotel as there was a revolution in progress; however, M. Pasquier, the governor-general, to whom we had a letter of introduction, sent his A.D.C. and car to fetch us, and we spent a strange evening in the Government Palace with M. Pasquier, two generals, an admiral, and the A.D.C. Outside the revolution was in full swing, and there was occasionally the sound of gun-fire. Inside all was peaceful and well-ordered. The dinner was delicious, the wine excellent, and M. Pasquier the most delightful host.

We hired a car and a driver and set off the next day down the length of Indo-China to Saïgon. The journey took the best part of a week, the scenery alternating violently between the steepest of steep mountains and the flattest of flat plains, with a little jungle thrown in every now and then, and a never-ending series of rivers across which we were ferried on creaking, insecure barges. We were deeply impressed by the admirable French colonisation which enabled us to procure excellent coffee and rolls in the remotest villages.

The night before we were due to arrive in Saïgon we stopped at a small village called Nah Trang. The rest-house was clean but primitive, and we went to bed early as we were getting up at dawn to make the last lap of our journey. At about a quarter to five, before it was light, I was wakened by Jeffrey demanding, in a shaky dry voice, a thermometer. I struggled out from under my mosquito net, lit a candle, and took his temperature which, to my horror, was nearly a hundred and four. I disguised the truth from him and told him it was just on a hundred and, having roused our driver and dressed as quickly as we could, we set off, hell for leather, for Saïgon. It was a hideous journey—our driver, none too good at any time, became demoniac when urged to drive fast. We slaughtered countless chickens and ducks, two dogs, a snake and a cat. Jeffrey was delirious part of the time, and I watched him anxiously for symptoms of coma, because my mind all the while was haunted by the memory of Lady Lampson and spinal meningitis.

We arrived in Saïgon in the full glare of midday. Every blind was down and there wasn't a creature moving. The streets were white with heat, and Jeffrey by then was almost unconscious. I got him into a room in the hotel and set off in a rickshaw, the hotel porter having directed me to a clinic, where I managed to persuade a pompous little doctor to rouse himself from his siesta and come with me.

The result of all this was that Jeffrey was moved into the clinic, with what the French doctor hilariously diagnosed as *'mal au foie —rien que mal au foie.'* He was given a few injections and some vegetable soup immediately, and why he didn't die I shall never know, because several weeks later when he was properly examined in Singapore he was found to be suffering from amœbic dysentery.

However, he lay in the clinic in Saïgon for close on a month, and finally emerged looking more like a hat-pin than a human being, but pronounced fit enough to continue our journey up through Angkor and into Siam. In the meantime I spent those four weeks in isolated splendour in the Grand Hotel. Saïgon is very small and is referred to proudly by the French as the Paris of the Orient. This, I need hardly say, is an over-statement. It is a well-arranged little town and it has several cafés and a municipal opera house, but it is *not* very like Paris.

I visited Jeffrey twice a day and discovered a pleasant little café and brothel combined which catered mostly to the lower-class mercantile marines and a floating clientele of tarts of all nations; apart from these distractions I spent most of my time sitting on a cane chair outside the Grand Hotel watching the *beau monde* bouncing up and down the Rue Catinat in rickshaws. The hotel orchestra played selections from *Tosca, Madame Butter-fly,* and the tinkling French operettas of the nineties every evening, and for a little while the scene took on a certain forlorn charm. But even this faded after the first few days, because it took only a very short while to know every single person that passed by sight.

When Jeffrey so strangely recovered from the ministrations of that doctor we set off to Angkor, where we stayed for ten days. We wandered through queer magnificent ruins; we watched the temple dancers in the vast courtyard of Angkor Vat, swaying and stamping to harsh music in the flickering light of torches and coloured flares; we drove through the jungle roads, coming upon villages still in the process of excavation, still in the grip of the jungle, houses with strong trees growing right up through them and grey monkeys chattering on the crumbling roofs.

From Angkor we motored to Aranya Pradesa, the Siamese frontier, over the most appalling road I have ever encountered; from there, after a night in a surprisingly German rest-house, we took a train to Bangkok, where we stayed for two weeks. The Phya Tai Palace, which had once belonged to the Royal Family, was now a hotel, cool, spacious and reasonably comfortable, although I must admit that I once woke up from my after-lunch siesta to find a majestic procession of red ants making a forced march from one side of the mattress to the other, by way of my stomach.

We saw all the sights the city had to offer, and they were many and varied, ranging from an emerald Buddha the size of a football to the Pasteur Institute, where they extracted the venom from snakes by the apparently casual method of seizing them by the neck and making them bite little parchment saucers.

(6)

During that holiday I think my spirits reached their lowest ebb on the first evening I spent in Singapore. I sat on the veranda of the hotel, sipping a gin-sling and staring at the muddy sea. There was a thunderstorm brewing and the airless heat pressed down on my head. I felt as though I were inside a hot cardboard box which was growing rapidly smaller and smaller, until soon I should have to give up all hope of breathing and die of suffocation.

My state of mind was not solely due to the climate. Jeffrey had been taken badly ill again in the little Danish freighter which had brought us from Siam, and I had just left him in the hospital, looking like death and waiting to be diagnosed. My imagination was busy wording, as gently as possible, the fatal telegram to his mother. I pictured her receiving it in the cool quietness of her Wilton Crescent drawing-room while I, in this God-forsaken hole, dealt sadly but efficiently with grisly funeral details; in fact, by the time my second gin-sling was brought to me Jeffrey was dead and buried.

Presently the thunderstorm broke and raged violently for about an hour. It was the most thorough-going storm I had ever seen. The sky split in two; the sea lost its smooth, oily temper and rushed at the hotel as though it wanted to swallow it up; and then the rain came. I recognised it as rain only because I knew it couldn't possibly be anything else; it certainly bore no resemblance to any rain I had ever met before. It fell like a steel curtain, and its impact on the roof of the veranda was terrific. Then, abruptly, the whole performance stopped. The sea relaxed, the skies cleared, the stars came out, and in the cooler air my imagination became less fevered. I drove up to the hospital after dinner and found Jeffrey enjoying a cigarette and an animated conversation with the night nurse.

The next day the doctors said that he had dysentery and would be able to leave the hospital in about a month if all went well. Once resigned to this enforced pause in our travels we both felt better, and while Jeffrey concentrated on his discomforts and treatments, I set out to discover what Singapore had to offer in the way of distractions.

The first and principal distraction I found was an English theatrical touring company called 'The Quaints.' They were appearing at the Victoria Theatre and their repertory was almost shockingly varied. They played, with a certain light-hearted abandon, *Hamlet, Mr. Cinders, Anthony and Cleopatra, The Girl Friend, When Knights Were Bold,* and *Journey's End.* I was taken to their opening performance of *Mr. Cinders* by the manager of the theatre and from then onwards I never left them. My chief friends among them were Betty Hare and John Mills, both of whom have worked with me a great deal since, and the general major-domo of the whole enterprise, Jimmy Grant Anderson. Jimmy was rich in quality; he was 'of the dust the theatre bore, shaped, made aware', his blood was the best grease-paint. I had met him before in a thousand people, but never so concentrated, never such triple-distilled essence. His mind was a prop hamper crammed to the lid with theatre finery. To him the sea and the sky were only painted on canvas, and not any too well painted at that. Behind the immediate Singapore act drop there were other scenes being set, there always had been and there always would be. I had the feeling that even after his own death he would merely retire, swearing, to some celestial dressing-room and take off his make-up.

There were other Quaints, a dozen of them. En masse we went

to supper parties and swimming parties after the show at night. Some of the more refined social lights of Singapore looked obliquely at us, as though we were not quite the thing, a little too rowdy perhaps, on the common side. I'm sure they were right. Actors always laugh more loudly than other people when they're enjoying themselves, and we laughed most of the time.

Intoxicated by so many heady draughts of familiar vintage theatre, I allowed myself to be persuaded by Jimmy to appear as Stanhope in *Journey's End* for three performances. The Singapore Press displayed gratifying excitement and my name glittered proudly in blue bulbs across the front of the Victoria Theatre. I learnt the part in two days and had three rehearsals. The élite of Singapore assembled in white ducks and flowered chiffons and politely watched me take a fine part in a fine play and throw it into the alley. The only cause for pride I had over the whole business was that I didn't dry-up on any of the lines. True, I became slightly lost during the second performance in a maze of military instructions, and commanded a surprised sergeant-major to take number eight 'platoolian' into the back trenches; and I was never actually certain which scene I was playing, and how long it was going to last, but Bob Sheriff's lines remained, on the whole, intact, although I spoke the majority of them with such over-emphasis that it might have been better if they hadn't. John Mills, as Raleigh, gave the finest performance I have ever seen given of that part, and Jimmy Grant Anderson was excellent as Trotter. The whole company was good and the production admirable. The outstanding failure was undoubtedly me. Of course, there were many excuses. Only two days to learn it, insufficient rehearsals, etc., etc.; all the same I should have been ashamed of myself for attempting anything as important as *Journey's End* in such circumstances. In discussing it beforehand it had seemed a lark, great fun, an amusing experiment; it wasn't until I got on to the stage in a temperature of about 115 in the shade, with the sweat rolling off me, that I began to be aware of my folly, and it wasn't, mercifully, until the three performances were over that I relaxed enough to realise my impertinence.

The third performance was a little better than the first two, and probably with a few weeks of hard work I might ultimately have played it properly. If it had been a bad play I should have accepted the lark at its surface value and been content that I had, at least, amused The Quaints; as it was, however, my retrospective embarrassment afterwards was mortifying and I have never quite forgiven myself.

Singapore's behaviour to me was beyond reproach, with the exception of one of the gentlemen of the Press, who was indelicate enough to hint that I was not quite as good as the man he had seen play it before. I saluted him, wanly, for his honesty.

(7)

I have often thought I should like to write a travel book. Not the *Through Tibet on a Bicycle* variety, nor yet the Richard Halliburton formula with pictures of myself swimming unswimmable rivers and straddling ancient statuary. Rather a casual travel book, in which the essence and charm of every strange place I visited would be recaptured in a few apt and telling phrases; in which I could devote pages and pages to gentle introspection; sketching lightly my opinions of Life, Love, Art and Letters on to incongruous backgrounds of mountains and deserts and shrill tropical vegetation.

My body has certainly wandered a good deal, but I have an uneasy suspicion that my mind has not wandered nearly enough. It is a well-trained mind, disciplined to observe, record and store up impressions without any particular wear and tear or exhaustive effort. It is capable of functioning quickly, and making rapid and usually intelligent decisions. It is at its best when dealing with people, and at its worst when dealing with the inanimate. Its photographic propensities are good, but something goes wrong with the developing, because the pictures it takes of landscapes and seascapes fade too easily. Faces, events and tunes remain clear, fragments of past conversations, also, and the sudden stinging memory of long-dead emotions. But visual experience, that glorious view when you reach the top of the hill, that moment in the Acropolis just before sunset, those pale dawns at sea, all these become smudged and half rubbed out until, frequently, not even an outline remains.

My travel book would be difficult to write, for, in addition to these defects, my mind resents certain kinds of information; it cannot or will not accept history for history's sake. Remote foreign churches, carved, sculpted and decorated by remote foreign monks centuries ago; ruins, museums and cathedrals, unless for some specific reason they happen to catch my imagination, leave no imprint whatsoever. In fact, many of the world's noblest antiquities have definitely irritated me. Perhaps the sheen on them of so many hundreds of years' intensive appreciation makes them smug. I feel that they bridle when I look at them. Once, in Ceylon, I saw an enormous sacred elephant sit up and beg for a banana; I don't believe it really wanted the banana, it merely knew what was expected of it. I have also seen the Pyramids give a little self-deprecatory simper at the sight of a Kodak. I have not, as yet, seen the Taj Mahal at all, but I feel that when I do it will probably lie down in a consciously alluring attitude and pretend to be asleep.

I freely admit that this blindness is perverse; perhaps it's a repressed complex, perhaps I was frightened by a Bellini Madonna when I was a tiny child, but there it is, complex or not, a permanent obstacle to a respectable travel book. On the other hand, although insensitive to history for history's sake, I am keenly responsive to travel for travel's sake. I love to go and I love to have been, but best of all I love the intervals between arrivals and departures, the days and nights of steady, incessant movement, when the horizon is empty and time completely changes its rhythm. Then I can sleep, wake, write, read and think in peace. It is in these hours I feel that, after all, there may be a chance for me, less likelihood of opportunities missed, less intolerable distraction. It is probably a temperamental defect in me that I can only catch this elusive quietness when moving, a maladjustment of my nervous system, but it is certainly the reason above all others that I go away, not to get anywhere, not even to return, just to go.

Jeffrey emerged from the hospital in Singapore more emaciated than ever, but definitely on the way to recovery. We lingered on a little. The Quaints left for Hong Kong and we celebrated their going with a party, waving them hazily into a small P. and O. at two in the morning. We went to a few dinners, picnics and cocktail parties, and finally went on to Ceylon by way of Kuala Lumpur and Penang. From Penang to Colombo we travelled in a Prince Line freighter; an enchanting few days, most of which we spent lying in a canvas swimming tank rigged up on the fo'c'sle.

At Colombo we were met by my brother Eric, in shorts and a sola-topi. We stayed with him in his bungalow in the hills for a few days, and then came down again to the Galle Face Hotel, where there was a jazz orchestra, curry, Cingalese waiters with elaborate combs in their hair, and, surprisingly enough, Cole and Linda Porter. They were on their way from Java and Bali, and looked splendidly immaculate. The climate did its best to flurry Linda's coolness, but without success; she remained serene and smooth, and bought a lot of emeralds. Meanwhile, a tremendous telegraphic bickering was taking place between me and Gertie Lawrence in New York. She had cabled me in Singapore, rather casually, I thought, saying that she had read *Private Lives* and that there was nothing wrong in it that couldn't be fixed. I had wired back curtly that the only thing that was going to be fixed was her performance. Now cables were arriving at all hours of the day and night, with a typical disregard of expense, saying that she had foolishly committed herself to Charlot for a new revue—could we open in January instead of September—could I appear in the revue with her, just to fill in—could I wire to Charlot to release her from her contract—that it wasn't a contract at all, merely a moral obligation—that it wasn't a moral obligation at all, but a cabled contract—that her lawyers were working day and night to get her out of it—that she would rather do *Private*

Lives than anything in the world—that she couldn't do *Private Lives* at all. In her last telegram she remembered to give me her cable address which, had she done so sooner, would have saved me about forty pounds. I finally lost patience and cabled that I intended to do the play with someone else, and I heard nothing further until I arrived back in England.

(8)

Our journey from Ceylon to Marseilles was accomplished in one of the older P. and O. ships—in fact she was so old that we expected her to hoist enormous bellying sails when a light wind sprang up in the Red Sea. The voyage started badly for me; I was awakened from a deep sleep at eight o'clock on the first morning out by the games organiser, who walked peremptorily into my cabin and told me that I was to play shuffle-board with Mrs. Harrison at eleven, and deck-quoits with Miss Phillips at ten-fifteen. I replied that I intended to pass most of the day in the lavatory and that if Mrs. Harrison and Miss Phillips felt like a little Russian bank or backgammon, he could tell them where to find me.

Owing to this reasonable outburst of irritation, both Jeffrey and I were considered snobbish and exclusive by our fellow-passengers and were, mercifully, excluded from most of the ship's social activities, with the exception of the fancy-dress ball at which I was invited to give the prizes. Here I disgraced myself again by giving the first prize to a woman who had been ignored by most of the ladies on board, apparently because they suspected her of coloured blood. Had I known this, I should have given her the first prize even if she had been a Zulu.

During that voyage I wrote an angry little vilification of war called *Post-Mortem;* my mind was strongly affected by *Journey's End,* and I had read several current war novels one after the other. I wrote *Post-Mortem* with the utmost sincerity; this, I think, must be fairly obvious to anyone who reads it. In fact, I tore my emo-

tions to shreds over it. The result was similar to my performance as
Stanhope: confused, under-rehearsed and hysterical. Unlike my
performance as Stanhope, however, it had some very fine moments.
There is, I believe, some of the best writing I have ever done in
it, also some of the worst. I have no deep regrets over it, as I know
my intentions to have been of the purest. I passionately believed in
the truth of what I was writing; too passionately. The truths I
snarled out in that hot, uncomfortable little cabin were all too true
and mostly too shallow. Through lack of detachment and lack of
real experience of my subject, I muddled the issues of the play. I
might have done better had I given more time to it and less
vehemence. However, it helped to purge my system of certain
accumulated acids.

(9)

Back in London again, the Far East receded swiftly. Once the
various presents had been doled out and the principal anecdotes
related, all memories fused in a highly coloured jumble.

I sat in the garden at Goldenhurst in the sunset, worrying about
pneumonia rather than malaria; I no longer shook my bedroom
slippers to see if there were any scorpions inside them, although
I must admit I was badly frightened one night by a daddy-long-
legs falling on to my face. Jungles, mountains and seas looked up
at me from snapshots. Yes, I had been there and there and there—
there was Saïgon, that suffocating little Paris of the Orient—in the
right-hand corner was the hotel terrace where I sat interminably
night after night—the little orchestra—*Tosca, Bohème, Veronique*
—the rickshaws passing back and forth—podgy French business
men in creased, tropical suits, clambering in and out—Jeffery in the
clinic, lying yellow and wretched under a mosquito-net. There
was the Tartar Gate in Pekin—I'd been through that—ice-cold
winds blowing across from the Gobi Desert—clouds of stinging
grey dust. Hong Kong harbour, unrecognisable in the photograph,
just a view, no suggestion of its reality—that gigantic island rising
out of the sea—the peak with white veils of cloud round it, as

though it had been washing its head—at night the millions of lights—the little ferry-boats chugging to and fro across the harbour. There was the Suffolk looking glossy and prim and overposed—there was the scuttle through which I stared at the China Sea—the cross marks my bedroom window. Indo-China—Siam—monks in faded yellow robes—temples and palaces with porcelain roofs—emerald Buddhas—silver mesh floors—cobras hooded and angry, snapping at bits of parchment—ships of all shapes and sizes —freighters, P. and O.'s, Dollar Line, N.Y.K., sampans, junks— Singapore—a thunderstorm like the breaking of the sixth seal— straight, flat streets lined with coloured shops—palms, flame-in-the-forest, hibiscus, poinsettias—the Victoria Theatre, with large electric punkahs eternally scuffling round and round, while I sweated and ranted in a British warm and full trench equipment— Kuala Lumpur, Penang, Colombo, Kandy, Aden, Suez—names on a map no longer, but places that I had been to; I—me—sitting here in a familiar garden—I had walked along those streets, eaten and drunk, gone to sleep and wakened up in those strange hotel rooms; crossed those wide seas; bumped over those far-away roads, and here I was again; the world was round all right, one small circle had been completed, perhaps Time was round, too. I remember going indoors, twirling the globe, and looking towards future journeys.

(10)

We played a short provincial tour of *Private Lives* before bringing it to London. Gertie had arrived back in England in gay spirits and, by hook, crook, love and money, managed to extricate herself from her moral, legal and financial obligations to Charlot. She seemed happily unaware that there had ever been any question of her not playing *Private Lives*. All the cables and muddles and complications hadn't existed. Here she was, eager, enthusiastic and looking lovely; the play was perfect, nothing had to be fixed at all. Gertie has an astounding sense of the complete reality of the moment, and her moments, dictated by the extreme variability of her moods, change so swiftly that it is frequently difficult to discover what, apart from eating, sleeping, and acting, is true of her at all. I know her well, better, I believe, than most people. The early years of our friendship set her strongly in my mind. I knew her then to have quick humour, insane generosity, and a loving heart, and those things seldom change. I see her now, ages away from her ringlets and black velvet military cap, sometimes a simple, wide-eyed child, sometimes a glamorous *femme du monde,* at some moments a rather boisterous 'good sort', at others a weary, disillusioned woman battered by life, but gallant to the last. There are many other grades also between these extremes. She appropriated beauty to herself quite early, along with all the tricks and mannerisms that go with it. In adolescence she was barely pretty. Now, without apparent effort, she gives the impression of sheer loveliness. Her grace in movement is exquisite, and her voice charming. To disentangle Gertie herself from this mutability is baffling, rather like delving for your grandmother's gold locket at the bottom of an overflowing jewel-case.

Her talent is equally kaleidoscopic. On the stage she is potentially capable of anything and everything. She can be gay, sad, witty, tragic, funny and touching. She can play a scene one night with perfect subtlety and restraint, and the next with such obviousness and over-emphasis that your senses reel. She has, in abundance, every theatrical essential but one: critical faculty. She can watch a great actor and be stirred to the depths, her emotional response is immediate and genuine. She can watch a bad actor and be stirred to the depths, the response is equally immediate and equally genuine. But for this tantalising lack of discrimination she could, I believe, be the greatest actress alive in the theatre to-day.

Adrianne Allen (Mrs. Raymond Massey) played Sibyl in *Private Lives,* and Lawrence Olivier, Victor. The whole tour was swathed in luxury. Adrianne travelled in a car, so did Gertie and so did I, the touring days of the past belonged to another world. Assurance of success seemed to be emblazoned on the play from the first, we had few qualms, played to capacity business, and enjoyed ourselves thoroughly. We felt, I think rightly, that there was a shine on us.

In London we opened in a new theatre, the Phœnix. We were an immediate hit, and our three months' limited engagement was sold out during the first week. It was an interesting play to play, naturally more interesting for Gertie and me than it was for Larry and Adrianne. We had the parts, or rather, the part, as Elyot and Amanda are practically synonymous. The play's fabric was light and required light handling. Gertie was brilliant. Everything she had been in my mind, when I originally conceived the idea in Tokio, came to life on the stage. The witty, quick-silver delivery of lines; the romantic quality, tender and alluring; the swift, brittle rages; even the white Molyneux dress. Adrianne played Sibyl with a subtle tiresomeness and a perfect sense of character, more character actually than the part really had. Larry managed, with determination and much personal charm, to invest the wooden Victor with enough reality to make him plausible. I frequently felt conscience-stricken over them both, playing so gallantly on such palpably second-strings. Gertie and I certainly had most of the fun and, with it, most of the responsibility. Our duologue second act when, for some reason or other, we were not feeling quite on the crest of the wave, was terribly exhausting. We both knew that if we let it sag for a moment that it would die on us. On the other hand, when it flowed, when the audience was gay and appreciative, when our spirits were tuned to the right key, it was so exhilarating that we felt deflated when it was over.

We closed, at the end of our scheduled three months, with the gratifying knowledge that we could easily have run on for another six. This arbitrary three months' limit of mine brought me a certain amount of criticism. 'It was a sin,' people said, 'to close a play when it was doing so well.' Some even prophesied darkly future catastrophes: 'A day will come,' they said, 'when you will bitterly regret this.' I am told that even Sir Cedric Hardwicke sprang into print about it. However, I remained convinced that that policy, for me, was right. Perhaps a day will come, as the Cassandras foretold; perhaps in later years, when I'm looking for a job, I shall indeed regret those lost grosses, but I don't really think that I will. I consider myself a writer first and an actor second. I love acting, and it is only during the last few years that I have become good, although, as yet, limited in scope. If I play the same part over and over again for a long run, I become bored and frustrated and my performance deteriorates; in addition to this, I have no time to write. Ideas occur to me and then retreat again because, with eight performances a week to be got through, there is no time to develop them. For me, three months in London and three months in New York once in every two years is an ideal arrangement. It is, of course, more than possible that I might write and appear in a play that wouldn't run three weeks. In that bleak moment, age permitting, I shall turn gratefully to a revival of *Private Lives*.

I spent Christmas week at Goldenhurst before sailing for America. Goldenhurst was growing; bedrooms and bathrooms were multiplying rapidly, so also was acreage. I could now walk proudly for quite a long way over my own land. Goldenhurst was a continual pleasure. Even then, in 1930, it was unrecognisable from what it had been a few years before. Now, of course, at the moment of writing, it has almost over-reached itself. It has completed its metamorphosis from a tumbledown farm house to a country estate. To do it justice, it hasn't got a self-made look. It has no vulgar 'nouveau-riche' mannerisms, it doesn't eat peas with its knife, but I am beginning to feel a little awed by it, especially when I come across its photographs in the smarter illustrated weeklies.

I employed that Christmas week by writing some numbers for a revue that Cochran was preparing. Two of them, 'Any Little Fish' and 'Half-caste Woman', were reasonably successful, although the revue—which I never saw—wasn't.

(11)

During the London run of *Private Lives* I discussed with Cochran the idea of doing a big spectacular production at the

Coliseum. I felt an urge to test my producing powers on a large scale. My mind's eye visualised a series of tremendous mob scenes —the storming of the Bastille—the massacre of the Huguenots— I believe even the Decline and Fall of the Roman Empire flirted with me for a little. Soon my imagination became over-crowded, and I began to simplify. These mass effects were all very well, but they couldn't sustain a whole evening; they should be, at best, a background for a strong story; at worst, padding for a weak one.

Cockie was enthusiastic and settled himself blandly to wait until I delivered him a more concrete proposition; meanwhile, history continued to parade through my mind, usually at night, when I was tired and wanted to go to sleep. Events, grand and portentous, battles, sieges, earthquakes, revolutions and shipwrecks, but no story, not the shadow of a theme. The Second Empire was the most tenacious of all; gaslight—chandeliers—richly apparelled courtesans driving in the Bois—Englishmen in deer-stalker caps climbing out of smoky trains at the Gare du Nord—the Empress herself, haughty, beautiful, crinolined; somehow a little synthetic —the whole scene a little synthetic—Winterhalter figures moving to Offenbach tunes. At the time perhaps a trifle shabby, but now, set in retrospect, charming. A sentimental, daguerreotype sort of charm, belonging to the past, but not too far away.

However, as an idea for the Coliseum it seemed too pale, too lacking in action; so away it went with the chariot-races and car-magnoles and blood-and-thunder, and I continued the search, until one day I happened to buy, at Foyle's in the Charing Cross Road, some ancient bound volumes of *Black and White* and the *Illustrated London News*. This was chance, and extremely happy chance. In the first volume I opened there was a full-page picture of a troop-ship leaving for the Boer War, and the moment I saw it I knew that I had found what I wanted. I can't explain why it rang the bell so sharply, I only know that it did. The tunes came into my mind first, tunes belonging to my very earliest childhood: 'Dolly Gray,' 'The Absent-minded Beggar,' 'Soldiers of the Queen,' 'Bluebell' (later this, but I neither knew nor cared). I played them on the piano immediately. G. B. Stern, who was coming to tea, found me in a state of high excitement; by then I had progressed, musically, quite a long way through the years; I'm not sure, but I think she entered to the tune of 'Tipperary.'

The emotional basis of *Cavalcade* was undoubtedly music. The whole story was threaded on to a string of popular melodies. This ultimately was a big contributing factor to its success. Popular tunes probe the memory more swiftly than anything else, and *Cavalcade,* whatever else it did, certainly awakened many echoes.

That afternoon in my studio, Peter (Stern) tottered a bit under the full impact of my enthusiasm, but she rallied after a while and, renouncing any personal problems she might have wished to discuss, obligingly retired with me to the beginning of the century. She remembered Mafeking Night, the Relief of Ladysmith, 'Dirty old Kruger,' One-armed Giffard, and newsboys—particularly newsboys—shrill Cockney voices shouting victories and defeats along London streets; cooks and housemaids running up foggy area steps to buy halfpenny papers; elderly gentlemen in evening capes stopping hansoms in order to read of 'Bob's' latest exploits. Then the illness of the Queen—newsboys again—the Queen's sinking—latest bulletin. She remembered vividly, graphically, and became as excited as I was. Later on I dedicated the published play to her in gratitude for those two hours.

My original story was different from what finally emerged, but the shape was the same, New Year's Eve 1899 to New Year's Eve 1930. Events took precedence first in my mind, and against them I moved a group of people—the bright young people of the nineties, the play was to finish with their children—the same eager emptiness, but a different jargon. After a while, I realised that the play should be bigger than that. I had flogged the bright young people enough, my vehemence against them had congealed, they were now no more than damp squibs, my Poor Little Rich Girls and Dance Little Ladies. Thirty years of English life seen through their eyes would be uninspired to say the least of it. Presently my real characters appeared in two classes. The Marryots, and Ellen and Bridges. Jane Marryot displayed a greater fecundity in my original conception, there were several more children than just

Edward and Joe; however, these fell away, still-born, into oblivion, discouraged by my firm determination to keep the whole thing as simple and uncomplicated as possible, and gradually the whole story completed itself in my mind.

I knew I couldn't attempt the actual writing of it until I had finished with *Private Lives* in New York. It would obviously require a lot of time, concentration and research, so I outlined it, in brief, to Cockie and promised it vaguely for the following year.

(12)

Private Lives was as gratifyingly successful in New York as it had been in London. Adrianne Allen was unable to come, and so Jill Esmond (Lawrence Olivier's wife) played Sibyl excellently, in a blonde wig. The New York critics resented the thinness of the play less than the London critics, and enjoyed the lightness of it more; in fact many of them came to see it several times. I think we retained, on the whole, the shine that we had started with; at all events, we strained every nerve to justify the almost overwhelming praise that was most generously lavished upon us.

I lived in a little penthouse on West 58th Street, with a lot of rather 'Ye Olde Teashoppe' furniture, a French cook, and an uninterrupted view of the Empire State building. Here, with the extremely twentieth-century sounds of New York in my ears, I embarked on my researches for *Cavalcade*. I had brought stacks of books with me from London, even the faithful bound volumes of the *Illustrated London News*. I started at an earlier date than 1899, feeling that to work slowly through the seventies, eighties and nineties would give my people a more solid background than if I just let them appear, untouched by any past experience whatever, in leg-of-mutton sleeves. For some of the later scenes of the play I could, of course, draw on my own memory.

The 1910 seaside scene—Uncle George and his 'Merrie Men' from Bognor would be useful there—the war scenes—'We don't want to lose you, but we think you ought to go,' 'On Sunday I walk out with a soldier.' I could remember Gwennie Brogden singing that in *The Passing Show* at the Palace. The Victoria Station scene—hospital trains coming in, leave trains going out— I remember that clearly—walking home from the theatre at night after the show, a sinister air-raid consciousness in the air—hardly any lights anywhere, the Mall ghostly and almost deserted. I often walked through Victoria Station, it was practically on my way, and there was always activity going on. It seems, looking back on it, more dramatic than I expect it actually was. In those days everybody was quite used to that interminable anti-climax. Khaki everywhere. Tommies laden with trench equipment. Tired officers in thinner khaki and Sam Browne belts—movable canteens on wheels—movable Red Cross stations, too—nurses, V.A.D.'s, chaplains, R.A.M.C. corporals, military police with red bands round their arms—groups of anxious civilians and always, always, the tarts mincing about on high heels, with their white fox furs and neat navy blues and checks—permanent grimaces at our national morality—hoping to squeeze a little profit from a few last drunken moments of leave.

Armistice night—I could certainly remember that—thousands and thousands of human beings gone mad—very effective on a revolving stage—yelling, dancing, fighting, singing, blowing squeakers. Then—later on—a night club; a gigantic noisy brassy night club—Dance Little Lady again—Twentieth Century Blues— a comment accurate enough and empty enough.

Jane Marryot took shape in my mind quite early. She seemed real to me and still does, a bit of my own mother and millions of others, too; ordinary, kind and unobtrusively brave; capable of deep suffering and incapable of cheap complaint. I was proud of Jane Marryot from the first.

In March I had a cable from Cockie saying that we couldn't have the Coliseum, but that we could have Drury Lane if I could guarantee him an opening date. This flurried me a bit, I have always loathed working to set time limits; however, I made a few rapid mental adjustments, bade a sad adieu to the revolving stage and cabled back that I would have the play completed and ready to open at the end of September.

Gertie got ill towards the end of our three months' run, so we closed the theatre for two weeks. This naturally put a little additional time on to the end of the run, and I arrived back in England to start on *Cavalcade* at the beginning of May.

(13)

It was a long time before I could settle down to the actual writing of the play. Mother was taken ill with appendicitis, and an anxious time ensued, during which concentration was impossible. It was then discovered, after a series of scenic conferences at Drury Lane, that certain structural alterations would have to be made, and a lot of new lighting equipment installed. Frank Collins, Dan O'Neil, William Abingdon, the Lane stage manager, all the heads of departments, the Strand Electric Company, Gladys and I, spent hours on end trying to solve, on paper, a mass of complicated technical problems. We planned the production so that there should be never more than thirty seconds' wait between any of its twenty-three scenes. The stage was divided into six hydraulic lifts. These had to be timed to sink and rise on light cues from the prompt corner; at the same moment, other light cues would cause the hanging parts of the scenery to be whisked up into the flies and simultaneously replaced. We installed a row of automatic lights along the front of the second balcony. These had five changes of colour and could be regulated by the electricians from the stage. The footlights were reconstructed so that they could silently disappear altogether for the big scenes, and rise into place again for the small interiors when needed. When all the estimates were passed and the work under way, Gladys and I retired to Goldenhurst and set ourselves to a rigid daily routine, until every word of the play and every scene design was completed. We worked from eight in the morning until five in the afternoon, with an hour's break for lunch. Gladys downstairs in the library, I upstairs in my bedroom. We passed through every emotional phase; the height of exhilaration, the depths of despair, and all the intermediate grades between. Fortunately our moods were, as a rule, mutual. On gay, successful days, when everything had gone well, we drove into Folkestone in the evening, relaxed and happy, and went to the pictures. At other times, when everything had creaked and stuck, when there had been no flow, we sat miserably in the garden, hardly speaking, convinced that we had bitten off a great deal more than we could chew, and sick to death of chew-ing.

At last it was finished; the dialogue all written and typed, the sets designed and coloured, the changes approximately timed, the dresses and uniforms sketched, individually for the principals, in blocks for the crowd.

While the scenery was being built, we took a short breather in the South of France, but the holiday, although outwardly peaceful, lacked inner tranquillity. The sun was hot; the sea blue. We drank a lot of Pernod, and watched brightly dressed crowds passing to and fro. They looked carefree and irresponsible, no recalcitrant hydraulic lifts haunted their sleep; no obstinate, unautomatic, auto-matic lights bedevilled them. The Alpes Maritimes, the smooth Mediterranean, the coloured houses, the harbours, the beaches, seemed to us to be only so many act drops, liable to rise at any moment and disclose a vast stage, dimly lit and crowded with odds and ends of furniture and mumbling actors. Most of the cast had been engaged before we left London, and on our return we dealt with the crowd auditions. This was a depressing business. We needed about four hundred, and over a thousand applied. Hour after hour we sat on the stage at a long table set against the lowered safety curtain, while an endless stream of 'out-of-works' passed by us. All of them professional actors or actresses; every one of them so in need of a job that the chance of being engaged as a super for thirty shillings a week was worth queueing up for. Many of them, at some time or other, had been comparatively successful; in fact we had several in our crowd who had actually played important parts on that very stage. The old ones were naturally more pathetic than the young; little thin old women, rather dressy, terrified of not being engaged, but quibbling a bit at the salary, asking time to think it over, then giving in suddenly —'Very well, I'll take it.' Pride was all very well, but times were hard, almost too hard to be borne.

They were tragic, those auditions, and they lay heavily on my conscience for a long while. I felt sentimentally ashamed at having succeeded so quickly, faced with those old lives who had worked all their years and never succeeded at all. I knew that thirty shillings a week was hopelessly inadequate, but the production was budgeted down to the last penny, and couldn't be put on at all if the crowd were paid any more.

I discovered, to my horror, that Cockie, in past moments of expansiveness, had promised three stage-struck society girls walk-ons in the show. There they stood, rather nervously, wearing excellently-cut clothes, good furs, and discreet jewellery. One of them whispered sweetly to me that she believed I knew her aunt. I told them, all three, that they were not the types I wanted, but Cockie intervened and insisted on engaging them. After a long argument I finally gave in on condition that for each of them I engaged two extra from the ranks of those who really needed the work.

In September rehearsals started. The carpenters and electricians were still in possession of the stage, and so I worked with the principals in the bar for the first ten days, getting all the dialogue scenes learnt and polished before I dealt with the crowd. As with *Bitter Sweet,* I felt a direct enthusiastic response from the cast. Everyone seemed to know his lines almost immediately, nobody was obtuse, tiresome or temperamental. I had lots of old friends with me: Moya Nugent, always efficient, gentle and utterly reliable; Maidie Andrews; Phyllis Harding; Betty Hare; John Mills, and several others. The newcomers seemed imbued with the same spirit; in fact the amount of work achieved in those first ten days was remarkable. Mary Clare played Jane with simplicity, tenderness and complete reality. Irene Browne was stylish and effective as Margaret. Una O'Connor and Fred Groves, as Ellen and Bridges, set themselves securely in the framework of the play from the first. Everybody was admirable, and the smaller parts were as expertly handled as the bigger ones. I woke up on the morning of my first crowd rehearsal frankly terrified. All night long a shouting mob of four hundred people had shared my bed, pushing and clamouring and asking me what I wanted them to do. I was in a bad panic, but the dreadful day had to be faced, so off we went, Lorn, Jack, Gladys and I, to the theatre.

I had decided to break the ice with the seaside scene, and it sat on the stage, complete in every detail, lowering forbiddingly at us as we filed into the front row of the dress-circle. Below us, in the stalls, was the full strength of the company, chattering and whispering. There was an extra buzz of expectancy when we came in, and then silence. I had thought out, in advance, a plan for handling such large numbers of people which, as it saved us endless trouble and time, I will explain. I had divided, on paper, the entire cast into groups of twenty. For each group there had been made a set of large plaques in different colours and numbered from one to twenty. Number one in each group was the captain, and was virtually in charge of the other nineteen. Each captain was responsible for his group having their plaques tied on before rehearsal started, and was also empowered to collect them at the end of the day and deliver them to the property master. This scheme, after a little preliminary confusion, worked splendidly. I could direct, through my microphone in the dress-circle, without the strain of trying to memorise people's names, entirely by numbers and colours: 'Would number seven red kindly go over and shake hands with number fifteen yellow-and-black stripe?' etc.

At that first rehearsal it naturally took a long time to get everybody correctly numbered and sorted. Finally, however, it was done, and there they stood, serried ranks of them, waiting for what was to happen next. That was the moment that I nearly broke. I had an insane desire to say, quite gently, into the microphone: 'Thank you very much, everybody, I shan't be wanting you any more at all'—and rush madly from the theatre. Fortunately I conquered this impulse and gave them a brief explanation of the scene. I told them that it was a seaside resort in the year 1910, and that when I blew a whistle I wished them all to walk about and talk and behave as though they really were at the seaside. There was the parade (number two hydraulic lift), the beach, the steps leading down, the small stage for Uncle George's Concert Party, sand castles for the children, bathing-machine and the bandstand. All they had to do was to use their imaginations and circulate until I told them to stop. I gave them full permission to use any by-plays and bits of business that they could think of, with the proviso that any undue over-acting would be discouraged. Then I arranged Uncle George's Concert Party round their small stage, grouped roughly the rest on the parade and the beach and then, commending my soul to heaven, blew the whistle. The effect was fantastic—immediately the scene came to life, whole and complete. People laughed and talked, promenaded to and fro along the esplanade, children patted their property sand castles, Uncle George besought the crowd to listen to his concert. It was a most thrilling and satisfying moment, and from then onwards I had no more fears.

We did the scene over again several times, until it was set. Little bits of excellent business crept in; a child burst its balloon and screamed, and its mother smacked it; an old lady collapsed in a deck-chair, and one young woman shut herself up in her parasol when she heard the noise of an aeroplane. The by-play was prodigious and hardly any of it over-done. I was considerably praised later on for my little touches of sheer genius in that scene, and few believed me when I replied that the only genius I had displayed was in blowing a whistle!

Scene after scene was accomplished in that way, and rehearsals progressed rapidly. There were several comic interludes and a few tragic ones. In time we grew to know the names of nearly everyone, numbered or not. One of our lighter diversions was the 'Shy Bride.' This was the locomotive in the Victoria Station scene. All it had to do was to advance, amid clouds of steam, for a few yards, on rollers, and stop at the buffers. This it resolutely refused to do. It went backwards, it went sideways, it tangled itself in the

With GERTRUDE LAWRENCE
in Private Lives
Phoenix Theatre, 1930

With GERTRUDE LAWRENCE, ADRIANNE ALLEN
and LAWRENCE OLIVIER in PRIVATE LIVES,
Phoenix Theatre, 1930

black velvets and the fog gauzes, but never, until almost the last dress rehearsal, did it come in on cue.

We had a full week of dress rehearsals which, although chaotic at first, gradually righted themselves. The whole thing was the most thrilling theatrical adventure I could ever have imagined. The play grew and lived just a little bit more each day. The first time the Queen Victoria funeral scene went without a hitch, we found ourselves crying. Suddenly, unexpectedly, the emotional content of the play caught us unawares; once set, of course, and rehearsed over and over again, the scenes became familiar and lost their sting, but there were always certain moments in *Cavalcade* that touched me however often I saw them.

Cockie came to rehearsals during the last weeks, and encouraged everybody, as he always did, with just the right amount of praise and criticism. Frank Collins and Dan O'Neil achieved miracles of stage management. Elsie April pounded the piano, sorted band parts, and evolved brilliant ideas for the blending of the popular tunes; in fact, everybody concerned with the production worked with untiring diligence and enthusiasm.

Gladys remained calm throughout. She had designed and ordered the entire scenic part of the production; sketched, planned and chosen about three thousand seven hundred costumes; selected and hired every stick of furniture; and managed to be at my side through almost every rehearsal. Without undue modesty, I can truthfully and most gratefully say that *Cavalcade,* apart from its original moment of conception, was as much hers as mine.

(14)

The first night of *Cavalcade* will remain for ever in my memory as the most agonising three hours I have ever spent in a theatre. This, I am sure, will appear to be an over-statement to any reader who happened to be present at it. But nobody in that audience, excepting Cockie and a few who had been concerned with the production, had the remotest idea how near we came to bringing the curtain down after the third scene and sending the public home.

The evening started triumphantly. The atmosphere in the auditorium while the orchestra was tuning-up was tense with excitement. Many people had been waiting for the gallery and pit for three days and nights. Gradually the stalls and dress-circle filled; Reginald Burston, the musical director, took his place. I came into my box with Mother, Jack, Gladys and Jeffrey, and received a big ovation. The overture started and we settled ourselves to wait, while the house-lights slowly faded. The first scene went smoothly. Mary was nervous, but played with experienced poise. The troopship, with our military band and real Guardsmen, brought forth a burst of cheering. The third scene—inside the house again—went without a hitch. Half the strength of the orchestra crept out during this to take their place on the lower hydraulic lift, on which they played for the theatre scene.

It was a very complicated change. The second two lifts had to rise so many feet to make the stage. The first lift had to sink and rise again with the orchestra in place on it. The preceding interior had to be taken up into the flies, and the furniture taken off at the sides. Two enormous built side-wings, with two tiers of boxes filled with people, had to slide into place on rollers, when the first lift had risen to its mark. All this was timed to take place in just over thirty seconds, and had gone perfectly smoothly at the dress rehearsals.

We sat in the box on the first night with our eyes glued on to the conductor's desk, waiting for the little blue warning light to show us that the scene was set. We waited in vain. The conductor played the waltz through again—then again—people began to look up at us from the stalls; the gallery became restless and started to clap. Neither Gladys nor I dared to move, there were too many eyes on us, and we didn't want to betray, more than we could help, that anything was wrong. I hissed at Jack out of the corner of my mouth, and he slipped out of the box and went down on to the stage. In a few moments he returned and said, in a dead voice: 'The downstage lift has stuck, and they think it will take two hours to fix it.'

Glady and I talked without looking at each other, our eyes still set on where the blue light should appear. She said, very quietly: 'I think you'll have to make an announcement,' and I said: 'I'll give it another two minutes.' Still the orchestra continued to grind out the 'Mirabelle' waltz, there seemed to be a note of frenzy creeping into it. I longed passionately for it to play something else—anything else in the world. The audience became more restless, until suddenly, just as I was about to leave the box and walk on to the stage—the blue light came on, the black curtain rose and the scene started.

From then onwards there wasn't a moment's peace for us. The effect of the hitch on Dan O'Neil and the stage staff had obviously been shattering. The company caught panic, too, and the performance for the rest of the evening lost its grip. I don't think this was noticed by the audience, but we knew it all right. That unfortunate accident took the fine edge off the play, and although the applause at the end was tremendous, we were heartbroken. I appeared at the end against my will, but in response to frantic signals from Cockie in the box opposite. It was one of the few occasions of my life that I have ever walked on to a stage not knowing what I was going to say. However, standing there, blinded by my own automatic lights, and nerve-stricken by the torment I had endured in course of the evening, I managed to make a rather incoherent little speech which finished with the phrase: 'I hope that this play has made you feel that, in spite of the troublous times we are living in, it is still pretty exciting to be English.' This brought a violent outburst of cheering, and the orchestra, frantic with indecision as to whether to play my waltz or 'God Save the King', effected an unhappy compromise by playing them both at once. The curtain fell, missing my head by a fraction, and that was that.

(15)

Lorn came in the next morning and plumped all the papers down on my bed. 'I think,' she said, 'that our little piece is a success!' We read the notices through carefully. Mounting pæans of praise—not a discordant note. Jack and Gladys appeared presently, and we had lunch at the Ivy, where our reception was most satisfactory. Abel gave us all cocktails and drank to us solemnly, trembling a little with kind, friendly emotion. Congratulations bombarded the table. Our little piece was a success. Such a success, indeed, that I knew the moment had come for me to disappear. It seemed to me that there was danger in the air— a private, personal danger. I was happy enough, more than happy, delighted, but somehow, somewhere, not quite comfortable. Everybody seemed to be more concerned with *Cavalcade* as a patriotic appeal than as a play. This attitude I realised had been enhanced by my first-night speech—'A pretty exciting thing to be English'—quite true, quite sincere; I felt it strongly, but I rather wished I hadn't said it, hadn't popped it on to the top of *Cavalcade* like a paper-cap. I hadn't written the play as a dashing patriotic appeal at all. There was certainly love of England in it, a certain natural pride in some of our very typical characteristics, but primarily it was the story of thirty years in the life of a family. I saw where my acute sense of the moment had very nearly cheapened it. The Union Jack stretched across the back of the stage—theatrically effective jingoism. 'It's pretty exciting to be English'—awareness of the moment, not quite first-rate, a nervous grab at success at any price. Fortunately the essence of the play was clear. A comment mostly, emotional at moments but, on the whole, detached enough. The irony of the war scenes had been missed by the critics—naturally, they couldn't be expected to see it in a time of national unrest with a General Election looming in the immediate future. The Queen Victoria funeral was good— dignified, reticent and touching—the Titanic scene excellent, too, in a different way—the 1914 outbreak of war was again touching, but there was irony here, the beginning of bitterness. 'My world isn't very big.' The Trafalgar Square scene, obvious, not quite psychologically accurate, but undeniably effective, all that noise and movement against 'Land of Hope and Glory.' Best of all the Toast speech—'Let's couple the Future of England with the Past of England. The glories and victories and triumphs that are over, and the sorrows that are over, too. Let's drink to our sons who made part of the pattern and to our hearts that died with them. Let's drink to the spirit of gallantry and courage that made a strange Heaven out of unbelievable Hell, and let's drink to the hope that one day this country of ours, which we love so much, will find dignity and greatness and peace again.'

That was all right. That was deeply sincere and as true as I could make it. I do hope, profoundly hope, that this country will find dignity, greatness and peace again—no cheapness there, that came from the heart, or rather perhaps, from the roots—twisted sentimental roots, stretching a long way down and a long way back, too deep to be unearthed by intelligence or pacific reason or even contempt, there, embedded for life.

With reasoning I felt better; better for myself, but sadder for poor *Cavalcade*. It was already becoming distorted and would, in time, be more so. 'A message to the youth of the Nation.' 'A Call to Arms.' 'A shrill blare on a trumpet,' blowing my decent, simple characters into further chaos. I could stay in England and cash-in if I wanted to, cash-in on all the tin-pot glory, but I felt that it would be better for me, and much better for my future work, if I went away.

(16)

On the twenty-ninth of October 1931 Jeffrey and I left for South America. It was a casual departure, without the strained courtesy of long farewells; in fact, there weren't any farewells at all. England slipped away into the mist behind us without waving a single handkerchief. A slightly complacent England, basking in pale sunlight and the ambiguous security of a vast National Government majority. I compared her in my mind to a gallant, unimaginative old lady convalescing after an abdominal operation, unaware of the nature and danger of her disease, and happy in the belief that it could never possibly recur, because all the doctors had told her so.

Seagulls followed the boat for a little way, screeching with what may well have been national pride, and as we rounded the harbour jetty we could see the whole of Folkestone greyly spreading over the hills. Small figures promenaded along the Leas, invalids probably, sad, flat women and rheumaticky old gentlemen in Bath chairs. There were nursemaids sitting in the shelters, easily distinguishable by the perambulators drawn up before them; other figures, too, huddled on iron chairs, seeking protection from the sharp wind in the shadow of the empty bandstand.

Far away to starboard, Dungeness point crept into the sea from the marshes, and nearer, dominating the picture, just before the cliff dipped towards Sandgate, rose proudly the Grand Hotel and the Metropole Hotel, sisters in impressiveness and flushed with gentility.

We were catching a small German-Spanish ship at Boulogne, for Rio de Janeiro—seventeen days of the Atlantic were ahead of us, not our well-known Atlantic of violence, wind and icebergs, but a gentle ocean growing hourly gentler, later becoming warm and phosphorescent under new stars.

We planned to be away about nine months. We had no itinerary. After Rio we intended to drift in whatever direction the spirit moved us; our anticipatory flights included jungles, orchids, lianas, turgid tropical rivers, squawking, coloured parakeets, vast mountains, Inca ruins, deserts and languorous Latin-American cities with white houses, green jalousies, and dark-eyed, attractive people sipping cool drinks on palm-shaded patios. Most of these things, we knew, would drop into place, modified a little, perhaps, by actuality, but glamorous enough on the whole. England receded a little farther, and only a few gulls remained with us.

The whole world seemed remarkably empty to me, probably because the last weeks had been so full. From the first night of *Cavalcade,* until this moment, I had been unable to put myself down at all. The tempo of everything had increased alarmingly. If I had been working all these years merely for the outward trappings of success, I had certainly achieved my destiny, and

[354]

there was nothing left for me to do but hop over the side of the ship and triumphantly drown.

I was almost surprised that my incorrigible sense of the right moment didn't force me to do it. I had had a lot of this 'right moment' business dinned into me just lately. There seemed to be a set conviction in many people's minds that I had dashed off *Cavalcade* in a few days, merely to help the General Election and snatch for myself a little timely national kudos. The rumour was fairly general that I had written it with my tongue in my cheek, in bed, probably, wearing a silk dressing-gown and shaking with cynical laughter. This I knew was partly my own fault—that good old Union Jack—'Land of Hope and Glory'—my redundant theatre sense over-stepping the mark a bit. But still, there it was— a louder success than I had ever dreamed—vulgarised a bit, but real and satisfactory within its limits. The apex had been reached the night before I sailed, the night immediately following the election results, when Their Majesties, the King and Queen, and the entire Royal Family had come to the play. A thrilling, emotional event, everything in its place. Sitting in our box, exactly opposite the Royal Box, Gladys, Jack, Lorn and I had heard the roar outside the theatre as the Royal Party arrived. The house was crammed to the roof, the dress-circle presented an unbroken line of diadems, tiaras, sunbursts and orders—people sat on the steps and stood in the aisles. When the Royal Family came into the box, the whole audience stood and the orchestra played 'God Save the King.' We stood rigidly to attention. I remember trying not to cry, trying not to let the emotional force of the moment prevent me from discovering what it was that was so deeply touching. I didn't succeed, the force was too strong.

The play started and went smoothly from the first; everybody played perfectly; none of the effects failed; even the 'Shy Bride' steamed in eagerly on time.

After the second act, Cockie and I were received in the ante-room behind the Royal Box. Six Royal bows, one after the other, were rather agitating, but we were kindly and graciously put at our ease. I repressed a nervous desire to describe to Their

Majesties the extreme squalor of that very ante-room in the early hours of the morning during our first lighting rehearsal, when Gladys and I had used it as a sort of combined rest-room and snack-bar. My mind's eye could still see curling ham-sandwiches in greasy paper—crumbling Banbury cakes and bottles of gin and tonic littering that smooth, correct table. I think Their Majesties were pleased with the play, and the Prince of Wales asked me several searching questions. I was a little too nervous entirely to enjoy the conversation, but I hope I acquitted myself favourably; at all events, it was a proud moment for me, and I set it gratefully in my memory.

The end of the evening was even more exciting than the beginning. When Mary Clare spoke the Toast speech, there was such a terrific burst of cheering that I feared the chandeliers would fall into the stalls. At the final tableau the audience rose again, and sang 'God Save the King' with the company. The curtain fell, and the Royal Family left the box, but the cheering persisted with increasing volume until, after a while, they came back.

Of all emotional moments in that very emotional evening, that, somehow, was the most moving; the Queen drew back a little, leaving His Majesty in the front of the box to take the ovation alone. He stood there bowing, looking a little tired, and epitomising that quality which English people have always deeply valued: unassailable dignity.

It had been a tremendous night for me; a gratifying theatrical flourish to my twenty-one years of theatre.

Twenty-one years since I had sung 'Liza Ann' unaccompanied to Lila Field, in a small bare room off Baker Street—a rich, full, and exciting twenty-one years—'Jam yesterday; jam to-morrow, but never jam to-day!' wasn't quite true of me. I had enjoyed a lot of immediate jam, perhaps a little too much. I didn't want it to cloy, I didn't want to lose the taste for it, but I comforted myself with the assurance that there were lots of different varieties. This was another holiday, another escape, another change of rhythm. In the months before me I should have a little breathing-space in which to weigh values, re-assemble experience, analyse motives,

THE SELWYN THEATRE, New York, 1931

and endeavour to balance the past and present against the future. I waved a loving au revoir to Mother, Gladys, Lorn and Jack, to my family and to my friends, and went below to have a drink with Jeffrey. When we came up on deck, there was no England left. Nothing but sea and sky!

INDEX

INDEX

INDEX

INDEX

INDEX

INDEX

INDEX

INDEX

INDEX

INDEX

INDEX